Reading *A Glorious Ride* will be one of the best investments of time you will ever make. Soak up the lived experience and learned wisdom… I wish it were around 40 years ago!

*Senator the Hon Eric Abetz*
*Former Leader of the Senate, Canberra*

After several midlife crises, both personal and professional, Tony became a committed Christian and thereafter devoted an enormous amount of time and money to supporting and running various Christian organisations around the world. His takeaway is that it is the striving for success that leads to the top.

*Hon Richard Alston*
*Former Senator, Minister, and Chairman Liberal Party of Australia*

Tony McLellan's fascinating and inspirational story is as exceptional as the man himself. From the Australian bush to some of the great and palatial places in the world, and from sorrow to faith, this is a story not to miss.

*John Anderson*
*Former Deputy Prime Minister of Australia*

Inspirational, motivational, spiritually anointed. Walking with Tony McLellan as he describes life's important truths compels one to seek to make a difference with the talents one has been given by God. Read this with a pen in your hand.

*Archbishop Foley Beach*
*Chairman GAFCON, Loganville, Georgia*

A must read for discerning and aspiring leaders. The secrets of
Tony's dynamic leadership unfold and blend into a mystery
of his intimacy with Jesus, culminating in a life
of service to a hurting world.

*David Bussau*
*Founder of Opportunity International and Senior Australian of the Year*

Christian leadership is a skill we must continually feed.
This book tells of one man's lifetime of practical leadership
experiences both successes and learning experiences.
It is full of good healthy food and therefore incumbent
on us all to read this book and learn.

*Phillip Cave*
*Chairman Excelsia College, Sydney*

You will cry, laugh out loud, shout in the victories and
commiserate in the low times. You will come face to face
with greatness. God's trust in Tony and Tony's overflowing
gratefulness to his Creator shine through.

*Dr Sam Chand*
*Leadership consultant and author of Leadership Pain. Atlanta, Georgia*

Rarely has one person risen to such heights of leadership
and accomplished so much, in so many countries,
through so many organizations. His story offers profound
insights into what is truly important and inspiration
to achieve all that God has for you.

*Rick Dunham*
*Dunham + Company, Dallas, Texas*

Tony McLellan is the man who doesn't know that
a goal is impossible. He sees looming mountains as
annoying bumps, vast chasms as petty streams, and
baffling complexity as a trifling puzzle.

*Calvin Edwards*
*Founder and CEO, Calvin Edwards & Company, Atlanta, Georgia*

Tony is a man of immense drive and ambition who brings
100% focus to whatever he undertakes. Possessed of a warm
and charming personality—and boundless optimism—Tony
quickly established rapport with a diverse range of people.

*Sheila Fennessy*
*Former PA at Barrick Resources, Toronto, Canada*

One epic read, the testimony of how this business leader's
midlife encounter with God inspired him to employ his gifts
to enrich others. Replete with instructive experiences and
pregnant with life lessons, this is a book that must be read.

*Dr David Furse-Roberts*
*Research Fellow at the Menzies Research Centre, Sydney*

A captivating story of faith, courage, resolve and a raw and
heartfelt insight into the realities of life. This is so much more
than another book on leadership. It is a book on life and
a lesson of learning to truly trust in Jesus.

*Mike Gore*
*CEO, Open Doors, Sydney*

Tony McLellan has lived a life well examined. His book has
many contours that tell a story worth reading. All who seek to
lead will benefit from Tony's wisdom: success in leadership is
found in the committed, generous service of others.

*Bishop Peter Hayward*
*Bishop of Wollongong*

The story of Tony McLellan's life a tale worth telling and no one could tell it better than he does. He is a man who learns from others, but without doubt his chief teacher has been none other than Jesus Christ.

*Archbishop Peter Jensen*
*Former Archbishop of Sydney*

It is hard to imagine that one man can accomplish so much in so many fields in so many countries. A wonderful raconteur with a well of stories, this epic is his greatest story of all.

*Julian Leeser MP*
*Member of Federal Parliament, Canberra*

A courageous exposure of Tony's and Rae's life and The Way they choose to follow. The Way they followed has brought them to greatness because they served and remain true and faithful in serving people well.

*Rev Carlos Mendez, Jr.*
*Minister, Life Anglican Church, The Ponds, Sydney*

Philanthropist, politician, passionate family man.…
the challenge of conveying Tony in a few short words is beyond me. Tony is a down-to-earth Aussie whose book is a manual for the value of humility and hard work in navigating a complex world.

*Corey Nolan*
*Former Managing Director of ASX listed, Elementos Limited, Brisbane*

There are a number of silent contributors to what made this country great and safeguard its future, and Tony is one of those. Building an institution like the Australian Christian Lobby was no simple feat. I quietly give thanks to God.

*Byron Pirola*
*Managing Director, Port Jackson Partners, Sydney*

A testimony to the energy, intellect, character and humbleness of this highly accomplished man. There are rarefied highs as well as staggering setbacks all serving to hone a man blessed by his Creator. Buckle up and turn the pages.

*Jeffrey S. Rawson*
*Chairman, Merrick Capital, Houston, Texas*

I couldn't put it down. It wasn't until I read these pages that I fully realised the gift from God we have in Tony. A story of incredible highs and devastating lows… essential reading for anyone who aspires to lead.

*Lyle Shelton*
*Former Managing Director, Australian Christian Lobby, Canberra*

Sometimes we admire people from a distance, but rarely do we have the opportunity to learn about the principles successful people followed. This is a book both to ponder and to enjoy… a real keeper.

*Dr John D. Woodbridge*
*Research Professor, Trinity International University, Chicago*

Published in 2021 by Wilkinson Publishing Pty Ltd
ACN 006 042 173
PO Box 24135, Melbourne, VIC 3001, Australia
Ph: +61 3 9654 5446
enquiries@wilkinsonpublishing.com.au
www.wilkinsonpublishing.com.au

Cover and book design by Tango Media.
Family tree design by Jade Karam.
Image of Concorde in photo section by David Parker/BWP Media/Getty Images.
Printed and bound in Australia by Ligare.

Softcover ISBN 9781925927702
Hardback ISBN 9781925927771

A catalogue record for this book is available from the National Library of Australia.

Visit www.agloriousride.net for more photos and reading material.

Follow Wilkinson Publishing on social media.

WilkinsonPublishing

wilkinsonpublishinghouse

WPBooks

# A GLORIOUS RIDE

*From Jumble Plains
to Eternity*

Tony McLellan
with Nick Cater

# McLellan Family Tree

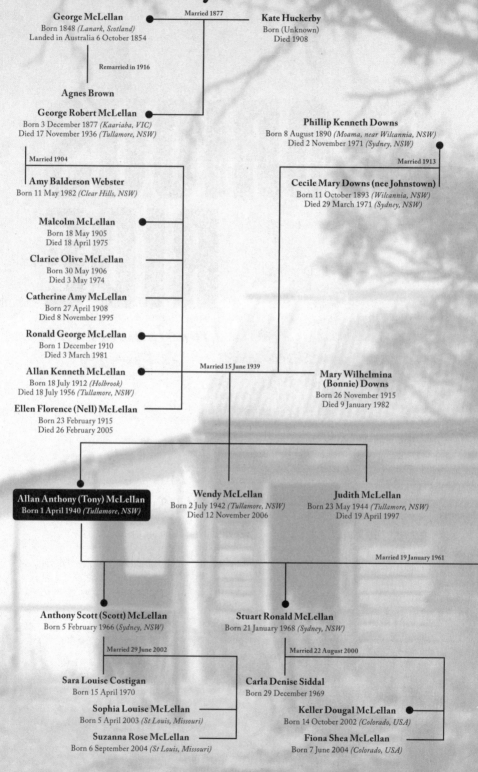

**George McLellan**
Born 1848 *(Lanark, Scotland)*
Landed in Australia 6 October 1854

Married 1877

**Kate Huckerby**
Born (Unknown)
Died 1908

Remarried in 1916

**Agnes Brown**

**George Robert McLellan**
Born 3 December 1877 *(Kaariaba, VIC)*
Died 17 November 1936 *(Tullamore, NSW)*

**Phillip Kenneth Downs**
Born 8 August 1890 *(Moama, near Wilcannia, NSW)*
Died 2 November 1971 *(Sydney, NSW)*

Married 1904

Married 1913

**Amy Balderson Webster**
Born 11 May 1982 *(Clear Hills, NSW)*

**Cecile Mary Downs (nee Johnstown)**
Born 11 October 1893 *(Wilcannia, NSW)*
Died 29 March 1971 *(Sydney, NSW)*

**Malcolm McLellan**
Born 18 May 1905
Died 18 April 1975

**Clarice Olive McLellan**
Born 30 May 1906
Died 3 May 1974

**Catherine Amy McLellan**
Born 27 April 1908
Died 8 November 1995

**Ronald George McLellan**
Born 1 December 1910
Died 3 March 1981

**Allan Kenneth McLellan**
Born 18 July 1912 *(Holbrook)*
Died 18 July 1956 *(Tullamore, NSW)*

Married 15 June 1939

**Mary Wilhelmina (Bonnie) Downs**
Born 26 November 1915
Died 9 January 1982

**Ellen Florence (Nell) McLellan**
Born 23 February 1915
Died 26 February 2005

**Allan Anthony (Tony) McLellan**
Born 1 April 1940 *(Tullamore, NSW)*

**Wendy McLellan**
Born 2 July 1942 *(Tullamore, NSW)*
Died 12 November 2006

**Judith McLellan**
Born 23 May 1944 *(Tullamore, NSW)*
Died 19 April 1997

Married 19 January 1961

**Anthony Scott (Scott) McLellan**
Born 5 February 1966 *(Sydney, NSW)*

**Stuart Ronald McLellan**
Born 21 January 1968 *(Sydney, NSW)*

Married 29 June 2002

Married 22 August 2000

**Sara Louise Costigan**
Born 15 April 1970

**Carla Denise Siddal**
Born 29 December 1969

**Sophia Louise McLellan**
Born 5 April 2003 *(St Louis, Missouri)*

**Keller Dougal McLellan**
Born 14 October 2002 *(Colorado, USA)*

**Suzanna Rose McLellan**
Born 6 September 2004 *(St Louis, Missouri)*

**Fiona Shea McLellan**
Born 7 June 2004 *(Colorado, USA)*

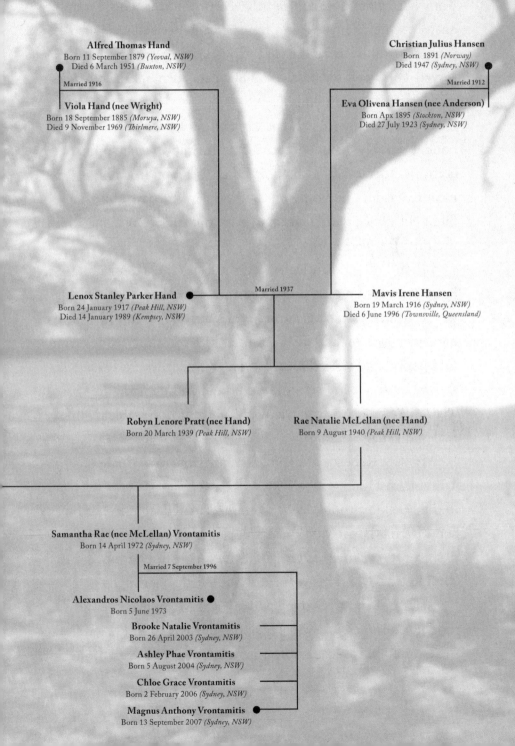

Key: ● = male

**Alfred Thomas Hand**
Born 11 September 1879 *(Yeoval, NSW)*
Died 6 March 1951 *(Buxton, NSW)*

Married 1916

**Viola Hand (nee Wright)**
Born 18 September 1885 *(Moruya, NSW)*
Died 9 November 1969 *(Thirlmere, NSW)*

**Christian Julius Hansen**
Born 1891 *(Norway)*
Died 1947 *(Sydney, NSW)*

Married 1912

**Eva Olivena Hansen (nee Anderson)**
Born Apx 1895 *(Stockton, NSW)*
Died 27 July 1923 *(Sydney, NSW)*

**Lenox Stanley Parker Hand** ●
Born 24 January 1917 *(Peak Hill, NSW)*
Died 14 January 1989 *(Kempsey, NSW)*

Married 1937

**Mavis Irene Hansen**
Born 19 March 1916 *(Sydney, NSW)*
Died 6 June 1996 *(Townsville, Queensland)*

**Robyn Lenore Pratt (nee Hand)**
Born 20 March 1939 *(Peak Hill, NSW)*

**Rae Natalie McLellan (nee Hand)**
Born 9 August 1940 *(Peak Hill, NSW)*

**Samantha Rac (nee McLellan) Vrontamitis**
Born 14 April 1972 *(Sydney, NSW)*

Married 7 September 1996

**Alexandros Nicolaos Vrontamitis** ●
Born 5 June 1973

**Brooke Natalie Vrontamitis**
Born 26 April 2003 *(Sydney, NSW)*

**Ashley Phae Vrontamitis**
Born 5 August 2004 *(Sydney, NSW)*

**Chloe Grace Vrontamitis**
Born 2 February 2006 *(Sydney, NSW)*

**Magnus Anthony Vrontamitis** ●
Born 13 September 2007 *(Sydney, NSW)*

# A WORD FROM THE CO-WRITER

Tony McLellan does not lightly accept the word "no" for an answer, which helps explain how he came to lead such an interesting and varied life. Tenaciousness is a quality that has served Tony well for more than 80 years, turning his journey into a story worth telling.

His persistence also helps explain my association with this book. I politely declined Tony's first invitation to help him craft his story, making the point that the good Lord in his infinite wisdom had only put 24 hours in the day. The argument cut no ice with Tony, however, and so I went along for the ride. I'm glad I did.

I found myself captivated with the story of Tony's childhood growing up on a property in western New South Wales where a can-do spirit is a matter of survival and nothing is handed to you on a plate. I pestered him for more stories from that period and visited Jumble Plains myself where I was shown around Tony's childhood home, unoccupied and somewhat dilapidated, by the property's current hospitable owners, Ros and Greg Baker.

My wife Rebecca and I made a pilgrimage to the Tottenham Hotel where Tony first encountered his wife Rae in the breakfast room. We called on Paula Clegg and her husband Richard, who described young Tony bouncing out of his flash sports car to cross Umang Street in Tottenham exuding confidence beyond his years and not a little charm.

After moving to Sydney and later to Melbourne, Tony rode the commercial property boom of the 1960s. He gained the reputation for leadership that launched his international career working on projects in the Pacific, Egypt, Europe, Canada and the United States. In crafting a series of fascinating anecdotes into a narrative, I was impressed by Tony's record-keeping, including a detailed itinerary or hundreds of international flights and a chronological list of the 41 homes the McLellans occupied on four continents over six decades of married life.

This story is much more than the story of a highflying globetrotter who shared flights on Concorde with the rich and famous. It is a story of man who discovered himself through self-reflection and grace. By the time he reached 50, Tony had achieved what counts in worldly terms as success, allowing for the ups and downs in his business fortunes. What was missing, however, was the spiritual dimension, the acknowledgement of a greater force, a guiding hand and a life lived for others directed by God.

Not everyone who reads this story will share Tony's faith and some may find his Christian interpretation of the world in the second half of the book somewhat challenging. As someone who's faith has wavered over the years, I sympathise, but would encourage readers to persist. Wrestling with these sections of the book has been enlightening for me, forcing me to draw on the understanding of scripture with which I was blessed in my younger years and thinking deeply about the meaning of discipleship.

Difficult as some of us may find it to surrender to faith, I share Tony's conviction that we must not shirk from the gospel's message or try to soften its edges. The modernisers who try to lower the barriers to entry into God's kingdom by watering down the more demanding aspects remove the very essence of faith. As Cardinal George Pell once memorably explained to me, offering the trappings of Christianity without acceptance of the Divine is like serving a glass of tonic without the gin.

Working as closely as Tony and I on a project such as this was either going to make or break our friendship. I am delighted to say that our friendship has only deepened as our understanding of one another has grown. My thanks go to Rae and Tony for their warm hospitality, to Rebecca for agreeing to join me on our summer journey to Tullamore, and to the Bakers, the Cleggs and many other solid folk who made us feel so welcome.

My aim was to ensure that Tony's decency, warmth and selfless devotion is illuminated on the printed page as brightly as it shines in the flesh. I hope you will enjoy taking this journey with him as I have.

Nick Cater
April 2021

# FOREWORD BY JOHN HOWARD AC, OM

A. Anthony (Tony) McLellan has had an extraordinary international career. Coming from a rural background in Australia, he has been the chief executive officer of large companies around the world. He has met many famous people and has dealt with the presidents of several countries. A self-starter who has founded many organisations, he is a leader in every sense.

Raised on his father's sheep station, Tony left school at 15, and assumed the management of the property when his father died. He quickly learned a range of skills associated with the land and, in particular, managing and motivating men. Tony has enjoyed a varied career in a range of industries and has been enriched by living in many countries. In sixty years of married life, his wife, Rae, has followed him faithfully—handling the responsibility for the well-being of their family as they have lived in 41 different homes.

Tony and Rae moved to the city so that Tony could study to become a valuer and begin his new career as an advisor to major corporations developing a number of landmark projects. His accomplishments are legion, including serving as the real estate consultant to the NSW Government on the redevelopment of the 24-hectare The Rocks area on Sydney's foreshore.

Later, he moved to Egypt to build a new city for 45,000 people. Pretty impressive for a boy who had to leave school at 15 when his father died. Subsequently, he became the founding President and CEO of Barrick Resources, out of which emerged Barrick Gold, which is now the world's largest gold company. While in just the last few years, he has founded Chrysos Corporation Limited in partnership with the CSIRO and the company is now on an international trajectory.

Tony has made an enormous contribution to the Christian not-for-profit world both in Australia and overseas. When he was chairman of Habitat for Humanity Australia, it was my honour to present his organisation with the Prime Minister's National Award for Excellence in Community Business Partnerships.

Always a powerful and evocative speaker, Tony set the scene for a number of Australian Christian Lobby events at which I was present and served it for nearly ten years as Chairman, helping it to grow from 3,500 supporters to over 200,000 today. When he retired, ACL honoured him with the title of Chairman Emeritus.

I personally had another connection with the "boy from the bush" when he was elected to the board of The Menzies Research Centre, the policy think tank associated with the Liberal Party. He was a great contributor for many years and I remember well his regular visits to my office when I was Prime Minister.

These memoirs capture the personal experiences and lessons learnt from leadership across a wide range of business and not-for-profit activities here and overseas. But as important, are those nuggets of advice and example that only a few experience, by observing closely, and through meeting those prominent leaders at the very heart of the business and political world.

Well worth the read.

# CONTENTS

## CHAPTER 1

# JUMBLE PLAINS

The Scottish farmer ponders upon the future of his son, and sees it most assured not by the inheritance of money but by the acquisition of that knowledge which will give him power.

SIR ROBERT GORDON MENZIES

The first secret to success in life is to choose your ancestors well. Mine were a family of pioneers from Scotland, and although I can't remember having much say in the matter, it was a pretty good pick. Scotland has contributed more than its share of leaders to the world, not least in Australia where enterprising Scottish migrants began stamping their influence from the early days of colonial settlement.

I may be biased, but to be born into Clan McLellan was a particular stroke of luck. *Mac Gille Fhaolain*, the Gaelic name from which McLellan derives, means sons of the servant of St Fillan, an Irish missionary who helped bring Christianity to Scotland in the 8th century. According to legend, St Fillan was ploughing a field in Ireland when a wolf attacked and killed his ox.

Undaunted, St Fillan harnessed the wolf to his plough so he could finish the job. I cannot vouch for the truth of that story, but do know that St Fillan's can-do attitude, the determination to do the best with what you've got, was imbedded in my ancestors' DNA.

My great grandfather George McLellan was born in Lanark in central Scotland in 1848. His father was a blacksmith. It would have been an isolated town in those days, seven years before the arrival of the railway to Glasgow, where farmers and townsfolk relied largely on their own wits.

George emigrated to Australia with his parents at the age of five, landing in Portland, Victoria aboard the *Indian Ocean* on 6 October 1854. He grew up to become a pioneering settler in the Goulburn Valley in Victoria, securing a block of land at Kaarimba in 1875. Two years later he married Kate Huckberby who gave birth to a son, George Robert, on 3 December 1877. Not content with taming one frontier, George went on to conquer a second at the age of 50, moving his family to Oaklands in the Riverina, then known as Clear Hills, in 1898. After the death of his first wife in 1908 he moved on again, taking up land in Kellerberrin in the wheat-belt district of WA. At the age of 68 he married Agnes Brown, a widow in her late 30s, living to the then ripe old age of 86. A newspaper obituary lauded him as "one of the best and progressive public men."

George's son George Robert, my grandfather, met his wife Amy Webster in Clear Hills, where she was renowned for playing the pedal organ in the local church. They were married in 1904 in a ceremony in the Clear Hills School of Arts and enjoyed a wedding breakfast held in the Clear

Hills Coffee Palace before departing for their honeymoon in Melbourne. Grandfather George followed in his father's pioneering footsteps, earning great respect in the community where he served as councillor. They had six children, Malcolm, Clarice, Catherine, Ronald, my father Allan Kenneth (born in Holbrook on 18 July 1912) and Ellen (Nell).

At the age of 50, Grandfather George moved to the Tullamore district in western NSW where he purchased Jumble Plains in 1927. The magnificent homestead in which I was raised was the product of Grandfather George's labour. It was he who felled and saw-milled the timber to construct a spacious home for his wife Amy and their large family, with sleepouts on three sides and a spacious ballroom with a decorative pressed metal ceiling and a hardwood dancefloor. He dug a deep well in the garden lined with bricks which would be fed by ceramic piping from the creek. It was fed to the house via a water tank supported on a galvanised steel platform four metres high. My grandfather added a golf course, a tennis court and a plethora of cottages and other outbuildings, including the shearing shed and shearer's accommodation.

Under the proprietorship of grandfather George, Jumble Plains was not just a productive farm but the centre for community events. The Jumble Plains golf tournament was a feature of the local sporting calendar, written up in the local newspaper. It was a favoured venue for school concerts, horse races, ballroom dances, and Empire nights with bonfires and fireworks. Jumble Plains is marked on most maps as it was a changing station for the horses drawing the Cobb & Co coaches, before the days of motor vehicles. To this day the mail is delivered right to the front door of the homestead, unlike most country properties which have mailboxes by the roadside, typically converted 44-gallon drums.

As a young child it was the only world I knew. I had no idea that my grandfather, who I never knew, had accomplished so much. Like most children, I took my surroundings for granted. This discovery later in life made me exceptionally proud. Like Robert Menzies, Rupert Murdoch and many other great Australian leaders, I was blessed with the good fortune to descend from Scottish migrants whose grit and determination helped build the Australia we know today.

My Grandfather passed away on 17 November 1936 at the age of 59 in Tullamore Hospital after an operation for acute appendicitis. An obituary in the Lachlander and Condobolin and Western Districts Recorder offers a glimpse of the measure of a man "both widely known and highly respected… who will be much missed in many circles."

> At an early age he showed keen business capacity, and as time went on became a very successful stock and station agent in partnership with others…
>
> His taste for the beautiful, as well as similar tastes by his good wife, resulted in adding beauty to the homestead and surroundings, until it was the home beautiful and of ideal comfort admired by all who visited it.
>
> The deceased was a good sport, in the best sense of the word. As a golfing enthusiast there seemed to be no limit to his energy and desire to forward the interests of the game.

Grandfather George's funeral was the largest ever held in the district, the newspaper reported, attended by a "colossal circle of friends" from as far away as Shepparton, Victoria. True to his Scottish Protestant ancestry, the funeral was held in the Tullamore Presbyterian Church.

The death of a person much admired has consequences for the living. His passing placed a tremendous burden on my father Allan who, at the age of 24 and unmarried, took the running of the estate and inherited the formidable responsibility of living up to his fathers' standards. While I never had the chance to talk to my father about it, I sense that he carried the fear of failing to accomplish that task to his grave. Death also gives us pause to think about our own mortality and the precious gift of life. The passing of a person under 60 would be considered an early death today. But since the average lifespan of an Australian born in the 1870s was 35, Grandfather George had beaten the odds.

My strongest connection with the generation that grew up before Federation was through Grandma Amy who lived to 82. She was a dour, but very kind lady who moved off the property into town, where she made an array of biscuits that we loved hoeing into whenever we visited her.

Grandma McLellan had a pedal organ in her home and played the organ at the red-brick Presbyterian church in Tullamore, in which there was a window and a pew in honour of my grandfather and my father. I have no doubt about the faith of my grandmother and think that grandfather George Robert was also a believer in God. My parents were not churchgoers, although I do remember going with them to a tiny weatherboard church in the bush not too far from Jumble Plains. I guess it may have been the funeral of a local grazier.

Later, Grandma was moved into an aged care facility in Sydney where she died on 26 September 1966, aged 84. She was buried alongside my grandfather in the Presbyterian section of the peaceful country cemetery surrounded by bushland outside Tullamore. Rae and I used to visit Grandma in the Killara facility from time to time after we moved to Sydney from the bush in late 1962.

In the late 1930s, my father visited Sydney with a friend from his days at Geelong College, Bruce Waugh. Bruce introduced him to an attractive young lady, and a champion swimmer, Bonnie Downs, who lived with her mother Cecile in a large, comfortable middle-class home in Haberfield. Not one to waste time, my father proposed to her and they became engaged three days later. A few months afterwards, on 15 June 1939, my father Allan Kenneth McLellan married Mary Wilhelmina "Bonnie" Downs at St Stephens Presbyterian Church in Macquarie Street, Sydney. Allan was 26 and Bonnie 23.

My mother moved to her new home in Jumble Plains where she and my father were sole occupants of the family estate until my arrival on 1 April 1940, a respectable nine months and 16 days after their wedding day. I'm told that as my parents drove up the hill to the Tullamore District Hospital, my mother asked my father, "If it's a boy what about 'Tony'?" Dad apparently responded, "Well, I only know two Tonys. One of these is in the madhouse and the other one ought to be!" So, Allan Anthony it was, or Tony for short. That day's edition of *The Sydney Morning Herald* offers a glimpse of the Australia I entered; a country in the early stages of a terrible war; Winston Churchill as First Lord of the Admiralty declaring Britain was not seeking war with Russia; Australia's new cruiser, HMAS Perth, greeted by cheering crowds in Sydney; coal miners on strike in NSW; and apple growers welcome a new innovation—corrugated cardboard packing trays. My sisters were also wartime babies: Wendy born on 2 July 1941 followed by Judy on 23 May 1944. Both Wendy and Judith (Judy) married and had families although, sadly, both died of cancer when they were in their fifties and sixties.

Jumble Plains was flat, red-soil country, timbered with Red Gums and Box trees. A creek ran past the back of the property, its banks edged with a thick stand of trees, which offered cool relief in the height of summer. In one part of the property, where the soil was lighter, large Cypress Pines grew. From this area, the timber was obtained for the construction of the homestead and all the outbuildings. Further out, the country was harder with Wattle trees and even Iron Bark, from which railway sleepers were made.

The summers were very hot, the winters icy. I can remember one year when we experienced ten consecutive days of over 115 degrees Fahrenheit (46 degrees Centigrade). One year, when Rae and I were living in nearby Tottenham, the temperature rose to 129 degrees Fahrenheit (54 degrees Centigrade). Worse, the nights were often unbearably hot too. During the summer, we all slept on the verandas which were gauzed in to keep out the mosquitoes. Because the country was open and the skies typically clear, the winter nights were cold. When the frost was heavy, puddles would freeze over. With long periods of drought and occasional flooding rains, farming in that country was seldom uneventful. Average rainfall was approximately 16" (400 mm), roughly a third of that in Sydney, although the "average" gives a false impression of the struggle farmers face to the west of the Great Dividing Range.

The year I arrived was one of the driest years of the century over most of southern Australia. The Nepean Dam in NSW dried up completely and water restrictions were imposed in cities on the East Coast. The drought in South Eastern Australia continued with little relief until it finally broke in 1947.

The rains and greening landscape brought a new challenge as the rabbit population exploded. With typical litters of five, by 1950 the initial twelve pairs of rabbits brought to the country in 1859 had increased to several hundred million. I well remember the battles we fought on Jumble Plains trying to control these pests. Apart from denying feed for livestock, rabbits were damaging the environment. The entire property of Jumble Plains was surrounded by a wire netting fence, with the netting buried in the ground. But rabbits quickly found that they could burrow under it. We created "rabbit trails" and set the trails with bait (usually carrots) laced with 1080 poison. We had contractors who set traps at the entrances to burrows. We ripped up as many warrens as we could. We burned logs that were being used as homes for rabbits.

As the numbers increased, one thing that was noticeable was the emergence of many different coloured rabbits, which I was told was a result of in-breeding. The longer the plague existed the more and more white, black, orange, and silver/ blue rabbits were to be seen. During the drought, we fenced in our tanks, which were the below-ground stock water reservoirs, to trap the rabbits. And I can remember catching as many as 1400 rabbits in each tank each night. They were bagged and taken back to the woolshed where it was my job to break their necks before they were slaughtered and sent off to the abattoir. I have never counted, but imagine I was personally responsible for the death of 100,000 rabbits.

The breakthrough came with the release of Myxomatosis by the CSIRO in 1950. As soon as it was available, we rushed to the Condobolin Pastures Protection Board and obtained our allocation of serum which we injected into about a dozen rabbits we had caught and placed in a hutch, located on the bank of the creek on our property. We were hoping that the many mosquitoes would help spread the virus. The rabbits in the hutch survived for 10-15 days and within weeks we began to see other rabbits on the property had contracted the disease. As I remember, within a year the rabbit plague was decimated with a notable increase to farm productivity. Within two years of the release of the virus, Australia's meat and wool production increased by $68 million.

Approximately 2,000 acres of Jumble Plains had been cleared for farming. This was rotated so that crops were never planted in the same paddock two years in a row. As a result, we probably farmed around 700 to 1000 acres a year. Approximately 20% of this would usually be sown with oats (which we harvested and stored for supplementary stock feed during droughts). The balance was sown with wheat for sale, the most popular breed in those days being Bencubbin, which was relatively drought resistant.

Before the days of bulk handling, we filled three-bushel jute bags from the harvester, or header. These then had to be sewn individually before being transported to the nearest silos at the rail head in Tullamore or Albert. If we had 700 acres of wheat that could be expected to yield, say, six bags per acre in a good season, resulting in over 4,000 bags to sew. In some years the yield was more like four bags per acre, although I recall our award-winning crop that yielded almost ten bags per acre. I did my share and therefore probably stitched over 1000 bags each year. A bag of wheat weighed 180 pounds and was typically lifted from the ground with a hydraulic loader onto the shoulders of a man standing on the truck who then stacked it three or four tiers high. Loading a lorry provided a good work-out for all the men involved. The harvest period involved intense work over long hours. We usually began in November and the rush was to complete it by Christmas. We aimed to get to the paddock by 6 am, fuel and grease the tractor and the header and be ready to start harvesting as soon as the dew had dried off and worked through until dusk. It was a seven-day-per-week job, unless we were interrupted by a breakdown or by rain. This meant I missed a few days of Sunday cricket at the beginning of summer.

The world beyond Jumble Plains seemed remote. The nearest large town was Dubbo, three hours journey in the 1937 Chevrolet car my father drove. My father had installed a radio set with a huge outdoor aerial, perhaps 20 metres tall, on which we were able to listen to 2CR, the ABC station that broadcast from Orange. The AM signal was crackly and unreliable, particularly during the day, but it did provide us with some contact with the outside world. One item my parents enjoyed when the reception was good was the serial, "The Lawsons" that came on at 1 pm over what was called "dinner" in the bush; "lunch" to the city slickers. Later, this was super-seded by "Blue Hills", with many of the same actors. One of the stars was the mother of a friend I met in Sydney 20 years later and have been in close touch with for 50 years.

A public stock route, known as the "Long Paddock", crossed the top end of our property. It was used by drovers to take sheep or cattle to Condobolin and was a legacy from my grandfather's presidency of the Lachlan Shire Council and involvement with the Condobolin Pastures Protection Board. I was given a stockwhip as a boy that later accompanied me around the world: to Egypt; to London; to Canada; to the USA, and finally back to Australia. Why, you might ask? I have no idea, but I am looking at it now on the wall of my office where it remains one of my most valuable treasures. When I pick it up, it revives memories of my days on horseback droving cattle to the railhead or drafting out animals in the paddock.

I learned how to handle firearms from a young age, begin-ning with a single-shot .22 Lithgow rifle at age 11. My father also had a range of other weapons, including a .22 repeater rifle, a .303, commonly used for killing kangaroos. My dad also had 12-guage double-barreled shotguns and a .410 shotgun. The 12-gauge was also used on kangaroos, if one could get close enough (typically on the back of a truck—how dan-gerous, when one thinks of it now)—and for wild wood ducks. The .410 was often referred to as a "ladies' gun" and was suit-able for killing snakes. As an aside, I learned many years later that the gauge of a shotgun is determined by the number of lead balls weighing a total of one pound that can fit snugly through its bore. Thus, 12 lead balls weighing a total of one pound would fit through the bore of a 12-guage shotgun. A

20-guage would need 20 balls; and so on. The .410 gun does not fit this model; its bore is simply .410 inches in diameter.

Later, I purchased a .22 Hornet, which was much more powerful, capable of taking out kangaroos and other pests such as foxes. Later when we lived at Warren, I sometimes went wild pig shooting in the Macquarie Marshes which I enjoyed in the knowledge that I was performing a valuable public service. Feral pigs destroy crops and pasture, as well as habitat for native plants and animals.

My passion for shooting stayed with me for a while, even when there were no longer pests around threatening our livelihood. When Rae and I moved to Sydney, I joined the NSW Gun Club, where I enjoyed clay pigeon shooting at Terry Hills. I took my handsome 12-guage Remington automatic shotgun to Egypt where I hunted ducks and pigeons on the Cairo canals. As I recall, no licence was required to import the Remington. I did have to obtain a gun licence when we relocated to London where my automatic shotgun was put to use shooting pheasant. The weapons followed me to Canada, and then to the USA. No licensing was required in those countries, although I do not believe I ever fired a shot in either of these places. Eventually, the two weapons were shipped back to Australia where they were seized by the authorities, due to the strict Australian gun licencing laws. I never bothered to claim them.

As a boy, I worked as a rouse-about both at Jumble Plains and at other shearing sheds. The rouse-about's job was to gather the fleece as soon as the last stroke was made and spread it on the grated table by throwing it. There, the wool-classer removed the skirtings, examined the fleece and decided in which category it would be binned prior to baling. The pieces of fleece that fell through the grid were called lox. The rouse-about then had to sweep up the tailings. Every now and then I would hear the loud call, "Tar boy!" from one of the shearers who had just cut a sheep. My job was to dab some "tar" or "dope" on the injury.

I was probably 14 or 15 when my father taught me the art of shearing. It is back-breaking work. First, you grab the sheep firmly and flip it onto its backside, sitting like a dog, leaning it back to your legs. Next you shear off the belly wool and begin a carefully-orchestrated routine, called the Tally-Hi technique. You stay close to the animal's body and try to avoid going over the same area twice which will reduce the value of your fleece. Starting with the chest, and lower neck area, you strike the blade down one flank and then part of the back. Shifting the sheep to the other side, you repeat the process. The prize is a single homegrown fleece, ready for a roustabout to throw on the wool table, an art in itself.

In the early days, shearing was done by hand shears. The most famous of the old-time blade shearers was Jackie Howe, who once shore 321 sheep in 7 hours 40 minutes. The navy-blue singlet worn by working men is called the "Jackie Howe" after this incredible man. Our shearing shed at Jumble Plains had a tally board behind each stand on which was recorded the record number of sheep shorn at that stand. A top shearer can turn out a daily tally of around 150, earning the shearer about $400 for the day.

One of the greatest shearers of this generation was Steve Handley. On the board, Steve Handley was only ever in full flight. After pushing a newly-shorn sheep through the chute into the counting-out pen, he would lurch towards the catching pen for another, grasp it firmly between his knees, and work it with his hand-piece. Less than two minutes later, he'd have another gleaming white merino added to his tally. And so he would continue, half-man, half-machine, from the first sounding of the woolshed bell at 7:30 am, to the final bell at 5:30 pm.

Handley was known affectionately as "The Chinchilla Killer" for his ferocious appetite for work and would regularly turn out a daily total of 250, sometimes 300, shorn sheep. "No-one's on par with him and he just keeps himself to a regime that I don't think that anyone could keep up with," his long-time friend and shearing contractor, Noel Dawson, once observed.

In the macho world of the shearing shed the fastest shearer, known as the "gun", holds a prestigious title. With his red carroty hair and imperious air, Handley would glare and glower at rival shearers on the board burning holes in them with his eyes. In his mid 40s, Handley sustained a serious back injury. The thought that he might never shear again was intolerable to him. Despite medical help, he spiralled into deep depression. A little while later, he was found dead, aged 49, at Charleville. I share this poignant story to remind us all that Australia is made up of a wide range of people. Some of them are Victoria Cross winners, some are Olympic stars, and some became champion shearers. Steve Handley was created by God for a purpose, and those of us who are more fortunate in many ways, should always be prepared to give honour and respect to men and women like that.

Having shorn a few sheep myself, I can really admire the

prowess of Steve Handley. As C.J. Dennis said in the immortal *Sentimental Bloke*, "I dips me lid" to that extraordinary man.

My father loved the bush and its people and it was from him that I inherited a love of bush poetry. He was particularly fond of Banjo Paterson, who wrote about the country area where we lived. Legend has it that Banjo met his friend Thomas Michael MacNamara, while he was shearing at Jumble Plains. MacNamara is said to be the model for Thomas Gerald Clancy, the hero of my favourite Paterson poem, *Clancy of the Overflow*. Paterson's first published poem appeared in *The Bulletin* in 1885 under the pen name of "The Banjo" after a race-horse his family had owned. He was a 21-year-old solicitor at the time, practicing in Sydney. In 1889, *The Bulletin* published the romantic bush ballad, "Clancy of the Overflow:"

> I had written him a letter which I had, for want of better
>> Knowledge, sent to where I met him down the Lachlan, years ago,
> He was shearing when I knew him, so I sent the letter to him,
>> Just "on spec", addressed as follows: "Clancy of the Overflow."
>
> And an answer came directed, in a writing unexpected,
>> (And I think the same was written with a thumbnail dipped in tar)
> 'Twas his shearing mate who wrote it, and *verbatim*, I will quote it:
>> "Clancy's gone to Queensland droving, and we don't know where he are."
>
> In my wild erratic fancy visions came to me of Clancy
>> Gone a droving "down the Cooper" where the western drovers go;
> As the stock are slowly stringing, Clancy rides behind them singing,
>> For the drover's life has pleasures that the townsfolk never know.

And the bush hath friends to meet him, and their kindly voices greet him

    In the murmur of the breezes and the river on its bars,

And he sees the vision splendid of the sunlit plains extended,

And at night the wondrous glory of the everlasting stars.

When the Boer War broke out in 1899, Banjo Paterson went to South Africa as a War Correspondent. He was in the thick of the action and became an expert on the use of horses in warfare. After returning from the Boer War in 1903, Paterson went to visit his fiancé in Winton and heard a local legend about a wanted man who drowned himself to avoid being captured. Paterson wrote a song about it, selling the rights to Angus and Robertson because he didn't particularly like it.

Oh there once was a swagman camped in the billabongs,

    Under the shade of a Coolibah tree;

And he sang as he looked at the old billy boiling,

    "Who'll come a-waltzing Matilda with me."

On 5 February 1941—exactly 25 years before the birth of our first son—Banjo, who was almost seventy-seven, finally laid down his pen and died. Like Banjo Paterson's Clancy of the Overflow, a sheep shearer who went to Queensland droving down the Cooper, I did my share of droving and there is something special about the sense of freedom—being on horseback in the open country. I think of the times, as a stock and station agent I went looking for stock being brought down from Queensland to the railhead at Warren, or simply feeding in the "long paddock" during times of drought. On finding a mob, I would get on a spare horse and ride around inspecting the animals so that I could report back to the owner. I have stopped and "magged" to drovers over the years, including those passing along the stock route through our property, Jumble Plains. I have driven our stock to the nearest railhead for shipping to the markets in Sydney. And I have loaded tens of thousands of sheep for trucking by trains to the main abattoir then in Riverstone (now a new genteel suburb of Sydney) from Tottenham and Warren. I have loaded many "special trains" of more than 30 wagons, each with over 100 sheep, on their way to slaughter. Assisting me was my amazing Kelpie/ Collie cross sheepdog, Jeddah, who would climb on the backs of the sheep urging them up the loading ramps into the train.

In my early days at Jumble Plains, the sheep were protected from lice by dipping them in a trough through which they swam. Typically, dipping was done shortly after the sheep had been shorn and their cuts had healed as the dip was a powerful concoction of arsenic. Later, we installed a spray dip in which the sheep were herded and then sprayed from both the top and bottom. The apparatus consisted of a large below-ground concrete well, from which the spray was drawn. Our unit had just been built and did not have a cover over the well.

We had started early at about 6 am one morning, and as the first mob was being sprayed, I tripped and fell in the arsenic laden well. I tried to grab the side as I slid down, ripping skin off both thighs and one shin and then dousing myself in the arsenic. I was lifted out by one of the men and immediately hosed down. I was bleeding quite a lot and there was concern that I may have absorbed some arsenic. I was rushed to the local hospital where the bleeding was controlled. The doctor then coated my wounds with iodine in order to prevent infection—which was common in those days. A dab of iodine stings, but when it was all over fairly extensive raw wounds it stings like hell. It was a practical lesson on the importance of workplace safety.

A child who grows up on a remote property like Jumble Plains, then 45-minutes' drive from the nearest thing that could be called a town, is inclined to imagine that an education is something you obtain elsewhere, whether at boarding school or university. Looking back, however, my first and most important lessons in life were taught in the family home and on the station where self-reliance and persistence are matters of survival. There is never a moment on a property when your work is finished. The only division is between tasks that must be performed right now, and those that must be done later. We might talk about running a station, but in actual fact the station runs you, seven days a week, from dawn to dusk, and frequently beyond.

As I was to learn later, the doggedness and staying power I learned on the land are the universal keys to success in life.

## CHAPTER 2

# A RUGGED EDUCATION

All men who have turned out worth anything have had the chief hand in their own education.

SIR WALTER SCOTT[1]

My formal education began at Pinefield Public School where there were never more than 11 pupils across Grades 1-6 crammed together in a one-roomed hut. I graduated as dux, which was hardly surprising since I was the only person in my grade. At the age of 11, my parents sent me off to board at The Scots College, Bellevue Hill. It was another world, one that filled me with wonderment and wobbliness in equal measure. I had graduated from a school with perhaps three or four boys from which to pick your friends to a college of 1000. I had never seen a cricket match for the simple reason that it would have been hard to muster one team of eleven, let alone two. A rugby match would have been out of the question. At Scots, I was standing at the edge of a lush-green oval watching games being played with skill and purpose overlooking Sydney Harbour in a city of 1.7 million people. It was

1    Letter to J.G. Lockhart, August 1825. Lockhart's life of Sir Walter Scott Volume 6, Chapter 2, 1837.

a chance to put a lesson my father had taught me into action: never be afraid. Later in life I was to learn from Anglican Bishop N.T. (Tom) Wright that "Don't be afraid" is the most frequent command in the Bible, frequently linked with the exhortation to take courage.

On the second night, I was lying in my bed unable to get to sleep, when Mr Dunn, the housemaster, crept into the dormitory and whispered, "Anyone awake?" I was the only boy who answered. Mr Dunn tip-toed over to my bed, leant over and said very softly: "The King is dead: long live the Queen." It was the first time I had heard the expression and it struck me as rather odd. (The phrase was first used when Charles VII ascended to the French throne after the death of his father, Charles VI, in 1422.)

It was Wednesday 6 February 1952, and King George VI had died from lung cancer and was succeeded by his eldest daughter Elizabeth. My father was a great admirer of King George VI particularly his courage and leadership during the War. I remember my dad telling me how Queen Elizabeth, later the Queen Mother, was asked why she did not leave London to be safer with her children in the country. She replied: "I will always remain with my husband, and he will never leave London." Her response characterised the extraordinary courage shown in Britain by a people who found themselves at the front line of a war on a scale that can barely be imagined by my children. We have much to learn from them, and much more to admire.

My four years at Scots were far from happy. I was awkwardly shy, lonely and frequently scared in the company of hundreds and hundreds of boys. In my early days at Scots, I was chosen for a roughing up by a group of older boys who tried to pin me down and coat my privates with black raven oil which is commonly used for dying leather. In the struggle, I managed to kick the jar of raven oil out of the boy's hand, which spilt all over his suit. It hardly helped my popularity.

At Scots College I knew a larrikin of the highest order. He was a flagrant troublemaker, but bright and very amusing. His name was Brett Whitley. I had won the school prize in geography and the following year was saddled with sitting at a shared desk with this young man. He was not the slightest bit interested in studying geography or, it seemed, anything else. Our teacher was a Mr. Peck, and Brett would call out behind his hand, "peck, peck, peck" throughout the whole lesson. Mr. Peck would wheel around and stare in my direction looking for the culprit.

Brett and I also played together in the Colts, the under 15 A Rugby team. He was the most amazing flanker (or break-away as we called them in those days). Why was he so good? Because he was absolutely fearless; completely unafraid. As a result, he was an incredible tackler. When one tackles one is always subconsciously concerned that you might hurt yourself, so you hold back a fraction. But not Brett—he went in "boots and all" with absolutely no concern for any pain he might suffer. We had some other stars on our team as well, but Brett was as good as just about anyone.

Brett won the school art prize and later went on to become one of the most famous Australian painters of the post-war era. His work reflected the larrikinism I remember so well from our school days and the fearlessness he would show on the rugby field. He was twice fought by his demons in life and died on 15 June 1992 from an overdose of opiates in a motel room at Thirroul, New South Wales. He was survived by his spirited wife Wendy who has worked tirelessly to uphold his legacy from the home they shared together in Lavender Bay, North Sydney.

Discipline was strict at Scots. I remember the feeling of terror when I was reported to the principal by our housemaster, Mr Dunn for coming back to school one Sunday evening wearing sports pants under my overcoat instead of the regulation uniform. The headmaster gave me four viscous cuts with the cane for my sin, the only consolation being that he reluctantly agreed to cane my hand and not my backside when I told him I had carbuncles. The experience made me bitter and I never regained my enthusiasm for Scots.

Despite everything, I did well at schoolwork and was in the A grade, receiving particular encouragement from my incredible mathematics teacher, Fred Pollock. I once created a graph of $y = x2$, which resulted in a parabola. Mr Pollock showed it off to the class. Mathematics became a passion, I later taught it to my valuation students and wrote a textbook on interest tables. I won the geography prize in my second year at Scots, which was presented to me on speech day by Sir Robert Menzies—much to my father's delight.

The end of term was always a relief. I would catch the 365 bus to Central Railway Station and board the Forbes Mail drawn by two steam locomotives to enable it to get over the Blue Mountains. The train departed at 8.30 pm and stopped the following morning in Parkes. There, I customarily enjoyed my favourite breakfast of lamb's fry and bacon, which was never on the menu at boarding school, before catching the rail motor coach to Tullamore where my parents would meet me and drive me home to Jumble Plains in time for lunch.

My education would have been a sacrifice for my father when you tally up the cost of private schooling, not to mention the loss of a pair of hands on the property. A faith in the power of education, however, is part of the Scottish tradition Sir Robert Menzies described in his Forgotten People radio talk.

> The Scottish farmer ponders upon the future of his son, and sees it most assured not by the inheritance of money but by the acquisition of that knowledge which will give him power; and so the sons of many Scottish farmers find their way to Edinburgh and a university degree.
>
> The great question is, "How can I qualify my son to help society?" Not, as we have so frequently thought, "How can I qualify society to help my son?"

My father was a Stoic, making virtue the highest good and enduring the hardships life dealt you with fortitude and patience. My father certainly did that, and he encouraged me to do so as well, even though he succumbed to those pressures by taking refuge in alcohol, which provided another lesson for me. My father's greatest gift to me was self-belief. He instilled in me the confidence I could achieve my goals, however ambitious they might seem, and whatever apparent obstacles might lie in the way.

In my early teenage years, one of the great frontiers of human achievement waiting to be conquered was the four-minute mile. Both my father and I became absorbed in the quest to run a mile, approximately 1609 metres, in less than 240 seconds. Many people, including my father, thought it impossible. The Australian runner, John Landy, and his British rival, Roger Bannister, had come to within a few seconds of the mythical four minutes, but there seemed to be some sort of a God-ordained barrier to achieving the feat. Some physiologists of the time thought it would be dangerous to the health of any athlete who attempted it. I remember listening with my Dad late at night to the live broadcasts of the mile races on the new cinders track in Helsinki in the 1952 Olympics on our crackling, static-filled radio. It was the first Games to be broadcast live by the ABC and was quite something to be listening in from the other side of the world.

At the end of 1953, Landy came within 2 seconds of achieving the target. As he boarded a BOAC flight in Melbourne on April 28, 1954 at the end of the Australian season preparing to run in Finland, the hopes of the nation went with him. Bannister, however, who had been following Landy's progress nervously from England, decided he couldn't wait for the next international meet. Unexpected, on May 6, Bannister employed two close friends as pacemakers in his attempt to break the barrier. Chris Brasher led Bannister through the first two laps, or the half-way mark, in 1 minute 58 seconds. Chris Chattaway, who later became an investment banker and with whom I subsequently did business when I lived in London, then took over. He led Bannister through the third lap in almost exactly even time: three minutes, naught point seven seconds. Now Bannister was on his own and had to maintain a pace of a fraction under sixty seconds for the last lap. Making a dash for the line, he broke through the tape in three minutes, fifty-nine point four seconds. The mythical barrier had been broken. Forbes Magazine rated it as the greatest athletic feat in the previous century-and-a-half.

Bannister's world record was only to last 46 days. On 21 June 1954, at an international meet at Turku, Finland, Landy knocked an incredible 1.4 seconds off Bannister's time to set a new world record of 3 minutes 58 seconds. The record was to hold for more than three years. H.J. Oaten, the athletics writer for the *London Evening Standard*, wrote "Perseverance ought to be John Landy's middle name."

Bannister and Landy proved the doubters wrong. The was no physical barrier to achieving the goal; the only barrier was their own self-belief. Nothing will scupper our plans more than fears or doubts we harbour about our ability to execute them. The lesson my Dad taught me was to believe in yourself, to put aside any fears or doubts about your ability to achieve what you have set out to do, and not to give up until you reach your goal. As athletes like Bannister and Landy know all too well, the definition of a loser is a winner who gave up trying.

Dad's life was blighted by his own personal demons. His drinking problem was a feature of my life as far back as my memory stretches. I recall him being taken away two or three times to an institution to help him cure the problem and remember visiting him with the family at one such place in Sydney. But always he fell back into the habit, drinking a bottle of spirits a day. When my father was on a binge, he sometimes became violent and often had little control of himself. I can remember calling my Uncle Malcolm to come from

Warren and man-handle him into a vehicle. My mother had a serious drinking problem, too, but she did not have the same predilection to violence.

In my fourth year at Scots, at the age of 15, I was recalled to the family property when my father became sick. Dad was taken to Tullamore District Hospital which was basic and ill-equipped. There was no such thing as dialysis and the world's first successful kidney transplant was three years away. In July 1956 I travelled to Sydney for an operation on an undescended teste. As I was recovering in hospital, we received news that my father was gravely ill and my maternal grandmother arranged to have me discharged a day or so earlier than planned. She then collected me and my two sisters from boarding school at PLC Croydon and helped us board a flight to Parkes. We were met by a neighbour, Stan Baker, who told us that my father was very ill. It was not until we reached Tullamore by car that we learned my father had died that morning, 18 July 1956, in a lonely hospital bed from kidney failure. He was to be buried that very afternoon.

And so, on a chilly July afternoon on what would have been my father's 44th birthday, I joined a large group of men with sombre faces in a procession of cars behind a hearse as it made its way from the Presbyterian Church in Tullamore to the cemetery on the edge of the town. Hundreds of men and women from the district and far beyond gathered for the memorial service. As was the practice of the times, only the men took part in the burial, standing heads bowed, hats off, around Dad's final resting place. I could smell the freshly dug earth in the air as they lowered the coffin of one of the town's most respected men into the grave.

As my Dad's casket disappeared below the surface, I burst into tears. I was ashamed because I'd always been taught that grown men don't cry. It felt like his final, frank and simple message to me: "Dry your eyes, son, and become the best man you can be. Then, when your time comes, you too can be laid to rest without regret." Engraved on my father's headstone is written, "Here lies a man." This is a perfect epitaph for an extraordinary man. At the age of 16, I resolved to honour my father by becoming the best man I could be, beginning by obeying his solemn instructions not to touch a drop of alcohol until I reached the age of 21.

I took as my motto the words of Alfred Lord Tennyson in his poem Ulysses: "To strive, to seek, to find, and not to yield." Tennyson wrote these words on the death of his very close friend, Arthur Hallam, and it was fitting that I should adopt them upon the death of my beloved father.

## CHAPTER 3

# A TIME TO DANCE

There is a time for everything, and a season for every activity under heaven.

ECCLESIASTES 3:1

Adulthood began abruptly the day we laid my father to rest in a country graveyard on the edge of town barely three months after my 16th birthday. My mother moved back to the city where my two younger sisters were at boarding school leaving me to manage Jumble Plains and its team of adult workers. It was a tough, three-year apprenticeship during which I became skilled at sheep shearing, wool classing, mulesing, castrating, mustering on horseback, farming and managing men. I slaughtered and butchered all the meat consumed on the property. Natural disasters were a frequent challenge: droughts, floods, bushfires and rabbit plagues.

The first thing I learned was the need for planning. I had mastered the basic skills. I knew how to prepare the rams for mating with the ewes and how to earmark, cut off the tails and castrate the male lambs. I could dip them and snip them, crutch them and shear them. My father had taught me the skills of Mulesing, drenching, and treating fly-blown sheep. What I did not yet understand was sequencing, for as Solomon in the Book of Ecclesiastes wisely explains, "There is a time for everything, and a season for every activity under heaven: a time to be born and a time to die, a time to plant and a time to uproot." (Ecclesiastes 3:1-2)

Managing finite time according to natural sequences is key to success in any career and indeed in life. In farming, the discipline of executing predictable tasks in an organised way leaves you better prepared to deal with those that are less predictable. And at Jumble Plains there were plenty of those. Within months of taking charge, Jumble Plains was hit by the worst flood anybody could recall as the creek that ran through the property backed up and overflowed. The Big Wet of 1956, caused by high rainfalls in Western Queensland and other parts of the Murray Darling catchment, caused record floods in river towns like Wentworth and Mildura and was judged South Australia's worst ever catastrophe. It seemed as if the surface water across our flat paddocks would never drain away. Five vehicles were bogged and abandoned in various parts of the property for months on end.

We had not long completed shearing when the floods came, stopping access for the trucks that would have taken the pressed bales to the railhead bound for Sydney. The sheep had been damp from the rain when shorn and so when the wool was eventually unpacked in Sydney eight months later, much of it was stained. This had a huge impact on the price we received. To add to the problems, we could not muster the sheep to bring them back in for dipping. The result was the lice caused extensive itching and the sheep rubbed off much of their wool trying to relieve themselves, damaging the following year's clip.

Necessity, as they say, is the mother of invention. For eight months we were forced to park our vehicles at the boundary gate and to walk or wade the last mile into the homestead. The problem was carrying in supplies. I discovered two old perambulators in the storeroom and turned one of them into a dual-wheeled vehicle to enable it to traverse the boggy ground. It passed the test, even when carrying fresh batteries for our 32-volt home lighting system. Like Noah, I brought the batteries in two at a time, making 8 return trips, a total of 16 miles.

I felt I could turn my hand to anything, even learning to play an instrument. In Sydney shortly before my father became seriously ill, I had fallen in love with an SML alto saxophone in the window of the then leading music store, Palings. It was a beautiful instrument, made in Paris by the firm Strasser Marigaux & Lemair and carried a price tag of 105 pounds, or around three and half thousand dollars in today's money. I raided my savings account and ordered it, imaging myself as the next Charlie Parker.

When it arrived, I followed the instruction in the accompanying manual to discover where to place my fingers and thumbs. I had no idea how to read music but I managed to figure out the basics and slowly began to pick up which notes to play. It was a little while before I realised that the alto saxophone was pitched in E flat and therefore all the music had to be transposed into another key. After a while I became reasonably fluent in this and could transpose on the fly.

My friend Brian, who lived on a property about 30 km away, was teaching himself to play the trumpet. From time to time we got together and tried playing some tunes. We were both big fans of Glenn Miller and learned a few of his popular songs from those days. We linked up with another friend, who fancied himself as a drummer, whose mother, fortunately, played the piano. Thus, began the Tullamore Modernaires, named after the Glenn Miller Modernaires. We soon had our first engagement at a ball in Tullamore.

When our pianist decided not to continue, I felt it was time to teach myself the piano. I purchased a book of chord symbols and was able to create the base and all the harmonies using that model. I therefore only had to read the melody, together with the chord symbol. After a few months I became quite proficient. During this time, we were flood bound and effectively trapped in the homestead and I therefore had lots of time to practice. Ambition got the better of me when I purchased a clarinet, which was pitched in b flat, requiring another transposition. I never learned to master it and performed on the piano almost exclusively.

In those days in the country, ballroom dancing was a huge social event. During the winter especially, each town had a range of balls sponsored by such organisations as the local hospital, the Catholic church, the Red Cross, and the Country Women's Association. Big events included the local picnic race club, but the feature was the Bachelors' and Spinsters' ball. Every town in the bush had a number of these events and there was no shortage of engagements.

After a while I got to know musicians in other orchestras and began the business of hiring them for individual events.

I would receive a call from the organiser of the Nyngan Golf Club to ask if I could play for its event next August. How many pieces would you like in the orchestra was my first question. The second was from when to when. Typically, we would have four to six musicians and be engaged from about 8:30 pm until 2 am. I would give a price and usually be engaged on the spot. I then had to round up the players who would be living in a range of towns and settle on their rates (which I well knew) and travel allowances.

Almost always, as the night wore on and people consumed more beers, the cry went up to stay on past 2 am. Often the organisers took the hat around and the dancers contributed money to keep us engaged. Frequently, we made more money in the next one, two and sometimes three hours than we did in the entire period prior to our scheduled two o'clock shutdown.

We then had the tiring drive back to our various homes, sometimes 100-200 kilometres. It was hard getting up the next day for work.

Later, while living in Nyngan, I drove the 170 kilometres to Dubbo every week to lead a small group at the famous Castlereagh Hotel lounge on Saturday night, returning to Nyngan the next day. In those days, people really appreciated the music and there was total silence whilst we played three or four numbers, when they clapped, before we launched into another bracket. On one occasion, I was invited to play at the Australia Hotel in Pitt Street, recognized as the most prestigious in Australia. The hotel was later replaced with the MLC Centre and as a memento I purchased the #1 barber's chair which I put in my cellar. One can only imagine which famous hotel guests might have sat in the chair over the years.

I had also developed a passion for cricket, which I began to play at Scots, where I learned the art of wicketkeeping. Back in Jumble Plains at the start of the 1955 season, my father introduced me to our local team, Topwoodlands, a mere 35km away. When my father became ill, I was able to get a driver's licence at age 15 and drove myself to the matches. I was invited to be the wicketkeeper for the Topwoodlands Colts, and was later appointed captain, leading out the team on ovals of graded red dirt. As a wicketkeeper, I had little problem coping with uneven bounces from cracks in the wicket, which was a concrete strip covered with coir matting. However, the first ball I received flew off the pitch and hit me in the chest giving me an awful whack. After the lush, irrigated turf of Scots, I was going to have to adapt to a faster pace

A love of cricket rarely desserts you. Later I persuaded the famous Arthur Morris to sign my application to join the Sydney Cricket Ground, but even with his endorsement, it was 19 years before I was finally admitted by which time we were living in Houston. I enjoy the pleasure of taking friends to key matches there and also using the reciprocal arrangement to visit Lords in London from time to time.

Tennis was perhaps an even more popular sport and form of recreation in the country in my days. We had our own court at Jumble Plains and I played a lot there with workmen on the property. I also played virtually every weekend in tournaments in surrounding country towns—often driving to and from the venue each day. In 1958, I won the under 19 doubles championship in Tullamore with Malcolm Dawes. When I lived in Tottenham, I was elected president of the local tennis club which also had its annual tournament, attracting players from far and wide. Later, when Rae and I settled in Warren in our first matrimonial home, I was elected president of the Warren Tennis Club. We also held an annual tournament and, I am proud to say, Rae won the ladies doubles with our long-time friend, Jill Parker. I regret to say my tennis prowess faded when, in my mid-forties, our teenage son, Scott, beat me in singles. We were living in Houston, Texas, at the time and I remember being humiliated.

Later, when we were living in Atlanta, Georgia, I was invited to play in the Grand Master Tennis Classic in Florida. A pro-am fund-raiser, held in March 1988, the players included many of the all-time greats of tennis, including a raft of Australians such as Fred Stolle, Mal Anderson, Owen Davidson and Roy Emerson. I was paired with Roy Emerson to play the opening match on the centre court in front of a packed stadium. At that time, Roy Emerson had won more grand-slams than any person in history.

I was nervous amongst such greats (Fred Stolle was in the opposite court). It was windy, and I hit up very badly. We tossed for the first serve and Emerson and I won. Roy Emerson immediately handed me the balls and said, "You serve." I tried to beg off, but Emerson insisted. I was petrified.

Nonetheless I went to the sideline to take off my track-suit in readiness. After removing my jacket, I pulled down my track pants. A few second later there was a roar from the crowd in the stadium. I was puzzled, but then looked down and realised that I had also pulled down my tennis shorts and was standing there in my underpants!

Among other professionals was Cliff Drysdale, originally from South Africa who was then a commentator on CNN.

After we had moved back to Australia, Cliff came and stayed with us in Sydney, inviting us as his guest to the Masters tennis tournament, which was won by Lleyton Hewitt.

Looking back at my teenage self, I see a young man fired by the conviction that nothing was beyond his reach. Despite the burden of managing a sheep property, thrust upon me at a young age, nothing could stop me becoming a dance band leader or captaining Australia in the Ashes if I really tried. For that good fortune I am indebted to my father, and the spirt of the Scottish pioneers he came from. I also had the fortune to come of age at a special time in Australia, a time of a booming economy and expanding opportunity. It was a country led by a man who like my father was born into a family of enterprising, industrious and inventive pioneers: Sir Robert Gordon Menzies. Menzies' Liberal philosophy began with the conviction that individual freedom was the foundation of a civilised society. The most important freedom of all, he said, was the freedom to do your best and make your best better. It was a freedom my father taught me to grasp with both hands.

Anthony de Mello, an Indian Jesuit priest and psychotherapist, tells a story I'm certain Dad would have appreciated about a farmer who found an eagle's egg which he put in the nest of a hen. The eagle hatched with the brood and grew up thinking he was a chicken, scratching the earth for worms and insects, clucking and cackling, thrashing his wings, never flying more than a metre or so into the air.

Years passed and the eagle grew old. One day he saw a magnificent bird above him in the cloudless sky. It glided majestically on the powerful wind currents, with scarcely a beat of its golden wings. The old eagle looked up in awe.

"Who's that?" he asked. "That's the eagle, the king of the birds," said his friend. "He belongs to the sky. But we belong to the earth—we're chickens."

If we are to succeed as leaders, we must not fear to believe we can be eagles. My father taught me the importance of self-belief. He encouraged me to put aside any fears or doubts about my ability to achieve what I had set out to do. His example emboldened me to strive to become a leader in new businesses, in different countries around the world. Contrary to popular opinion, Nobel Prize-winning economist James Heckman's research reveals that innate intelligence plays, at best, a one to two percent role in a child's future success. Instead, success stems from conscientious self-discipline, per-severance and diligence. You cannot control luck, but you can control how conscientious you are; how diligent you are; how persistent you are.

In my early fifties after experiencing some leadership success, I had the good fortune to have a private lunch with one of America's most famous head-hunters. This man was responsible for recruiting some of the top people in the USA. When I asked him what he looked for in a person meant to fill the shoes of the chairman of Citibank, or the president of General Motors, his answer was simple: someone who began work early. He was much less interested in whether the prospect had a degree from Harvard or had captained a top college football team. Rather, he looked for someone who was out working at a young age.

Many leaders come from broken families and through necessity have had to get out and get things done. As a result, they generally mature quickly, cannot countenance failure and are driven to succeed. They are not afraid to "have a go," and most of all they have persistence. When I reflected on this I thought about my own circumstances.

Looking back on my life now I believe my successes stemmed largely from an unrelenting determination to succeed, combined with perseverance and a willingness to work hard. These characteristics were laid down during my upbringing on the family sheep station, and even more so after being forced at a young age to take on huge responsibilities.

You may not be smarter than everyone else. You may not be as talented as others around you. You may not have the same connections, or the great education of your peers. But you can substitute intelligence with hard work—and, over time, hard work bears fruit. You can always be more persistent than others. You can always be more disciplined, and discipline, science says, will have the biggest impact of all on your pursuit of success.

Interestingly, according to research, conscientious spouses perform more household tasks, exhibit more pragmatic behaviour and promote a more satisfying home life. I was ignorant of that fact 60 years ago, as I sped around western NSW from the sheep dip to the cricket pitch to the dancehall. Indeed, I had no idea who my spouse might be. I was about to find out.

My three years of running Jumble Plains taught me the best and the worst of living on the land. We had recovered from the setback of the floods and the wool market was strong but the estate taxes following my father's death were punishing. After 32 years in the hands of three generations of McLellan's, the property had to be sold. I became a stock and station agent and auctioneer starting with the Australian Mercantile Land & Finance Company Limited in Sydney.

I was sent to Young—a large livestock sales centre—to learn auctioneering. I was excited at the opportunity. I purchased some slick, fashionable clothes, hoping to make an impression on my new work colleagues and headed for Central Station in Sydney to catch the train to Young. After an all-night journey in the middle of winter, I stepped off the train at Young Station in the early hours of the morning, with the frost thick on the ground. The manager of the Young Branch was kind enough to meet me at the station and take me to my hotel which became my home away from home for the next few weeks. After a shave and a shower, I walked the few doors to the company's office in the main street.

The manager was keen to get me started. He began by gathering the team in a large room to introduce me to my new co-workers. "Well, Tony", he began, "why don't you share with us all the news from Head Office." I was flattered. I puffed myself up and took a commanding position on the cold, linoleum floor in the centre of the room. My feet were cold from the journey and the frost, so I casually placed a foot on the kerosene heater set at full-on. After speaking for a minute or two someone blurted out, "What's that smell?" The acrid odour of burning rubber was thick in the air. It was the crepe soles on my new—oh so chic—desert boots melting on top of the heater. As I pulled my foot away there was a loud sucking sound as the foam rubber stuck to the cold linoleum floor. As I retreated, I left a trail of foam rubber across the meeting room floor. It was an inauspicious beginning.

After Young, I was invited to open a new office in Nyngan, where I was the second-in-command. The branch did well and after a couple of years I was invited to manage the WH Bertram stock and station agency in Tottenham. It involved a lot of travel on rough country roads over a wide area. Apart from inspecting and selling sheep, I also assisted a local trader in buying wool from properties, principally in the Far West, having completed a course and qualified as a wool-classer. On one occasion I drove 629 miles (more than 1,000 kilometres) over rough bush roads and tracks in one day, inspecting 13 mobs of sheep and selling 12 of them.

Apart from my business activities, I was president of the Tottenham Tennis Club and also captain of the Topwoodlands Colts cricket team. Both these activities involved quite a lot of travelling during the weekends. I was living at the Tottenham Hotel and when I was in town ate in the dining room. I had a large round table in the corner which I shared with the local bank teller and others from time to time.

On Monday morning 5 October 1959, I was late for breakfast and found an attractive young lady seated at "my" table. I was taken aback. The only strangers who joined us were normally travelling salesmen. When the young lady left, my bank teller friend told me she was a new schoolteacher in town. At lunch we introduced ourselves and started a hesitant conversation. The young lady, whose name was Rae, had arrived on the Saturday night before, following a 16-hour train ride from Bathurst. She had joined the other two teachers in town. I also learned that she was about to move into a boarding house around the corner.

That night, after dinner, I went upstairs to the lounge where I played the piano for an hour or so, as I often did. On her way to her bedroom, Rae stopped by the lounge and complimented me on the music. I shall never forget: at that moment I was playing the romantic, slow-waltz, "Ramona", which has remained a favourite of ours ever since. I seized the opportunity and invited Rae to drive with me out to see some old friends—about a 50-kilometre trip over corrugated dirt roads through bush with lots of kangaroos. Almost instantly, she said she would come, although later she revealed she was quite frightened. I had known the family we were planning to visit ever since I was a boy—the parents were friends of my late father and mother. The son, Brian, was a trumpet player in several of my orchestras.

We had to pass through many farm gates before we arrived at the relatively new homestead, and enjoyed a pleasant, relaxed evening. Brian and I played some music, we had a cup of tea and some supper and headed back home reasonably early. I did not drink alcohol in those days; indeed, my father had promised me that if I did not smoke or drink before I was 21, he would give me 1000 pounds. When my father died, my mother honoured the promise by buying me a new Austin Healey 100/6. It was simply magnificent and was the talk of the town.

I learned that Rae had had an amazing life. She was born in Peak Hill in Central West NSW on 9 August 1940. Her parents had separated when Rae was only a few months old and her mother returned to Sydney with Rae's older sister, Robyn. We have never found out why, but custody of Rae was left to her 24-year-old father, Lennox Stanley Parker Hand, who immediately passed Rae to his parents, Alfred Thomas and Viola Hand, who raised Rae as their own daughter, first in Peak Hill, then at Regents Park in Sydney and later in the tiny town of Buxton, in the Southern Highlands of NSW. Rae's grandfather was born in Yeoval, NSW, on 11 September 1879 to Thomas and Martha Ann Hand and died on 10 March 1951, when Rae was 10 years old. Her grandmother, Viola Hand (nee Wright), was born in Moruya, NSW, on 18 September 1885. She was one of eight children—six girls and two boys—whose parents owned a dairy farm. She died on 9 November 1969, when Rae was 29 and we were living in Melbourne at the time. Alfred Thomas and Viola Hand were married in 1916 in Auburn, NSW.

Rae's grandmother grounded Rae in the fundamentals of faith and life. Indirectly, so much of who I am and what I have accomplished I owe to that wonderful Christian woman. Although raised in modest circumstances, Rae learned to stick to it and, inspired by her wonderful Christian grandmother, she learned that when times are tough we need to pull our-selves up by our bootstraps and get going. Rae applied herself with great intensity. She skipped a year in school, graduated from Balmain Teachers' College and was in front of her first class as a certified schoolteacher at age 18. After a few months as a relief teacher in Oberon, Tottenham was her next appointment. It was there we first met.

Apart from ballroom dancing, tennis was the most pop-ular activity of people from the bush. I happened to enjoy it as much as anyone and was president of the local tennis club in Tottenham, and later Warren where we lived. In the town of Trangie was a young lady (17 at the time) Lesley Turner, who was a budding world tennis champion. Lesley, over two decades from the late 1950s to the late 1970s won 13 major titles, including the French singles championship twice (on one occasion beating Margaret Smith Court in straight sets). She also won seven doubles championships at all four majors, together with four mixed. In 1997, she was inducted into the Hall of Fame. Coming from the little country town of Trangie, Lesley made all of us from the bush so proud.

On the road to Trangie, where I was to lead my dance orchestra, Rae and I crossed the Bogan River at Dandaloo, a township immortalised by Banjo Paterson:

> On western plains, where shade is not,
>    'Neath summer skies of cloudless blue,
> Where all is dry and all is hot,
>    There stands the town of Dandaloo—
> A township where life's total sum
> Is sleep, diversified with rum.

As we scooted along the long dirt road in my Holden utility (pickup) I saw an unusually large black snake crossing the road ahead. "Let me show you how we handle this," I said to Rae. I jammed on the brakes and skidded over the snake breaking its back close to its tail. Having pulled up, I walked nonchalantly back to the snake, asking Rae "Have you ever seen anyone crack the head off a snake?"

"No," she replied, "but be careful."

My plan was to grab the snake by its tail, swing it around over my head and then crack it like a stock whip. As I reached down to grab its tail, however, it suddenly reared up, standing at least a metre high, spun 180 degrees and struck at me. I leapt back just far enough so that it hit the ground with a loud crack only centimetres from me. I abandoned that plan and set about the snake with a large branch from the side of the road. Once I was satisfied that it could do no harm, I picked up the now dead snake by its tail, swung it over my head and cracked its head off, which flew into the bush. Satisfied I had made a good impression, I got back into the utility to drive on to Trangie. Suddenly Rae let out a loud scream. There on the dashboard in front of her was the forked tongue of the snake. How it got detached from the snake's head and found its way through the open window in the vehicle is anyone's guess.

Our courtship continued and involved quite a lot of ball-room dancing, with me frequently leading the orchestra. Rae became recognised as an outstanding dancer and she was asked to judge ballroom dancing competitions all over the region. On one occasion I remember us driving 240 kilometres to a dance where Rae judged the competition. We then had to drive 240 kilometres back to Tottenham at two o'clock in the morning on rough, corrugated country roads with the ever-present danger of hitting a kangaroo.

Rae and I became engaged on her 20th birthday on Friday 9 August 1960. On the Saturday night before, we had a rare dinner celebration with my mother, my stepfather, my maternal grandfather—and his family—whom I had only met on three or four occasions. The dinner was to celebrate my grandfather's 70th birthday on 8 August and our forthcoming engagement the following day. It is no surprise that both of Rae's parents were somewhat nervous about our forthcoming marriage at the age of 20. Their marriage at a similar age only lasted three years before they were separated. The great blessing is that our marriage has lasted 60 years.

We were married on 19 January 1961 at All Saints Church, Parramatta, followed by a reception at Oatlands House, Dundas. Back then, long before emails and text messages, the standard form of communication was a telegram. The job of the best man was to read to those attending the wedding reception the pile of congratulatory cables. One we received which I shall never forget was simply:

CONGRATULATIONS STOP
TOPWOODLANDS COLTS BOWLS
ANOTHER MAIDEN OVER STOP

We spent the first two nights of our honeymoon in the newly built Chevron Hilton in Macleay Street, Potts Point, then regarded as the height of international luxury. Each room came with a remote-control TV and built-in radio in a panel attached to the desk. The ensuite bathroom with gold fittings, including the toilet seat-cover, added to the sense of opulence. It was just as well since it was costing us 9 pounds a night, almost half my weekly salary. On the second night we bought front-row tickets to see the American singer and actor Robert Goulet. During the evening the singer of French-Canadian ancestry came over, leant down, and kissed Rae's hand. She has never forgotten that and swears that she didn't wash it until after Goulet's death in 2007.

Our first matrimonial home was a tiny weatherboard and fibro-cement home in Warren, for which we paid 3000 pounds. There I managed one of the largest private stock and station agencies in New South Wales, specialising in Merino stud rams. Active in our local community, I was elected president of the tennis club and captain of the local cricket team. I was later appointed captain of the Far West under-25 representative cricket team. Located at the end of the railway line, Warren was a centre for much traffic in livestock. Large mobs were often driven down from Queensland to the nearest railhead of Warren. I remember once getting a call at 6 am on a Sunday morning asking if I could find a mob of 1000 "bally" steers being driven from Queensland to Warren. I promptly headed off, tracing the stock-routes before finally finding the mob. I rode around on horseback checking them out, and when I got back home reported back to the owner in Queensland.

Our life in Warren was busy—as it always seemed to be. We returned from our honeymoon at the end of January 1961, so that Rae could take up her teaching duties in the first week of February. I reported to my Uncle Malcolm, the principal of the firm, Lane & Fuller. Not long after, on 31 March, Ron Gorman, who was, in effect, the second in command, committed suicide in his apartment above the offices. On my 21st birthday, therefore, I stepped in as Malcolm's deputy. Later, Malcolm had a major heart operation in Sydney and was out of the office for several months, leaving me in charge.

Approximately 18 months after we were married, Rae had become pregnant and developed unexpected symptoms, for which she had numerous gamma globulin injections. She was admitted to the local hospital where, after three months of pregnancy, she gave birth to a hydatidiform mole, a pre-cancerous tumour that enlarges in the uterus much more rapidly than a normal pregnancy. Fortunately, the sister in charge at the local hospital immediately diagnosed Rae's problem and she was rushed by ambulance to Dubbo Hospital for a D&C procedure. There she was nursed by Joy Hood—my previous girlfriend before I met Rae—who cared for Rae in a very kind and gracious way.

Rae was warned against falling pregnant again for at least two years and she decided to return to school teaching and encouraged me to move to Sydney. I saw the chance for new opportunities including resuming my education that had been hurriedly abandoned when my father became ill. Two months later, my snake-cracking days were over and we were off to the big city.

## CHAPTER 4

# REACH FOR THE SKY

Keep your eyes on the stars, but don't forget that your feet are necessarily on the earth.

THEODORE ROOSEVELT

The Sydney to which we moved in 1962 was young and ambitious, a city of more than two million that was fast going up in the world. The 26-story AMP Building on Circular Quay was just being completed and at 384 feet (117m) was the tallest building in Australia. It signalled the start of the high-rise construction boom that would transform the urban landscape, make and break fortunes, and provide a start to a professional career for a determined, energetic boy from the bush like me. The vibrant demand for commercial and retail space reflected structural changes in the economy and the transition of the city into an international financial centre. Between 1958 and 1976, 210 new buildings were constructed in central Sydney, 84 of which were built after 1971.

Rae applied to be transferred as a teacher from Warren to Ashfield where we moved in August so she could take up her appointment from the beginning of the third term in

September. We rented a brand new two-bedroom apartment in Benalla Avenue, within walking distance of Rae's school and the Ashfield train station. My maternal grandmother was living a short distance away in an apartment on Frederick Street where we visited her from time to time.

I had become interested in property valuation, encouraged by Rae, and in my impatience to qualify, I made up my mind to do two courses at the same time, one organised by the Real Estate Institute in conjunction with the University of Sydney and the second by the Commonwealth Institute of Valuers which was entitled, The Valuation of Real Estate and Landed Interests.

I was offered a job in the property department of The Mutual Life and Citizens' Assurance Company Limited at North Sydney, a train ride from Ashfield. My office was in the company's landmark, modernist 12-storey building on Miller Street that towered above everything around giving it sweeping views across the harbour to the city and Circular Quay. The completion of the building in 1957 marked the start of North Sydney's growth as a centre for business. The building was opened by the Prime Minister, Robert Menzies, a Victorian born and bred, who wore his pride for Melbourne on his sleeve. On taking in the view from the top floor he declared that it had given him "such a new conception of Sydney that quite frankly I'm beginning to like the place." Before long, North Sydney had become the third-largest commercial centre in the country after the Sydney and Melbourne CBDs.

The senior executive was Terry Farrell, an outstanding man, and great mentor. When I told him that I intended to study land valuation he was very supportive.

I attended classes three or four nights a week either in the city or at the University of Sydney, which made for long days. I also set up a study group of fellow students at our apartment each Sunday morning, that was very helpful. In addition, I typed out extensive notes of what we had been told by the lecturers. I worked 50 plus weeks a year like this, sitting for exams at the end of each year. I was fascinated by the subject matter, which included law, surveying, building construction, interest tables and a host of other subjects and was committed to my studies. My first results were very satisfactory, having passed with honours. As we progressed, I became even more focused and intense in my studies, working late at night and every weekend taking no holidays.

On 23 November 1963, the day President John F. Kennedy was assassinated, (22nd in Dallas) we moved into our recently purchased home at 51 Thornleigh Street, Thornleigh. This was a brand new three-bedroom home a short walk from Thornleigh railway station and was on a tiny 40' x 120' lot. We had bought it for 4,000 pounds, the equivalent of around $120,000 today, although it would sell for close to $1 million on the open market in 2021. My employer, MLC, loaned me 100% of the cost on staff terms with an interest rate of 2 1/2 %. It was a lovely comfortable home, which provided a study for me and a spare bedroom for our first son, Anthony Scott, who arrived home from hospital on the day Australia converted from pounds, shillings and pence to decimal currency, 14 February 1966. We did a lot of work in the garden and were able to sell the house for a substantial gain when we decided to upgrade to a larger property when our second child, Stuart, was due. We moved into our new home, which we had purchased for $20,000, at 35 Wyvern Avenue, Chatswood, in May 1967. The profit on the sale of our Thornleigh home, together with the proceeds from the sale of our first matrimonial home in Warren, provided a substantial deposit on the purchase of our next home on the border with Roseville. This large home had sweeping views to the Blue Mountains and was on a large 10,000 square feet lot. Again, the debt was provided by MLC.

My intensive studies continued, passing my examinations with honours each year. In the final year, I won all the prizes, including the Val Donowa Award and the F.K. Sampson Memorial Prize. I was the only student who completed both courses without failing in any subject. In those days, you had to repeat the entire year if you failed in one subject. At my graduation, I was presented with the award by Bert Eastwood, the Valuer General of NSW, who told me I had obtained the highest grades since 1929. The year following my graduation, 1966, the Valuer General approached me and encouraged me to apply for the job of Valuer General of Sarawak, an appointment being sought by the British Overseas Foreign Service. This was very flattering to a young man who had just graduated. Eastwood assured me that if I were willing, he would be able to see me appointed. My responsibility would be to set up a valuation department, recruit the staff and then proceed to value every parcel of land, indeed every square inch, of Sarawak, to enable taxes to be levied. No small task for a 26-year-old "boy from the bush". After discussing it with Rae, I said, "Yes", and we began to make plans. We had our medical shots, required in those days. We then learned that President Sukarno of Indonesia had begun dropping paratroopers into

Malaysia. Rae got frightened and we decided not to move with our new baby, Scott. I have often thought of where the move to Sarawak might have led us, as opposed to the career I then pursued. Spending time in Sarawak years later, whilst on a cruise, only added to the intrigue.

Soon after graduating, I was elected the youngest director ever to the board of the Commonwealth Institute of Valuers, later the Australian Institute of Valuers and Land Economists. Appointed Chairman of the Legislation Review Committee; Chairman of the Fees, Standards and Ethics Committee and Convener of the Annual Conference. I was a keynote speaker at a number of conferences, including in Rotorua, New Zealand, and at the Real Estate Institute. It gave me an extensive set of letters to add to my CV: FCIV, REIV (Aust), QRV and LGV. Later, I was appointed a Member of the NSW Government Valuation Board of Review and in 1974 was elected a Justice of the Peace. I was invited to lecture to students in a variety of subjects, including the law relating to the resumption or compulsory acquisition of property and also the employment of interest tables in valuation. I enjoyed both these subjects intensely, and even wrote a textbook on interest tables. Later, I also was appointed by the Sydney Technical College to coach and grade correspondence students. One of the students I had was a man with whom I had indirectly done business but who was then in Goulburn prison for fraud.

In September 1967, I took up a position with the international firm of real estate consultants, Richard Ellis Sallmann & Seward, in their Sydney office. Within a year I was made a partner and invited to open the firm's office in Melbourne. That is when my real estate career took off. We purchased a new four-bedroomed property at North Balwyn, Melbourne, and moved to a new city, which we really enjoyed. My partners included Ken Menzies, the son of Sir Robert Menzies, Australia's longest serving Prime Minister. In Melbourne, I developed a number of landmark commercial projects in Melbourne city, St Kilda Road, and Toorak. During my time in Melbourne, I also launched the firm's new office in Adelaide in 1969. There, I was personally appointed as consultant to the Premier of South of Australia Steele Hall

The overriding feature of my life was long hours of work. All the feasibility studies were done manually with no electronic spread sheets. If an assumption (say the rental rate) changed, the numbers had to be erased and re-calculated. Doing these in pencil was therefore the norm and one always had an eraser in your pocket.

I was not into "clubbing", although that was considered important in sectors of society in Melbourne. Our *modus operandi* was home entertainment. Rae is an absolute master at that, and we have hosted hundreds, if not thousands, of dinner parties in all the 40+ homes in which we have lived over the years. Many of these have been focused on business. We even had formal dinner parties when the ladies wore long gowns and the men dressed in tuxedos. We managed to live in very nice, although not ostentatious, homes—made much more attractive by Rae's skills as an interior designer at which she practiced professionally for many years.

It was not until we moved to Melbourne that Rae got her first car. I drove a Valiant Regal, which was very comfortable without being too "showy". Later on, in Sydney I acquired my first BMW coupe, and then a Mercedes sedan. At one stage, when we lived in Houston, I remember buying matching top-of-the-line Mercedes; a sedan and a convertible. Rae's convertible later got car-jacked when we lived in Atlanta.

When we returned to Sydney and our two sons became old enough, we all had motorbikes and did trail-bike riding every weekend. This came to an abrupt end, however, when showing off on my friend's new motorbike, I tore my cruciate ligament, which was unable to be repaired.

Now, at our age, we each have beautiful cars (a Lexus LX-570 and a BMW M4) but they are nowhere as near important to us that they once were. Cruising is more our thing these days.

The highlight of our time in Melbourne was the promotion of the redevelopment of Melbourne's Civic Square, then the largest real estate project in Australia's history—from conception, through design drawings, preparation of cost estimates, feasibility studies, marketing, securing the financial backing from a client in London, to tender—all in thirty days. As a result, I was featured in a page three story in *The Australian*, "A skyscraping plan in 30 days flat." The article described me as having come from the country but eight years ago. "The hectic 30 days included a week's visit to London to seek the development proposals to the financial backers Star (Great Britain) Holdings Limited. The firm is also involved in negotiations for construction of a 60-storey hotel in Melbourne and an $18 million hotel and apartment complex in Kings Cross, Sydney."

It was no small accomplishment. In thirty days, we designed the proposed development, had the quantity surveyors estimate its costs, prepared detailed feasibility studies, packaged the lot up and headed to London where I had arranged a meeting with a new prospective client, Star (Great Britain) Holdings. We travelled on a BA VC-10, stopping endlessly (or so it seemed) in Sydney, Nadi, Honolulu, and Los Angeles, where we had time to freshen up with a shower and change of clothes. Back on the plane, we headed to New York and eventually to Heathrow, London. I was travelling with the architect and two assistants and we were all exhausted when we finally checked into the Hilton Hotel on Park Lane.

Unfortunately, we left in the taxi all the drawings rolled in a cylinder and did not realise our mistake until we had checked in and settled in our rooms. It was panic stations! Without the drawings, we would have little to show my client the following morning. Trying to trace a London black taxi in a fleet of 25,000 was an impossible task. As luck would have it, the architect had given the taxi driver a big tip when he dropped us off and when he spotted the plans an hour or so later he came back to the hotel and dropped them off. The doorman had been alerted and immediately brought the plans to the room and the architect rushed down and gave the taxi driver an even bigger tip. It was a miraculous escape from what could have been a disaster.

Our meetings with the clients went well and they committed to bid for the project, which we later submitted and for which were awarded the development rights.

I returned to Australia separately from the others, first flying to New York on the brand-new PAN Am Jumbo. When checking in, the lady told me that I may have been the first Australian passenger on what was an absolutely extraordinary plane. The First Class was packed with Americans—many in Texas hats—who all rushed upstairs to the bar as soon as the seat belts had been switched off. The enduring memory was, however, the enormous size of the plane.

At age 29, I was elected senior partner and returned to Sydney. There I conceived and negotiated Australia's largest commercial office lease contract and advised on the development of several landmark projects.

I serviced a range of major company clients, including the then world's largest property company, Hong Kong Land. I had many trips to Hong Kong on behalf of Hong Kong Land and others, including Jardine Matheson. Working with the managing director of Hong Kong Land and his colleagues, I purchased the site for its new Mandarin Hotel in Sydney and also lodged a bid for several projects in the Rock area. At one stage, I was approached to consider becoming the next managing director of Hong Kong Land, when Vernon Roberts retired, and Rae and I spoke about the possibility of moving there. One of the attractions was that the boss lived in one of only about 50 houses on Hong Kong island. I always stayed in the exquisite Mandarin Hotel, which was owned by Hong Kong Land and a short walk to the Hong Kong Land offices. Rae and I visited for a week or so, staying in the Excelsior, investigating the possibility of moving there before deciding to stay with what I had.

One of those who had encouraged me to take on the role in Hong Kong was Arthur Little, an extremely personable man with wide property development and building experience. He was married to the charming Molly. They spent much of their time on Pittwater.

Arthur and I frequently enjoyed lunch with Jeffrey Penfold-Hyland, the great grandson of Christopher Rawson Penfold, who emigrated to South Australia in the early 19th century and established the Penfold wine company. Naturally, Geoffrey always offered Penfolds to the guests. In those days Grange Hermitage sold for around $10 a bottle, the equivalent of around $60 at today's prices, and I used to buy it from Geoffrey by the case. Perhaps I should have kept it since a 1976 vintage would sell for four figures at auction today.

Arthur was a marvellous raconteur. One day he told the story of some land he had in Adelaide, which he had sold to a subdivision developer, whose name was Berg, as I recall. The developer had signed a note for a substantial part of the purchase price and he called Arthur to ask if he could roll it over for another year. "No", said Arthur, "I would like the note to be settled when it falls due."

Berg proposed that they meet in Melbourne to discuss the issue and offered to put up Arthur at what was then regarded as the most luxurious hotel in Australia: the Intercontinental on Exhibition Street. Arthur was met at the airport by a chauffeur and taken to the hotel where Berg had reserved a luxurious corner suite. As he was hanging up his clothes there was a knock at his door and there stood an attractive 25-year-old lady. "Mr. Little", she began, "Mr. Berg has asked me to provide any assistance you might need over the weekend." Arthur turned to me and said very intently, "Tony, you know I am a married man, so I turned and addressed her sternly. 'Young lady,' I said, 'I will give you 24-hours to get out of this room.'"

At Hong Kong Land I got to know Robin De Morgan, who was then the CFO, and we have been friends ever since.

On a trip to Sydney, Robin visited Rae in hospital on 13 April 1972, the night before she was scheduled to have an induction. Robin was a party to the selection of the name Samantha, should it have been a girl (which it was).

In addition, I was appointed real estate consultant to Metropolitan Properties, which was also interested in developing in The Rocks. In the meantime, the company flew me, together with Rae, to Singapore for a few weeks as we considered projects there, including in partnership with Shell, and also Tan Sri Khoo Tek Puat who later purchased Southern Pacific Properties from Peter Munk's group.

I also acted for the Duke of Westminster's Grosvenor Estates, on whose behalf I made the most expensive land sale in Australia for the National Australia Bank's Sydney head office. I also consulted for the AMP Society on the development of the Centrepoint project—which was then the tallest building in the southern hemisphere.

During the 1970s, whilst senior partner of the Richard Ellis organisation, I acquired anonymously a substantial part of a whole central business district block on behalf of the Metropolitan Water Sewerage and Drainage Board (now Sydney Water). The acquisition was not announced until 1981, by which time I was living in Toronto, Canada.

Featured on the front cover of Rydges business magazine, I was described in an extensive article as a young "new breed" real estate consultant who "has already made a name for himself in the competitive world of real estate development." The first to predict a downturn in office occupancies, I was pilloried in some sections of the press, but later vindicated when my forecast came to pass due to the significant acceleration in the development of new office space in the early 1970s.

In a rare honour I was appointed by the NSW Government as its real estate consultant for the redevelopment of The Rocks area—a historic 24-hectare site on the harbour in downtown Sydney. This was a huge undertaking with all the modelling done manually in those days. The irascible Jack Mundey, the secretary of the NSW Builders' Labourers Federation oversaw the imposition of the first of a series of Green Bans on the redevelopment of the Rocks.

In 1973, I incorporated Camenae Corporation in partnership with a major financial institution owned by the Commercial Banking Company of Sydney Limited. In the face of a severe recession, in less than three years I built Camenae into Sydney's leading developer of home units and town house complexes. At the same time, I incorporated a successful marketing company, A. Anthony McLellan Pty Limited, which marketed and sold over 90% of Camenae's new home units and townhouses.

Ever since I left the land, I have worked at least 60 hours or six days a week. This has been a big factor in my successes, but left me too little time with my family, including our young children, and to care for my wife. It was not until I was 47 that I came to my senses and started paying attention to my spiritual life, although, even at 81, I still spend too much time in the office.

The word "perseverance" is defined in most dictionaries as "persistence", or "determination". The difference between perseverance and obstinacy is that one comes from a strong will and the other from a strong won't.

I had first met Peter Munk when I invited him in 1975 to a board room lunch in my office at Camenae Capital Corporation in Sydney. Peter had recently moved to Sydney to assume the chairmanship of Travelodge Australia Limited, in which his company had a substantial interest. I had done business with Travelodge over the years and was keen to meet the new chairman.

It so happened on that day I had some other impressive guests, including Justice Rae Else-Mitchell, the chief judge of the Land and Valuation Court; Charlie Oliver, the President of the Australian Workers Union, who had shorn sheep on our family property in western New South Wales; Dick Bird, the NSW Valuer General; Leon Carter, the town clerk of the City of Sydney; and a number of other interesting personalities.

## CHAPTER 5

# AN EGYPTIAN MIRAGE

Nothing in the world can take the place of persistence. Talent will not; nothing is more common than unsuccessful men with talent. Genius will not; unrewarded genius is almost a proverb. Education will not; the world is full of educated derelicts. Persistence and determination alone are omnipotent.

PRESIDENT CALVIN COOLIDGE

The day after our board room lunch, Peter Munk called and told me it was the most stimulating lunch he had ever been to and he invited me to meet with him privately so we could get to know one another better. Peter had recently moved to Sydney to assume the chairmanship of Travelodge Australia Limited, in which his Hong Kong-based company, Southern Pacific Hotel Corporation, had a 58 per cent share. I had done business with Travelodge over the years and was keen to get to know the new chairman, a charismatic Hungarian-born Canadian businessman, investor, and philanthropist.

At our subsequent meeting in Peter's office in York Street in the city, Peter told me about an extraordinary project he was planning in Egypt. He was aware that I had been a consultant on several major development projects, including the redevelopment of the 60-acre Sydney Rocks area. The New South Wales Government had sought applications for this prestigious position but I was "too busy" on other matters and did not apply. Later, I was personally approached by a member of Bob Askin's Liberal government and offered the role of real estate advisor to the Sydney Cove Redevelopment Authority for the entire project.

Peter outlined his project, known as Pyramids Oasis, on the outskirts of Cairo, a new city that would house 45,000 people on a 10,000-acre property by the Great Pyramids of Giza, the oldest of the Seven Wonders of the Ancient World, and the best preserved. The project was planned as an integrated residential/tourist complex and was to have a Robert Trent Jones championship golf course, five hotels, a tourist village, commercial centre, 6,500 villas and 5,500 apartments. The development required the clearing of the site near the pyramids at Giza, which in recent years had been blighted by the unregulated construction of ramshackle buildings, considered by the Government to be aesthetically and culturally incompatible with the site. In its place, Southern Pacific Properties planned to develop a unified and architecturally harmonious complex, designed by a team of world-renowned architects and town planners. Structures were to blend with the desert, respecting traditional architectural forms.

I marvelled at the audacity of the scheme, conceived by Southern Pacific Properties Limited in response to an invitation from the Egyptian Government of President Anwar el-Sadat. It was a time of great optimism in the Middle East that culminated with the signing of historic peace accords with Israel in January 1974 and September 1975. Only two years earlier, the countries had been at war in the Sinai Peninsula. As well as boosting tourism, Pyramids Oasis was planned as a vehicle for Arab and western investors seeking opportunities in Egypt that were then opening up in the wake of the epic peace deals.

Cairo's ability to continue growing in importance as a Middle-Eastern business and financial centre would have been enhanced. In addition, significant employment opportunities were anticipated from both the construction and the long-term operation of the complex.

When Peter asked if I would be prepared to give him some advice on this massive undertaking, I was both fascinated and flattered. I immediately accepted his offer to fly Rae and me to London to examine the drawings, and from there to Cairo to inspect the site and meet senior government officials and ministers.

I returned to Sydney mightily impressed. I delivered my thoughts to Peter at his home in Vaucluse, including some warnings about a number of issues I thought may prove to be troublesome. Peter was grateful for the advice and then asked a blunt question; "Would you go to Egypt and become the managing director of the project?"

"How nice of you to ask, Peter," I replied, "but I have a wife and family and sit in the corner office at my development company with fifty employees. I am very comfortable where I am and with what I am doing." But Peter persevered. Over a couple of weeks, he talked me into taking on an enormous business challenge that dwarfed anything I had done in my life.

On top of everything, I had to pack up the family and move to a foreign country. Rae, ever the pragmatist, and I set about the task of mastering Arabic.

We discovered Egypt as a country both burdened and blessed from its history. For thousands of years Egypt had been dominated by foreign powers. The Romans, the Ottoman Empire, the French and the British in the late 19th and 20th Century. On July 23, 1952, the armed forces led a popular revolution against the incumbent monarchy and three days later King Farouk abdicated. Prime movers in the uprising were Gamal Abdul Nasser and Anwar Sadat, but the senior General, Mohamed Naguib, was appointed as the figurehead President of the new Republic, to be replaced by Nasser a year later. Almost exactly two years after the *coup d'état*, on July 27, 1954, an agreement was signed with Great Britain to withdraw from Egypt, after 72 years of occupation.

Then, on October 31, 1956, in great nationalistic fervour, Nasser nationalised the Suez Canal, causing one of the great fracases of the 20th century. The Israelis launched an all-out blitzkrieg into Sinai and the British and French occupied the canal zone, against the wishes of the US secretary of state, John Foster Dulles. This vital waterway was blocked for years by the bombing of vessels in passage, and through the laying of mines. Nasser embarked on a frantic drive of pan-Arabism, trying to unite disparate parts of the Arab world against the common enemy, Israel. This was undertaken in spite of the fact that Egyptians don't generally regard themselves as Arabs. It was, however, sufficient to excite the Syrians and Jordanians in June 1967 to join Egypt in launching a disastrous six-day war against Israel.

Three years later, on September 28, 1970, President Nasser died of a massive heart attack. What followed were rare scenes of unbelievable adulation. An estimated 10 million people turned out in Cairo for the funeral; the body was almost snatched from the gun carriage and had to be moved to an armoured car, and thousands were killed in the crush or were drowned in the River Nile. The following month, on October 16, Sadat was elected president, 10 months after he had assumed the post of vice president under Nasser. In 1975 he was named "Man of the Year" by *Time* magazine. He was subsequently re-elected president by a landslide, using the popular method of scoring favoured by quasi-dictators. (The proposition is put to the general population seeking an affirmative vote. To the "yes' vote is added all those who did not vote, resulting in an assumed "yes" vote typically in the high nineties).

Among the steps president Sadat took which affected Southern Pacific Properties' relationship with Egypt included the passing of Presidential Decree 90 of 1971, whereby Egypt agreed to adhere to the Washington Convention. Later came the unexpected expulsion of many of the Soviet workers on 16 July 1972. Then on 6 October, Egypt launched a surprise attack on Israel, restoring Egyptian pride with "the glorious Sixth of October war."

Egypt was still suffering after the 1973 war—with Cairo blacked out much of the time—and it was in its infancy as a host to foreign investment, when, in February 1974, Southern Pacific Properties was invited to visit Egypt to discuss with Egyptian officials a possible investment in the tourist sector. In 1974, Law 43 was enacted, which was the embodiment of Sadat's "Open Door" policy through which Egypt aggressively sought foreign investment, offering favourable tax treatment, a special exchange rate, repatriation rights and, of particular interest to Southern Pacific Properties, guarantees against the sovereign risks of expropriation, confiscation or nationalisation, the fate of many projects under the Nasser regime.

Under its agreement with the government, Southern Pacific Properties and the Government Tourism Organisation, EGOTH, formed a new entity known as Egyptian Tourist Development Company (ETDC) to undertake the Pyramids Oasis project. The Egyptian Government designated the project a "national priority." Southern Pacific Properties commenced detailed field studies and in September 1974 submitted a comprehensive project proposal for the development of a tourist area on the Pyramids Plateau, including hotels, tourist villages, artisan's markets, a conference centre, an Egyptology centre, a golf course and recreational facilities including public gardens, an artificial lake and sports installations. A similar tourist city at Ras El Hekma was also planned to exploit the Mediterranean coast on a year-round basis.

The development was approved at the highest level of government. The Prime Minister spent several hours reviewing all aspects of the project concepts which were then personally presented by Southern Pacific Properties' chairman to President Sadat on September 22, 1974. The President gave his enthusiastic approval.

A Heads of Agreement outlining the parties' general obligations was executed the next day, on 23 September 1974.

The agreement provided for the formation of an Egyptian joint venture company to be incorporated under the provisions of the Investment Law. The capital was to be owned 40 per cent by the Government Tourism Organisation and 60 per cent by SPP (Middle East) Limited, a subsidiary of Southern Pacific Properties Limited.

By the terms of the Agreement, the Minister of Tourism undertook to obtain title and possession of the sites for the projects and to transfer usufruct title to the Joint Venture. (Usufruct title is a form of leasehold title, which reverts to the grantor at the end of the term—in this case the Egyptian Government—after 99 years.) SPP (Middle East) undertook to obtain the necessary financing, as well as the technical expertise required for the planning, construction, management and marketing of the project.

This was the state of the project when I took up the reins in 1975 at the tender age of 35. I was appointed managing director of SPP (Middle East) Limited and its Joint Venture entity, Egyptian Tourist Development Company, responsible for developing the project. I arrived in Cairo in April 1976 with no staff and no office. Rae and I learned to speak basic Arabic before we left with the Professor of Semitic Studies at the University of Sydney, who visited our home five or six nights per week for two to three hours per night. We even took him with us to Fiji for a two-week holiday, where we sat around the pool chatting in Arabic. The trouble was that it was the wrong kind of Arabic. It was only when we arrived in Egypt that we realised we'd been taught the classical tongue, the version spoken in Saudi Arabia and the Gulf States and rather different to the "slang" spoken in Egypt. There people clip off many of the prefixes and suffixes in a simplified form of Arabic.

First, I had to find an office. I leased a house on Pyramids Road, about halfway between downtown and the Pyramids Oasis site. One early lesson on the way many Middle Eastern people negotiate was that even a signed agreement does not act as a deterrent to the other party coming back repeatedly to try to renegotiate the deal. As employees were installed in the new premises and office machines connected, we had a blackout caused by the power overload. The resourceful bawab (gatekeeper) obtained two corn cobs from a cart in the street, chewed off the corn and inserted the cobs into the fuse box and the lights magically came back on.

When I first arrived in Cairo in 1976, one of my first tasks was to assist Prince Nawaf ben Abdul Aziz al Saoud, a wily member of the Saudi royal family, to assess his potential shareholding in SPP (Middle East) Limited, the majority owner of the Pyramids Oasis project. The Prince was a member of the Saudi royal family and the previous Governor of Mecca. I met with the Prince and his team of advisors, including Naiel El Bably, at the Sheraton Hotel every day for a month in May 1976 to work through all the planning, the approvals documents and the financial forecasts. Although the Saudis were keen to invest in Egypt, Prince Nawaf had had prior investments nationalised by President Nasser in the 1950s and was therefore cautious—rightly so as it turned out. Baghdadi, the Prince's advisor, suggested that the Prince obtain political risk insurance from Lloyds of London. I met an insurance broker in Cairo, Salah El-Dine, who was able to arrange the cover. I also had a number of meals with the Prince.

Before he left to return to Saudi Arabia, Rae and I hosted a party for the Prince in Ali Ashour El Gabry's tent in the desert near the Pyramids. We had dancing horses, belly dancers, whirling Dervishes, all accompanied by Arab musicians. It was a spectacular evening.

By the end of 1976, most of the detailed engineering design and specifications for the first phase had been completed. Extensive soil tests had been carried out and field survey work begun. On 1 June 1977, Ministerial Decree 96, issued in terms of Laws 1 and 2 of 1973, approved the Master Plan as well as the detailed planning of the first phase of the development. With this last approval, the very next day we awarded a contract for building of the first phase of the project. Construction work began on the site on 2 July 1977.

Approximately four kilometres of sealed road was laid and a further two kilometres formed and graded. Some 2000 metres of sewerage pipes, plus about four kilometres of water mains were installed. The principal water storage reservoir of more than one million litres capacity was nearing completion. More than 400,000 cubic metres of earth had been moved, including the excavations for the artificial lakes and the golf course. The land surveying was virtually completed.

We created an enticing video of our plans, produced in Toronto, and engaged Omar Sharif for the voice over. Anyone who saw Dr Zhivago will not forget Sharif's dulcet tones, tinged with a slight but charming accent. He was magnificent. Born and raised in Egypt, Sharif was regarded a national treasure. One of our leading sales agents, Sophie Sarwat, knew Sharif and invited him to dinner one evening. Rae and I were invited to join Sophie and a handful of her friends. (Rae was especially thrilled for she was secretly in love with Sharif, having admired him and his roles on the big screen.) Rae was disappointed, however, when she found Sharif had dandruff and bitten fingernails, two of her pet hates. On the other hand, he had the most gorgeous smile, beautiful soulful eyes and was the most charming conversationalist.

Work was completed on the US$29 million Pyramids Oasis George V Hotel, including final design and contract documents. A management agreement was completed with THF and firm fixed-price tenders for construction were received from major international contractors. Financing and investment insurance was well in hand by way of a Eurobond issue, to be managed by a leading Kuwaiti underwriter.

The plan for the tourist village was for a project of 240 two-bed units. I priced the land for the tourist village at $50/square metre. Consultants had been appointed and designs for the second 4-star hotel were completed and contracts negotiated with operators. Detailed working drawings and specifications for a range of twelve villa designs had been finalised and sites reserved for the first phase to be constructed. I also drafted a Building Guidelines Manual which was published to assist lot purchasers with their villa design and construction. A complete village consisting of villas, townhouses, apartments, shops and offices was designed by the famous François Spoerry and a model had been built.

Agreement had been reached with the Egyptian telecommunications authorities to form a joint venture corporation to provide international telephone and telex services via satellite direct to the project. In total, the Joint Venture had spent over US$9.5 million on development costs. In accordance with the agreed plan, marketing of the villa lots commenced in early 1977 and approximately 400 sales with a net value of US$9.65 million had been completed.

By now I had become used to being told by the locals who used to say to me, "But that is not the way we do it in Egypt." My response; "My friend, you have had this land for 4000 years and done nothing with it. If we are to build a new city here now, you must allow me to do it my way." We also pushed ahead with our second project in Ras El Hekma, Marsa Matruh, on the Mediterranean coast. On a trip there, we took a detour west towards the Libyan border from Alexandria through the tiny railway stop of El Alamein where three battles were fought in 1942. The Australian 9th Division played a key role in two of these combats, enhancing its reputation, first established defending Tobruk in 1941, which proved decisive in preventing Rommel from capturing Cairo and the Suez Canal.

Life in Cairo was good. The people were exceptionally hospitable and we enjoyed socialising with both Muslims and Christians, who in those days intermingled freely.

On the other hand, doing business was difficult. The bureaucracy was overwhelming and there was little appetite for getting things done. Corruption was rampant, even in small transactions like getting a driver's licence, where paying a bribe was standard. For example, without my attendance, an office assistant obtained for me a report from an optician that I had passed the eyesight test for which he paid LE5. I was also shocked when I was informed by my driver that I needed to tip the policeman at the end of our street each month. Later I learned that a policeman's wages were LE14 per month and a few tips of LE1 were needed to help he and his family survive.

Although one can manage in Cairo with just English, we found our basic knowledge of Arabic was a great help, both in business and socially. When we took our kids for a walk, for example, we were able to purchase teen shorky (prickly pear fruit) off the street barrows. People respected that we had made the effort. With employees it was a great help in ensuring the message was clearly understood, and I made a practice of always giving important instructions in both English and Arabic. In more isolated parts of the country it made it possible to communicate with the locals.

One weekend, we took a long drive off the beaten track. We visited the Meidoum pyramid and climbed up inside with a torch—down 260 steps and then up old wooden steps. On our way home we suffered a blowout of a rear tyre. We didn't want to continue without a spare because punctures were common. We eventually found a sort of shop where we hoped to buy a spare tube, but no such luck. However, the owner had seen this problem before. The tube was badly torn, but he slowly and patiently hand-sewed on a large rubber patch, which he then vulcanised. In the end we didn't need it on the trip back home to Cairo, but it was comfort to know we had it aboard.

Rae's main recreation was horse riding, which she did virtually every day. The stables were quite close to the sphinx and the views she enjoyed were magnificent as you can imagine. On one occasion our family and some friends all rode on horseback out into the desert and camped overnight by the Saqqara stepped pyramids. We climbed the major one the next morning as the sun came up. We returned by lunch time, a little saddle sore. I went pigeon (hamam) and duck (butt) shooting at Fayoum and bagged 11 ducks. Being an old country boy, and a former member of the NSW Gun Club, I had my own 12-guage shotgun. Rae marinated the ducks and served them to much praise at a large dinner party we hosted. Guests included Adnan Khashoggi's man in Egypt, George Clarke, and his girlfriend Jenny Hill, Malcolm Dougal, the First Secretary at the British Embassy and his wife Elke. The party went on until 3:30 am.

Invitations to a private dinner were usually timed for around 9 or 10 pm. Drinks were served from the moment you arrived, but the food was not brought out until midnight. Everyone then ate, and left immediately afterwards. Lunch was usually taken around 3 pm, and was commonly followed by a nap. Some then returned to the office for two or three hours from about 6 pm to 9 pm.

Because I was responsible for such a high-profile project, said to be the most important since the Aswan Dam, we were entertained extensively, including at several embassies. Cairo was reputed to have the largest number of foreign embassies in the world, outside London and Washington, a product of its geography and strategic significance. Once we attended the Philippines Embassy, hosted by Marcelino and Nicole Lilligan, and after dinner we were each presented with a pen and invited to sign our name on the beautiful white linen tablecloth. This seemed a strange thing to do. When I asked about it, Nicole brought in a tablecloth used at a number of previous functions, with dozens of signatures which she had embroidered in colourful threads. It was enchanting.

From time to time we went to Alexandria for the weekend, usually by train, and often as the guest of Adel Abdul Ghaffar, our apartment landlord, who was one of the most hospitable and gracious people we have ever met. We sometimes spent the weekend in Athens, which was a little over an hour's flight from Cairo. On one visit we were in an antique shop, which we had visited previously and the owner approached us and struck up a conversation. This led to an invitation by Spanos and his wife Catherine to dinner, joined by a friend who was visiting from Australia. We were picked up from our hotel in Constitution Square and driven at break-neck speed in a tiny car to the foothills of Athens. There, we entered the restaurant through a butcher shop with scores of carcases hanging in rows. Our hosts selected a lamb which was barbecued and served with lemon and complemented by beautiful fresh salads on the veranda overlooking Athens with its night lights.

We loved the atmosphere, the meal and the retsina and we finally got down to two small pieces of lamb. Rae innocently asked: "What is that?" Our host chatted to his wife in Greek and then acknowledged, "They are the man things." My friend from Australia and I had one each. On weekends we would often play tennis at the Mena House hotel, which was made famous when Winston Churchill stayed there during the war prior to his meeting with Joseph Stalin.

There is no "P" sound in Arabic and commonly the "B" sound is used in its place. At the Mena House hotel there was an area near the Mena House tennis courts on which parking was forbidden. The hotel had erected a large sign "NO BARKING" which we would always greet by pretending to bark: "woof woof!"

Shortly before we left Australia for Cairo, Gough Whitlam had been deposed as prime minister by the Governor General Sir John Kerr who we were later to host for a private dinner in our apartment in London. Following this dramatic firing of the Prime Minister, there was an election, which Malcolm Fraser of the Liberal Party won in a landslide.

A few months after our arrival, the Australian Ambassador Robin Ashwin and his Japanese wife, Okche, invited us to attend an embassy cocktail party in honour of Gough and Margaret Whitlam who had embarked on a six-week, 16-country overseas trip. Whitlam, then Opposition Leader, was the most senior Australian politician to visit Cairo since Robert Menzies' ill-fated mission during the 1956 Suez Crisis. The Egyptians treated him like royalty, driving him to the Pyramids with a police escort of 20 motorbikes. Whitlam's young assistant Richard Whittington was surprised when he was approached later in the hotel lift by one of the police motorcyclists in the hotel lift. He was asking for bakhsheesh (a tip). Welcome to Cairo. Gough seemed aloof and clearly bored by the Embassy function. Margaret, however, was absolutely charming, and spent a long time with Rae chatting about our children and their education. Margaret seemed genuinely interested in the everyday aspect of living in a strange city and Rae has never forgotten how friendly she was. Margaret was an unusually tall woman and the trick question going the rounds of the pubs was, "Why did Gough always take Margaret on his overseas trips?" And the answer: "Because she is the only one who can kick-start the 747!"

In March 1977 we experienced an extraordinary trip to Upper Egypt. We flew from Cairo to Luxor and there boarded the SS Lotus on the Nile River. First we visited the Karnak Temple which was absolutely spectacular and later returned to the Temple that evening for the Son Et Lumiere. Early the next morning we again visited the huge Karnak Temple at Thebes (the old name for Luxor). We then travelled by ferry across the River, and by taxi to the Valley of the Queens and Kings and the Temple of Queen Hatshepsut. We saw the fabulous tombs of Rameses VI, Tutankhamun and Seti I. After lunch on board, we sailed down the Nile River to a mooring for a visit to Dendera. This was followed by an early start the next morning for a trip to Dendera Temple— the most fabulous of all—returning to Luxor via Kom Ombo. We left the next morning for a return flight to Aswan to see the magnificent ruins that were going to be flooded by the Nile, following the building of the Aswan Dam, but were saved and reconstructed on high ground. We finally returned to Cairo by plane.

President Sadat, the undisputed leader of Egypt at the time, a remarkable leader, but he was far from immune from the political pressure of some extremists and could not find a quick solution to the wealth gap that was feeding unrest among the poor. In January 1977, the Government increased the price of some staples, such as bread, sugar and tea. The country erupted in spontaneous rioting. Bread (aish baladi) was increased by 33% to two piastres, and sugar was doubled to two piastres a kilo. An emergency decree was declared on our 17th wedding anniversary, January 19th, imposing a 4 pm curfew. We lived in the Abu El Futuh apartment building directly opposite the presidential palace on the Nile River, and watched as tanks took up position outside our front door. The absence of the constant cacophony of car horns as a result of the decree was particularly eerie. The peace was broken only by sporadic gunshots.

The following day, on her way out to ride her horse by the Pyramids, Rae and her driver were met by a wall of protestors who appeared to be attacking the nightclubs along Sharia Al Ahram (Pyramids Road). Rae's car turned back quickly. Most of the staff at our office hid their cars and then closed the building. On my way home my driver chose back lanes to avoid the main thoroughfare, but we ran into a crowd of protestors who thumped my car before we were able to roar off. That afternoon Rae opened the windows on our balcony overlooking the presidential palace and immediately the huge gun on a tank swung around and pointed directly at her on the seventh floor. She slammed the window shut and dashed back inside. The riots were quelled in a couple of days, but we feared for our safety and especially the safety of our children. At one stage we feared they might have been trapped at their school on Zamalek Island in the Nile River with the bridges blockaded.

The Government had little choice but to rescind the proposed price increases, resulting in an LE750 million hole in the budget. On 9 November 1977, President Sadat startled the world when he announced that he would travel to Israel to speak before the Knesset, the Israeli Parliament. This was an enormously courageous, ground-breaking action which would begin a new era in the peace-making process after decades of fighting. Soon afterwards, US President Carter hosted the two leaders, Menachem Begin of Israel, and President Anwar Sadat, for the signing of the Camp David Accords on 17 September 1978.

These moves emboldened the opposition to Sadat. He had earlier allowed for opposition parties to form and for them to publish their own newspapers. One of the two main groups was extreme left wing in philosophy and the other right wing in its policies. Amid the unrest, however, we could hear warning bells for our project.

Both opposition parties objected to our project on the grounds that it was wrong for foreigners to enjoy majority ownership, even though 40 per cent was owned by the Egyptian Government through the Government Tourism Organisation and, after 99 years, the entire project reverted to Egypt.

The project would undoubtedly have brought prosperity to the country and jobs and opportunity for the dispossessed. The economic transformation of former Communist and developing nations in subsequent years has demonstrated the remarkable ability of capitalism to bring an end to poverty. Yet in the heated political atmosphere of the 1970s, Egypt was caught in a proxy battle in the wave of Arab nationalism, and our project appeared to be in serious trouble.

CHAPTER 6

# WRESTLING THE GORILLA

You don't quit when you're tired. You quit when the gorilla
is tired.

ROBERT S STRAUSS

On 28 May 1978, an Egyptian newspaper reported that the
President of the Arab Republic of Egypt had decided to
cancel the Pyramids Oasis project. It was just over two years
since Rae and I had flown into the country buoyed by high
hopes, imagining how the development could help transform the Egyptian economy as a step on the road towards a
peaceful and prosperous future for a people we had come to
love.

There was a feeling of inevitability about the news, despite
President Sadat's endorsement for the project in his May
Day speech, which we all listened to, four weeks earlier when
he urged his opponents to stop criticising the Pyramids
Oasis project. In February 1978 the project was debated in
the People's Assembly, with the Minister of Tourism and
the Minister of Economy strongly defending it. In April,
President Sadat explicitly criticised the People's Assembly and

its Speaker for putting in doubt a project duly approved and committed by the Government.

Yet by then the development had become hopelessly politicised, caught in a proxy-war between the President and his opponents who played to popular emotions resistant to any hint of foreign interference, whatever the national benefits. The project was publicly attacked and criticised from various quarters, some claiming that unscrupulous profiteers were planning to despoil the centrepiece of the Egyptian people's cultural heritage. There was more than a hint of vested interest; the opponents included entrepreneurs profiting from their illegal occupation of part of the Pyramids Oasis site who would have had to relocate. They formed an unholy alliance with those who opposed any commercial development near the antiquities site and ideologues hostile to foreign investment in general. They were joined by both left-wing and right-wing politicians, who saw an opportunity to oppose a project sponsored by the Sadat Government under its "open door" policy.

The newspaper article followed a decree from the Minister of Culture and Information declaring the land surrounding the Pyramids to be public domain and casting into doubt the validity of the transfer of the land from the Government Tourism Organisation to the Joint Venture. The following day, the General Investment Authority withdrew approval of the project and a week later, on 5 June 1978, the Ministry of Tourism instructed the joint venture to stop work on the project. The Giza Court in Egypt sequestered all the assets of the joint venture and then placed the company in judicial receivership. Finally, on 19 June 1978, President Sadat issued Presidential Decree 267, cancelling Presidential Decree 457/1975 which designated the lands on the Pyramids Plateau for touristic exploitation and enabled the Government Tourism Organisation to acquire ownership and transfer the usufruct title to the Joint Venture.

All work in process was stopped, the contract labour force demobilized and millions of dollars-worth of equipment and partially completed work effectively abandoned. The project team, made up of specialists in engineering, finance, surveying and marketing, was disbanded. SPP (Middle East) Limited's equity interest in the joint venture was rendered entirely valueless and its loans to the joint venture were unable to be repaid, due to the joint venture's insolvency. In addition, SPP (Middle East)'s valuable development contract was termi-nated, resulting in loss to SPP (Middle East) of not only its contractual expectancy, but also of more than three years of planning and performance entirely devoted to this major development.

At that time, there were 1000 people engaged on Pyramids Oasis, including a large number of expatriates from many parts of the world, mainly professionals from the engineering, town planning, surveying, and architectural disciplines. Everyone was nervous, and virtually all of the expatriates got themselves into a panic. They were concerned about how they would be returned to their countries, what would happen to their children, who would pay for the air tickets, who would take care of the leases on their homes. Only one man said, "I will stay with you as long as necessary to ensure an orderly demobilisation, and make sure that the assets of the com-pany are properly protected." Leaders must be prepared to persevere. We desperately need men and women who will do what it takes when the chips are down. As a leader, I have learned that, when times are tough, there are few who will do what is necessary. We must constantly remind ourselves that the hardships of life are not sent by an unkind destiny to crush us, but to challenge us. We must persevere.

The effective nationalisation was a huge shock at the time, although, on more mature reflection, one could see the dilemma facing the Government. Was this major international project worth more than trying to bring peace and stability to Egypt—particularly Cairo? Unwinding the operations was a major task, undertaken in a complete legal vacuum. What was going to happen to the hundreds of employees? What about the millions of dollars in the bank? Who was going to take care of the massive machines and other equipment, including plant held up at the docks?

The President announced that there would be compensation. By whom and for how much? No one seemed to know. Hundreds of individual investors had already paid 90% of the price of their land, but the building of the infrastructure to service the land was now stopped and they would not be able to get title. How would they be compensated?

There was no criticism of SPP by the Government which always defended the company and the project. In fact, shortly after Pyramids Oasis was cancelled, the Government expressed a wish for the joint venture to proceed with the second project at Ras El Hekma on the Mediterranean coast. Our confidence was fast evaporating, however. It was difficult to see how we could trust a Government that had not honoured its contractual commitments or its obligations under the Foreign Investment Law. It was disappointing, but hardly surprising, that the Government subsequently failed to make any offer of compensation to SPP for its losses, despite statements by the Prime Minister that investors' rights would be preserved. It was, to be sure, a considerable setback for SPP, but it was an even more serious setback for Egypt, reinforcing its reputation for sovereign risk and deterring the foreign investment the country and its people so badly needed.

Before leaving Cairo in August 1978, I arose before dawn with our two sons, Scott, aged 12, and Stuart, 10, to climb the Great Pyramid of Cheops, the oldest and largest of the three pyramids in the Giza pyramid complex. It proved to be a bigger challenge than it first appeared, even with the assistance of a guide. It stands at 146.5 metres (481 feet), 10 metres higher than the top of Sydney Harbour Bridge, and was the tallest man-made structure in the world for more than 3,800 years. As we watched the sun rise over Cairo, I thought about Egypt's rich ancient civilisation and the many Egyptian friends we had made in a nation that despite its problems is rich in achievement and promise.

We returned to London to where we had been living before the crisis. It had been a convenient base for travelling whilst I was seeking capital, principally for the major hotels and tourist village. I had concentrated on the Middle East, especially the Gulf States including Kuwait, Dubai, Abu Dhabi, and Bahrain.

While living in London, Rae and I never missed an opportunity to host a dinner party at our home with whoever might breeze by. Three years after meeting Gough Whitlam at a reception at the Australian Embassy, Cairo in 1976, we jumped at the chance to entertain his nemesis, the former Governor-General, Sir John Kerr, who had retired to London. Following the events of 1975, Sir John Kerr asked the Queen if he could retire early, stepping down in December 1977 after only three and a half years in office. He had withstood the public protests and demonstrations of 1976, with his final year in office, 1977, relatively free of controversy.

My Uncle Ken (a former head of the Attorney General and Justice Department) suggested we invite Sir John and Lady Kerr, whom he knew well, to dinner. We hosted them in our home on 6 July 1979. Other guests included Ken and Marie Downs, David Gilmour and his friend Jill Sweeney, and Jan Paulsson and his girlfriend Veronique.

Sir John gifted me his autographed biography. He said that the dismissal of Whitlam was dramatic despite his careful planning. Before the other guests arrived, Sir John told me privately that during their fateful meeting in Government House at approximately 1 pm on 11 November 1975, Whitlam threatened Sir John with dismissal. By convention the Prime Minister instructs the Queen who should be appointed Governor General. Whitlam told Kerr that if he did not resign he would instruct the Queen to replace him as Governor General.

As Whitlam got up from the Governor General's desk, apparently to call the Queen, Kerr handed Whitlam a letter which he had pre-prepared and which was lying face down on his desk. The letter terminated the Whitlam government with immediate effect, and Whitlam's reign as Prime Minister was, *ipso facto,* at an end.

Kerr then invited Whitlam to call the Queen, but ventured that as Whitlam was no longer Prime Minister but merely the Honourable Member for Werriwa, the Queen would be unlikely to accept his advice! (In any event, it was the middle of the night in Britain.)

Gough Whitlam, in his *The Truth of the Matter*, outlined a slightly different sequence of events, although the essence of his dismissal remains the same. Whitlam's commission as Prime Minister was terminated by the Governor General.

Some in the media reported that Sir John had used the Queen's reserve powers. He did not. He actually used the powers that devolved upon him as Governor-General, under section 64 of the Australian Constitution, which states:

> *The Governor-General may appoint officers to administer such departments of State of the Commonwealth as the Governor-General in Council may establish. Such officers shall hold office during the pleasure of the Governor-General. They shall be members of the Federal Executive Council, and shall be the Queen's Ministers of State for the Commonwealth.*

As Sir John later said, "The decisions I have made were after I was satisfied that Mr. Whitlam could not obtain Supply. No other decision open to me would enable the Australian people to decide for themselves what should be done."

I moved back to our Sloane Street office which gave me a chance to become more closely acquainted with my chairman, the incomparable Peter Munk. He was born into a wealthy Jewish family in Hungary in 1927 and fled on the famous Kastner train that transported over 1600 Jews safely to Switzerland in June 1944, shortly after the Germans had occupied his home country. He arrived in Toronto at the age of 20. He said of his adopted Canada, "This is a country that does not ask about your origins but concerns itself with your destiny."

As we sifted through the pieces of our shattered Egyptian joint venture, Peter encouraged me to become involved as a main board director in the parent company, Southern Pacific Properties, which owned a chain of 69 hotels and resorts. This involved trips to Australia, but my initial focus was serving as president of the Tahiti Beachcomber Hotel and Resort in French Polynesia. I managed to acquire the minority interest in the property from the Roman Catholic church and then repositioned it in the market while I obtained planning consent for a major condominium development. It is a long way from London to Tahiti, which I travelled innumerable times. The routine was London/Los Angeles a 12-hour non-stop British Airways flight followed by a few hours layover in LAX, before taking a UTA eight-hour flight to Tahiti, arriving at 5 am the following morning. It was tiring, but I was younger in those days and I had done it many times.

In the European summer of 1979, Peter asked me if I would be prepared to move to Toronto, Canada, to build an office for the firm. We loved living in London and had a magnificent five-bedroom apartment in "Harley House" on Marylebone Road backing onto Regents Park, which we had purchased and renovated extensively. Nonetheless the challenge of a new city and a new county was stimulating and I agreed. We packed up and moved in August 1979, stopping in Nassau, The Bahamas, for a break and then took the kids to Disneyworld before flying on to Toronto. There is much to like about Toronto. It is clean. It is safe and in the Summer it is great to have family bike rides all over town on the flat topography. The winters are cold, and so it is important to rug up and learn to deal with the snow that stays on the ground for four months.

The move also saved me 10,000 km on my frequent return trips to Tahiti, for which I was grateful.

Meanwhile, during our time in Toronto, I was always on the lookout for innovations that could help us drive more value from our hotel business. The idea of timeshares was just taking off in the United States which offered the chance to buy a vacation licence for a specified season and number of weeks rather than outright ownership. I didn't know much about it, but I got in touch with a lot of people in the US who came on board as consultants and helped me complete the feasibility studies. I joined the Canadian Timeshare Association and I put together quite a big plan to do that with a number of properties. Peter was mildly intrigued by it, but unbeknown to me, he was working on other plans.

On 24 July 1980, nine months after we moved into our new Toronto office premises, Peter called me out of the blue and asked if I was free. "I am just finishing one thing, but can meet you in ten minutes or so," I replied. "Well, I am with David (David Gilmour was Peter's business partner of 25 years) in the Four Seasons Hotel in Room 1210." As I walked the 100 metres from my office to the hotel, I wondered what on earth this could be about. Were Peter and David scheming to lay me off?

As soon as I entered the room Peter told me that he and David had decided to sell their chain of 69 hotels and resorts and get into the resources business. "Wow," I said, "that is a bold move." "Yes," said Peter, "and we want you to be the President!"

I was flabbergasted, "But, I don't know anything about resources or mining." Peter responded by assuring me that I was a leader, totally trustworthy, and driven to get things done. I was, of course, chuffed, but told Peter and David I would like to discuss the proposition with Rae. Over dinner, we jointly concluded that I should "give it a go" and, indeed, if I had declined, that that may have been the beginning of my last days with the company. I accepted the challenge and immediately formed Barrick Resources Corporation, negotiated the shareholders' agreement and secured the commitment of the founding minority investors, Norman Short of Guardian Capital and Joe Rotman of Pan Cana Minerals. Out of that emerged Barrick Gold, the world's largest gold company.

I travelled to Denver, Colorado for a crash course in geology and extraction of oil and gas and to Houston for a course in resource investment. I was determined to make a success of it.

In late December 1980, we drove from Toronto to Quebec City to spend Christmas/New Year in the famous Chateau Frontenac hotel on the banks of the St Lawrence River. Quebec City is the oldest city in North America and still has the remains of its original walls. It was a wonderful experience—especially as we were joined by long-time friends, Gerald and Susan Lancaster. Several went skiing on Mt St Anne; others of us enjoyed the fine French dining in a range of reasonably-priced restaurants. It was very cold and on Christmas day I took the three children skating on the rink adjacent to the hotel. The doorman warned me as we walked out that it was too cold out there, but foolishly we stepped outside. Within minutes we came running back. The doorman was relieved to see us inside. He told us that the ambient temperature was minus 40 degrees, and with the wind-chill factor was minus 80 degrees! (I subsequently learned that the Centigrade and Fahrenheit scales cross at minus 40 degrees.)

Peter was the smartest businessman I have ever worked with and he taught me an enormous amount, for which I shall remain indebted all my days. And he will always be remembered by me as a great encourager, backing my judgement in the legal action that was beginning to unfold against the Egyptians. I shall never forget Peter's willingness to change his mind, a surprisingly rare quality in business. Lesser leaders fear changing course as a sign of weakness. Not Peter, who was immensely smart, but at the same time sincerely humble. Often, he would say things such as, "Tony, I have been thinking over the weekend and believe we should make a bid for so-and-so." You could take it as read that it would be a smart idea, but it wouldn't always land there.

An hour later, after I had read over my mail, I might go upstairs to his office and say something like: "Peter, I have been thinking about your idea and wondered whether it might be better if we proposed a merger rather than an outright acquisition."

"Tony," he would say, "that is a much better plan; I like it." Peter was always searching for the best solution, irrespective of from where it came. He was never too proud to change his mind: I always felt free with him. Peter was the same with drafting correspondence; continually looking for the best solution and always willing to accept suggestions. On one occasion we spent a whole day in our office in Tulsa Oklahoma, drafting and redrafting a one-and-a-half-page letter to Hispanoil, the Spanish national oil company. The object was to secure a meeting with their president to discuss a major joint venture. After endless drafts we sent it off and were successful in securing our meeting.

During my time with the Barrick Group, I travelled almost constantly. Indeed, whilst living in London, I went through Heathrow airport 50 times in one year. Later, when we moved to Toronto, I spent 35% of my nights away from home in a foreign country. Appreciating what this meant to the family, Peter made a bold suggestion that I have never heard of before or since. He told me how grateful he was for my dedication and offered to pay for Rae to join me on my travels whenever I chose. I was thrilled. We had a resident housekeeper and it was not difficult for Rae to get away at short notice, which was often required. We always travelled first class, including in Concorde whenever we could, and stayed in suites in some of the best hotels around the world.

Rae was keen to join me. "I will be going to Paris on Thursday; would you like to come?" "Yes!" she would say enthusiastically and off we would go in the Concorde.

After a year, I made a crude estimate of the additional cost of Rae's travel and found it to be about $50,000. This was especially generous since it was a tax-free gift to me. But if Peter had suggested he pay me a bonus of $50,000, I would have scoffed. I would have considered it paltry, when set alongside my salary. It was, however, appreciated more than any money and was an enormous motivator. Why other companies don't do something similar is hard to fathom. It was yet another example of the genius of Peter Munk.

Our dispute with the Egyptian Government played out constantly in the background during this exciting time in my career, periodically occupying large chunks of my time that I could ill-afford to surrender. It became apparent early on that as the initiator of the project, SPP (Middle East) Limited of which I was managing director had a claim under Egypt's Foreign Investment Law. The contract with the Government of Egypt provided that any dispute was to be settled at arbitration under the auspices of the International Chamber of Commerce (ICC), based in Paris.

We held seemingly endless, tedious meetings with the government over many weeks without much progress. After many months of detailed preparation, we were ready to file a claim and on 27 November 1978 I notified the Prime Minister and the Minister of Tourism of our intention to do so. I duly filed the formal claim with the International Chamber of Commerce in Paris on 1 December 1978. We sought an award for reimbursement of SPP (Middle East)'s loan to the joint venture, together with all interest; repayment of all amounts due and owing by the joint venture to SPP (Middle East) or Southern Pacific Properties; the fair market value of SPP (Middle East)'s shareholding in the joint venture, now lost due to the actions of the Government; plus all costs, legal fees, and other out-of-pocket expenses reasonably incurred by SPP (Middle East) in protecting its interest or in prosecuting its rights.

We did not request an order of specific performance for the Government's breach. We acknowledged that the Government of Egypt must be free, as a sovereign state, to do as it pleased with projects in Egypt. Southern Pacific Properties merely sought damages for the breach of the Government's solemn contractual engagements, undertaken by its ministries and agencies, upon which we had relied to our detriment. The filing of our claim startled the Egyptian Government, who responded irritably, insisting that they would only continue with the "negotiations" if we withdrew the claim. Against our lawyer's advice, and under pressure, I agreed to suspend the claim filed at the ICC, pending further discussions. These proved as futile as the initial rounds. In an endeavour to keep the possibility alive I informed the Minister by telex that we were willing to discuss a proposal his people had made previously within an overall settlement. The Minister replied on 7 May confirming a meeting with him on 14 May. I travelled to Cairo and stayed from 13 to 18 May 1979, but the Minister was not prepared to meet with me.

On 14 May I met with Gamal El Nazer, Minister for Economic Development, and later Hafez Ghanem, Minister for Tourism. These meetings were ostensibly to discuss a settlement of the Arbitration case, but led nowhere. I later had further meetings with EGOTH and Minister Hafez Ghanen. Afterwards, I delivered a letter to the Prime Minister, followed by a further meeting with the Minister of Tourism. It became clear to me that I had made a mistake in trusting the Egyptian government to negotiate an honourable settlement and reinstated our claim at the ICC.

After endless delays by the Egyptians, the first arbitration hearing began in the ICC's hearing centre a stone's throw away from the Champs Elysees in Paris. The first thing I did was to ask for the lights in the courtroom to be dimmed so we could run a projector to show a film of President Sadat on his knees examining the model of our project and clearly endorsing what we were planning to do. The Egyptian defence team was outraged and protested loudly. The hearings dragged on requiring me to travel to Paris every six weeks for yet another hearing or meetings with the lawyers. We even had a hearing in Cairo itself, where the arbitrators inspected the site. It was a tiring, protracted business, and required intense concentration, which was difficult with all the other things with which I was then involved. Initially, we had launched the action when I was living in London. After my employer asked me to open our new office in Toronto, Canada, the fight continued from there. By this time, I had been appointed President of the predecessor of Barrick Gold and so I hired a lawyer in our office to work under my direction, to manage the whole case.

President Sadat's life ended tragically in a shower of hand grenades and bullets on 6 October 1981 at the annual celebration of the crossing of the Suez Canal and the taking back of the Sinai Peninsula, at the beginning of the Yom Kippur War. He was murdered by members of the Egyptian Islamic Jihad. The case continued. On many occasions we tired of it all, and as the legal bills grew, we asked ourselves, "Is all this worth it? Aren't there more important things for us to do?" But I was determined that we should persevere to ensure justice was done. Eight years later we were vindicated and received a massive award in our favour. Naturally we were elated, even though, as we strongly suspected, the Egyptians did not honour the award. As I facetiously said at the time, our demand for payment must have gone astray in the notoriously unreliable Egyptian postal system.

I refused to give up. After trying to access the decision makers through back channels, we decided to take pre-emptive action. We seized some ships being constructed in The Netherlands for the Egyptian Government, and at the same time also managed to freeze substantial deposits of Egyptian funds in the British banking system. This certainly got the Government's attention, and whilst they did not send us a cheque, they decided to appeal the arbitration award (which, technically, was final and non-appealable) to the French Supreme Court. Their defence against the award was—you guessed it—sovereign immunity.

It was a bizarre case. The dispute was between the Government of Egypt and a Hong Kong public company, and had nothing to do with France. We argued for Paris as the site for the arbitration because the lawyers we had employed were based in Paris. The Egyptians also liked Paris because it was a pleasant place to visit during the hearings. Thus, Paris it was, even though there was absolutely no connection with France, with French law, or with anything to do with the French. Notwithstanding this, the French Supreme Court, known as the *Cour de Cassation*, decided to hear the Egyptian Government's plea. How on earth it thought it had jurisdiction is beyond my untrained mind. Remember too, that we had argued our case for eight years before winning a huge judgement. The *Cour de Cassation* nonetheless decided after a day's arguments that the arbitration award should be over-turned on the basis of Egypt's sovereign immunity.

We could have walked away with our tail between our legs and $5 million of wasted legal fees. But we decided to fight on. Since the perfidious French courts had declared the arbitration award null and void, we took another look at Egypt's Foreign Investment Law and discovered that we had the right to take it to the International Centre for the Settlement of Investment Disputes (ICSID), an organisation attached to the World Bank. Fortunately, both Egypt and Hong Kong were subscribers. The circus moved on to the World Court at The Hague where it took a year or so to establish the ICSID's right to hear the dispute before we could start arguing the merits of the case.

Finally, the ICSID arbitrators determined that we had been wronged and that compensation was due. The parties then agreed to reconvene in Paris to hold hearings on the quantum of the damages. Although I had managed the entire case I had not testified at any of the hearings, but it was decided that as I had been the managing director and because of my degrees in valuation I should be the one to give evidence on the damages done to SPP (Middle East) Limited. Although I had gathered an enormous amount of data—first as managing director of the joint venture, and then during the many years working on the case—I spent several intense weeks in collating and sorting it, and in analysing it every which way. I prepared charts and graphs showing the history of the success of the project up until it was nationalised.

At the hearing on damages, I was called to demonstrate to the court the losses we had suffered. After nearly two days, I finished and the Egyptians were invited to question me. They didn't ask a single question and I was able to step down from the witness box. The Egyptians then declined to provide any evidence that might indicate lesser damages. I don't know whether it was pride, or incompetence, but it seemed absurd to me that they did not submit any argument at all that might have discredited my testimony. We waited several more months before we received the result. The court had awarded us damages far greater than the initial award. Additionally, the judgement spoke strongly against the actions of the Egyptians. So far, so good. But could we now collect?

Again, we made formal demands. Again, no response. We opened up a number of back channels through people who claimed they could influence the Government to pay. No success. I then visited the World Bank headquarters in Washington, DC, and made the case that unless the World Bank stepped in and put pressure on Egypt to honour its own foreign investment law, further overseas investment in that country would be at risk. I indicated I would uncover our position and warn anyone that, if they invested in Egypt, they could not rely on the protections they might imagine they would receive under Egyptian law.

Before long I received notification from the lawyer appointed by the Government of Egypt to represent it in finalising the matter, Lloyd Cutler of Wilmer, Cutler and Pickering of Washington. Interestingly Lloyd Cutler had just been advising President Clinton concerning his recent affair with Monica Lewinsky. By then we were living in Atlanta, Georgia where Cutler arranged to visit me at our home. Rae served us a pleasant lunch and then Cutler and I adjourned to my office and library where he laid out the Government's proposal, which amounted to a substantial discount on the face value of the award. I thereupon called a board meeting of the directors of SPP (Middle East) Limited, including Prince Nawaf ben Abdul Aziz from Saudi Arabia and Essam Khashoggi. The directors were scattered all over the globe—one in Toronto, one in London, one in Paris and one in Hawaii. We all agreed to accept the proposal outlined by Cutler. I conveyed our decision to Lloyd Cutler, who had left the room whilst we discussed the matter. We shook hands, signed a simple document, and a few days later the money was transferred to our account more than 14 years after the nationalisation of the project.

I forged many close personal bonds with the legal team headed by William (Laurie) Craig and Jan Paulsson of Coudert Freres in Paris over the years of non-stop litigation. Laurie wrote a very nice letter acknowledging the support the team had received:

> I know that you will feel slight satisfaction that the SPP cases are already known as benchmarks in international litigation and will be recorded in international law case books and commentary for years to come . . . I did want to share these thoughts with you and acknowledge your hard work and tremendous enthusiasm in the project which kept us all going.

Subsequently I have been asked to speak about the experience to audiences which were always impressed with the complexity and scope of the issue we litigated. I received this testimony after giving a talk to lawyers at the World Trade Club:

> Please accept my thanks both personally and on behalf of the World Trade Club for your fascinating presentation at the panel on international arbitration. Yours was a highly unusual experience, measured by almost any standard. The scope of the project itself must be unique. The duration of the controversy, its political nuances, the frequent reversals of fortune—surely not many arbitration situations are similar! You did a fine job in setting the technical questions against the historical/political background. The whole story would make an excellent book.
>
> —Paula Lawton Bevington
> Senior Vice President, Servidyne Incorporated

After more than 60 years as a leader I have learned that you must persist with the task in hand if you wish to be successful. So many of our achievements in life come from a belief in what we can accomplish. We must have confidence in the worth of our vision. Courageous determination and perseverance will help you realise your personal ambitions, remembering that the hardships of life are sent to challenge us, not sent to crush us.

My former minister, Rev Dr Michael Youssef, teaches that we must persevere, lest we abrogate God's work in our lives and cancel his plans for our future.

During the long battle to achieve justice there were many occasions when we were tempted to give up, but I was determined to persevere. Robert S Strauss, a towering figure in US politics, colourfully described chairing the Democratic Party during the Richard Nixon era as being 'a little like makin' love to a gorilla. You don't quit when you're tired, you quit when the gorilla's tired.'[2] The expression has since been applied to sporting and business situations where you don't have the luxury of quitting. The Pyramids Oasis project and its long aftermath taught me the hard way: The alternative to persevering is getting crushed.

2   Washington (DC) *Star-News*, December 1974

## CHAPTER 7

# FASTER THAN A SPEEDING BULLET

Shoot for the moon. Even if you miss, you'll land among the stars.

NORMAN VINCENT PEALE

Any feelings of deflation I might have felt at the abrupt end to our Egyptian joint-venture were as nothing to the excitement and anticipation of what might lie ahead. My chairman, Peter Munk, had experienced one spectacular corporate collapse with the Clairtone Sound Corporation Limited, a producer of high-end audio equipment that was lauded for its inno- vation in the 1960s that became a victim of its own success. The lessons he drew from that experience were to guide him for the rest of his career. He encouraged us to treat setbacks as learning opportunities, a philosophy that is common to all great business leaders. As a wise man said, smart people learn from their mistakes, but really clever people learn from other people's mistakes. Henry Ford, who was bankrupted twice before he founded the Ford Motor Company, said the only real mistake is the one from which we learn nothing. It is a lesson that applies not just to business, but to every aspect of life.

The Pyramids Oasis project had expanded my horizons as to what could be achieved with a bold vision, an appetite for risk and a good book of contacts who might be persuaded to take your call. By then mine included Adnan and Essam Khashoggi, the enigmatic Middle Eastern deal makers whose Triad Corporation had provided the capital for the acquisition of Southern Pacific Properties Limited by Peter Munk and his partner David Gilmour. Their stake in Pyramids Oasis was not inconsiderable, and it was my responsibility to keep them informed of developments. I also had extensive contact with Triad's representative in Egypt, George Clark, and his girlfriend Jenny Hill. George was helpful in introducing me to the Indian conglomerate Tata, which was interested in one of our hotels at Pyramids Oasis.

Adnan Khashoggi had a personal fortune in the billions and was not shy spending it. The TV series Lifestyles of the Rich and Famous followed him as he visited a handful of his 35 homes aboard his yacht and jet. It showed glimpses of Khashoggi's retreat at Marbella in southern Spain, an entire mountain with seven villas, and a 1,300-acre hunting preserve. The Spanish mansion laid claim to possess the world's largest outdoor marble disco floor. His duplex in the Olympic Tower on Fifth Avenue, valued at a cool $25 million in 1984, boasted a Jacuzzi with a panoramic view of the New York skyline. It was directly opposite our office in the Rockefeller Center on Fifth Avenue. His sumptuous $70 million yacht "Nabila" starred in a James Bond film, "Never Say Never Again" and was later sold to an ambitious New York property developer by the name of Donald J Trump. I spent countless hours with the Khashoggi brothers in their homes all over the world.

Journalists repeatedly referred to Adnan Khashoggi as an "arms dealer," a reference to his involvement in the sale of vast quantities of military equipment. The Khashoggi name is of Turkish origin and is a translation of "spoon-maker." Adnan and his two brothers, Essam and Mohamed, had formed an entity known as Triad (or "three"), but Mohamed was no longer involved. I did, however, meet with the Khashoggi's sister, Samira, at her home in Cairo in March 1978.

For my first four months back in London working in our Sloane Street office, preparing our arbitration case against the Egyptian Government was pretty much a full-time job. I had my first strategy meeting with Adnan and Essam Khashoggi in their office in London on 5 February 1979. I briefed them on the arbitration claim against the Government, which I had filed on 1 December 1978 at the International Chamber of Commerce (ICC) in Paris. The claim was in five leather-bound volumes in slipcases, which had cost 1500 pounds to print and bind. We also discussed how Adnan and Essam might be able to assist in brokering a settlement.

By then I had become involved in Southern Pacific Hotel Corporation, a Hong Kong-listed company, that owned a chain of 69 hotels and resorts. Peter and his business partner David Gilmour had acquired control of SPHC with the help of capital from the Khashoggi brothers. Many of them were badly underperforming. Much of the portfolio stemmed from SPP's takeover of the Australian-based Travelodge group in the mid-1970s. They were great assets but were afflicted by the mistakes of the previous owners. Others might have seen that as a problem but Peter encouraged me to think of it as an opportunity. New ideas were needed, and tough decisions were required and Peter asked me to join the board and do what I could to help.

My role involved trips to the Sydney operational head-quarters, but my initial focus was serving as president of the Tahiti Beachcomber Hotel and Resort in French Polynesia, a property built by Travelodge in 1974 with high ambition that had never achieved its potential. The strategy I developed was to reposition it further upmarket while I obtained planning consent for a major condominium development. The first thing I learned about Tahiti was that it was a long way from anywhere and was not on the major airline routes, which was a big part of the Beachcomber's problem. Another issue was the fact that less than 10% of Americans have passports, which are required for entry into French Polynesia and the market for the Tahiti Beachcomber was therefore severely limited in the USA. Most other nearby countries allow entry to USA citizens without passports, such as Canada, Mexico, the West Indies, The Bahamas and so on.

French Polynesia was more than 15,000 km from London, which made it a serious commute. On one occasion when returning from Tahiti in October 1979, I flew via American Samoa to Honolulu to look at development projects and paying a visit to Essam and Layla Khashoggi at their magnificent home fronting Waikiki Beach. By then the Khashoggis had a substantial interest in Southern Pacific Properties and I needed to keep them up to date.

The Tahiti Beachcomber was partially owned by a Catholic order, whose interest was managed by a prominent

London investment bank. One of my first steps was to purchase that share to give us flexibility to make the necessary radical decisions. I decided to seek approval for a major development of condominiums on the surplus land which afforded magnificent views across the water to the island of Moorea.

I first met with Frances Sandford, the president of French Polynesia, on 21 March 1979. We were joined at dinner in Sandford's home by Jan Paulsson, my French lawyer, and Janine Languesse. President Sandford supported our plans and we subsequently received official approval on 25 May 1979. On 10 April 1979 I visited Paris to meet with Caisse Centrale to renegotiate our bank loan, and on 21 October 1979 I proposed the acquisition of the majority interest in the property managed by J. Henry Schroeder Wagg and Company Limited, on behalf of the Roman Catholic Church.

Following a meeting with the lawyers in Paris on 25 June 1980, the complex transaction with J. Henry Schroeder Wagg was closed in London on 30 June 1980. After implementing these major structural changes, the value of the property rose dramatically. As a result, when the chain was sold to Tan Sri Koo Teck Puat, the value was higher than the rest of SPHC's properties put together. We resold it one year later at a profit of $8 million.

Being able to call upon the help of the Khashoggis, with the knowledge and experience of the oil and gas industry, was invaluable as we worked to get Barrick off the ground. In late 1980 I again met with Essam in his New York apartment on Fifth Avenue for lunch with Milton McKenzie and Duane ("Swede") Nelson, the chairman and president of Viking

Petroleum, Inc., based in Tulsa, Oklahoma to discuss our interest in acquiring a controlling interest in the company. I'll never forget the date, 6 December. Two days later, John Lennon was shot dead outside the Dakota, barely two kilometres away across Central Park on West 72nd. The meeting with the Khashoggis led to my finalising a merger agreement between Viking Petroleum and Quadrangle Petroleum two months later on 23 February 1981.

The pace of my life seemed to be accelerating exponentially. My journey from managing an ambitious development project in Egypt, to running a resources company and chasing international exploration deals had taken just a few years. In 1981, I crossed the Atlantic 15 times, 14 of them flying 18 km above the surface of the earth at twice the speed of sound. I fell in love with Concorde the moment I stepped aboard for my first flight in November 1978. Of the many miles I flew over the years, the trips on Concorde never failed to excite, as almost everyone who had that privilege would agree.

On one Concorde trip from London on BA 003, I found myself sitting alongside a handsome man who was being pestered by other passengers for autographs. I discretely asked the hostess who it was. "That's Christopher Reeves, the actor," she told me, "Superman." When I returned to my seat, Superman and I struck up a conversation. He was a warm and charming person who loved his family. He was reading the script for his next movie. Having experienced the acceleration of Concorde to Mach 2 with Reeve, I can testify that the comic book hero of my childhood could indeed fly faster than a speeding bullet, although he was a warm and charming person, apparently unspoiled by fame.

His bravery following the accident in which he was thrown from a horse during an equestrian competition breaking his back is something I shall always admire. It was a reminder that a beautiful life can be snatched away in a microsecond and causes me to reflect on what I am doing with mine. We saw him later in his wheelchair. I was sad to hear of his passing in 2004.

On another occasion, Rae and I were on the Concorde flight BA 001, which left at 10:30 am from New York to London. Also on board were Paul and Linda McCartney. Rae had a long conversation with Linda, who she found absolutely charming.

The journey from New York to Paris or London was about three and a half hours, as opposed to seven or eight hours in a Jumbo. The practical effect of this is that we could take a flight from Toronto at, say, 7 am to LaGuardia airport, jump into a taxi to J F Kennedy airport to catch the Concorde and land at Heathrow by mid-afternoon Toronto time, and collect our luggage at around 8 pm in London. A taxi ride to our hotel (we commonly stayed at the Dorchester on Park Lane) and we could be tucked up in bed by 10.30 pm. It was so much easier to adjust to the different time zones than on the overnight flight from Toronto to London which sometimes stopped in Montreal. The reverse journey was not dissimilar. We would depart London or Paris, as the case may be, at around10.30 am, and, with the five-hour time difference (six hours in Paris) arrive in New York before we left at approximately 8:30 or 9:00 am. We could spend the day in New York, or could catch a flight back to Toronto and be home by lunch time.

As an aside, if Concorde passed a Jumbo flying in the same direction, Concorde would be travelling at 10-20,000 feet higher but, staggeringly, at 700 mph faster.

The plane was quite small with one class only in two cabins and a total of approximately 100 passengers, seated 2+2. The aisle was too narrow for a trolley (which was a feature of British Airways first-class service) and our meals were brought to us on trays. The plane was quite noisy when taking off, and after one minute and 40 seconds the afterburners were turned off and the noise dropped dramatically. It almost felt as if we had stalled, and as we taxied to the runway, the pilot warned us to expect this sensation. There was no sound or vibration when we went through the sound barrier. An unexpected feature of Concorde was the way the small windows got quite hot, or at least very warm, from air compression on the outer surface. Indeed, the whole fuselage heated up, lengthening by as much as 12 inches.

The plane climbed to a height of about 56,000 feet which provided an awe-inspiring view of the earth, with the curvature clearly to be seen. I was once invited to the cockpit (that occasionally happened before 9/11) and saw the curvature even more clearly. Then, as we approached our destination, I could see Great Britain appear over the horizon. The nose could be made to droop to provide the pilot with a better view during take-off and landing.

Sadly, on 25 July 2000, AF 4590 Concorde crashed on take-off at Charles de Gaulle airport when all aboard were killed. Following the accident, passenger numbers decreased, compounded later by security concerns arising out of the September 11 attacks. In 2003, Air France and British

Airways announced they would cease all Concorde services, seizing the opportunity to halt further losses.

Rae had a first supersonic experience in July 1981 when we flew to France for a series of extraordinary business meetings. After overnighting in Paris, Rae and I flew to Nice, and then by helicopter to Monte Carlo, where I met with Adil Ozkaptan, Woody White, and Adnan Khashoggi to discuss my negotiations in Turkey in connection with the proposed oil exploration licence. We had the full royal tour of Adan's spectacular 83-metre yacht, the Nabila, where we met with Brooke Shields and her mother, after which Adnan offered to take us to Cannes for lunch. A Riva speedboat was lowered over the side and we sped off at 45 knots across the Mediterranean. We returned by helicopter to Nice and then flew to London which was in the final stages of preparing for the wedding of Prince Charles and Lady Diana Spencer that very day. We began watching the ceremony on television in the Concorde departure lounge, and because of mechanical problems we had to return to the lounge twice before finally departing, allowing us to see more of the televised ceremony. During the flight the passengers were presented with a range of gifts, including a slice of the wedding cake and a souvenir menu.

In August and September 1981, I found myself in Turkey pursuing the acquisition of exploration rights for oil and gas along the Black Sea coast. Thanks to the introduction by the Khashoggis, I had a series of meetings with the Minister of Tourism and Energy, Turgut Ozal, who later became Prime Minister and afterwards President of Turkey. He was a great economic reformer.

Since it was the summer holidays in Canada, my family had flown over with me—giving the kids the chance of their first flight on Concorde. We stayed in Istanbul, with my having a brief visit to Ankara, the capital. We were hosted by the Turkish Government on a number of tours throughout Istanbul, the Bosphorus and the Black Sea. Later we flew to Izmir and then drove to Bodrum where we rented a sailing boat to explore the Aegean and Mediterranean coast. It was a magnificent trip. When we docked at Marmaris, we were met by Adnan Khashoggi's private DC9 which picked us up and flew us back to London. As we approached Heathrow Airport, our daughter Samantha was invited to sit in the navigator's seat in the cockpit and I took a photograph of us about to land into the dusk of an autumn evening, guided by the runway lights. After overnighting in London, we travelled back on Concorde the next morning in time to get the children home for the start of their school term.

Securing the Turkish exploration licence had become a top priority for me. It was a potential game-changer for our fledging resources company. The Khashoggi's experience in the oil business was invaluable and they bent over backwards to help, opening doors at the highest level. Things were moving fast. Oil stocks were riding high at the start of the 1980s and we were not the only ones looking to acquire assets. In September 1981, barely a week after returning with the family from Europe, I was in the air again, this time for a brief visit to Tulsa to deal with the emerging issues at Viking and then by private jet to the Bahamas to dine with the other Barrick Group directors and their spouses on Essam Khashoggi's yacht, which was moored at Nassau. Rae flew in from Toronto to join me. Essam's yacht was spectacular like his brother Adnan's in the South of France. Rae told me that the bathroom she visited was covered entirely by sheets of lapis lazuli.

There weeks later I was back on Concorde, stopping off for a day of meetings in London before flying to Ankara for more discussions with Turgut Orzal concerning our exploration licence, assisted by Khashoggi's colleague Adil Ozkaptan. By now we were getting to the sharp end of negotiations, and as I flew back to Toronto via Frankfurt I knew it wouldn't be long before I was back. In early December, Rae joined me on the Concorde to London where I caught up with Essam Khashoggi at his property on the outskirts of London before flying to Ankara for further meetings with Turkish Government officials.

We returned via Paris where we stayed at the Intercontinental Hotel, a beautiful building facing on to the Place de l'Opera built in 1862 in the prescribed style as part of Baron Hassumann's grand reconstruction of Paris. Breakfast at the hotel's renowned Cafe de Paix was somewhat fancier than the one served in the Tottenham Hotel in western New South Wales where Rae and I first met. Her company, however, was no less charming after 22 years since we met in the hotel at Tottenham. Our jet-setting lifestyle, rubbing shoulders with the rich and famous, did nothing to change Rae's down-to-earth, country attitude to life, or change her sense of being incredibly blessed into a thought of entitlement.

The Khashoggis were generous in their hospitality and knew how to impress. Meetings with them almost always required juggling international flights and hotel bookings.

Over the years I had many meetings with Essam and Adnan Khashoggi, in London, Essam's country property outside London, New York, Santa Barbara, Monaco, The Bahamas, Paris, Tulsa, Houston and Honolulu. The locations were always exquisite and provided a wonderful place to demonstrate to customers and clients the wealth and connections of the Khashoggi empire. The people I took to these meetings were always impressed and did not doubt for a moment the ability of the Khashoggis to deliver on their promises. The Khashoggis opened doors for us in Egypt, in Turkey and in Tunisia. My chairman and I also met with the president of Hispanoil, the Spanish national oil company, in Madrid, assisted by the Khashoggis. After the Barrick Group purchased the Khashoggi's interest in SPP we saw less of them. But it was a wonderful experience mixing with these famous people, who always treated me with courtesy and respect.

While we were staying in Paris in December 1982, Rae and I were whisked by private jet to Tunis, courtesy of Essam Khashoggi, for the day. After a tour of the souk, where we purchased a large Tunisian pot, we met for afternoon tea with President Bourghiba's son and his wife at their home. Barrick Resources, of which I was president, had a joint-venture with Occidental Petroleum drilling for oil off-shore of Tunisia. President Habib Bourgiba was president of Tunisia for 30 years from 1957-1987. We returned to Paris in the Khashoggi jet that evening. The following morning, we travelled by Concorde from Paris to New York, where we connected with a flight back to Toronto. At check in we asked for the large Tunisian pot to be booked through as accompanied luggage, but the check-in clerk was reluctant in case it got damaged.

Since the plane was relatively lightly loaded, she suggested we carry it on board and strap it in a seat like a passenger. It must surely have been the most expensive means of transporting a piece of baked clay across the Atlantic, but fortunately we were not charged for the extra seat, nor for the seat it occupied on our one-hour flight home from New York to Toronto after nursing it gently in the back of a New York taxi for the connection at La Guardia airport.

Rae and I celebrated the 20th Christmas of our married life in Peter and Melanie Munk's house near the Caledon ski slope on the outskirts of Toronto. We were carrying out renovations on our own home at 199 Douglas Drive, Toronto, and Peter's offer to lend us his house was especially welcome, Caledon is a place where a white Christmas is all but guaranteed and we were able to enjoy a quiet, traditional Christmas together after a year of frantic travelling. During our time in London, in 1977 we took some old Australian friends on a driving tour of Europe, which we all really enjoyed. One of our stops was in Klosters, Switzerland, where we stayed in Peter and Melanie Munk's beautiful chalet from which they enjoyed skiing.

We had always considered Christmas a family time, but like so many expats living far from home, the family gathering around the dinner table on those occasions spanned just two generations. In any case, my mother Bon and I had grown distant after the death of my father, and she had never built a close relationship with my children.

The death of her husband, and my father, when my mother was only 41 must have been a dreadful shock. Shortly after Dad's death, she moved to Sydney to live, occasionally visiting Jumble Plains. On one such trip she met a man who had visited on spec in the hope of buying scrap metal. He was Sydney ("Sam") Giles, with whom my mother fell in love. They were married in St Stephens Presbyterian church in Macquarie Street on 19 August 1959, the very same place where she had married my father 20 years before. This time, however, it was me who gave my mother away. The couple moved into my mother's house at 19 Helen Street, Westmead, with my two younger sisters, Wendy and Judy.

In January 1963, after we had relocated from Warren to Sydney to live, Rae and I went to Peak Hill for the wedding of friends Ron and Jill Parker from Warren. During our time away, my stepfather Sam Giles had a dreadful accident while using his power saw to gather firewood. He lost his right arm and his left leg was severed, causing him to fall to the ground. In the first micro-surgery in Australia, his leg was sown back on. On 15 February 1963, the Sydney Sun newspaper published a front-page picture of Sam Giles in hospital with the heading: "Miracle of Wiggling Toes." My mother's marriage to Sam was virtually at an end but she stuck by him, visiting him every day in hospital until he was discharged a year later. We never saw Sam afterwards.

My mother moved to Wagga Wagga where she met a banker, Kenneth Chisholm Mallett, a widower then in his mid-50s. They married on 23 April 1966 at St Andrews Presbyterian Church, Wagga Wagga making Ken my second stepfather. Ken died in March 1987 when he was 75.

My mother's excessive drinking continued, which caused many difficulties for those around her.

When we travelled to Australia from overseas, we always made it our business to arrange to meet with my mother—usually flying her to Sydney for some meals, a night at the theatre, or whatever. It was never particularly intimate, but at least we felt we had made contact.

Shortly after the Christmas in Caledon, we returned to Toronto, staying at the Four Seasons Hotel while our renovations were being completed. The phone rang and the voice on the other end told me they were calling from the Australian High Commission with some bad news. My mother had died in Wagga Wagga, Australia, the day before on 9 January 1982, of cirrhosis of the liver, no doubt due to her heavy drinking over many years. I managed to contact my sister, Judy, who was also living in Wagga Wagga, wondering how quickly I could catch a flight home. Judy told me my mother had already been cremated after a short memorial service.

Family relationships are seldom uncomplicated and my relationship with my mother and my sisters certainly was. My mother was hardly wealthy, but for reasons that died with her she chose not to leave a single thing to either my sister Wendy or me, not even a photograph, but to hand it all on to our sister, Judy. I look back on my relationship with my mother with considerable sadness, in part for my own sake, but mainly for my children and grandchildren. Having experienced the incredible bond of love one feels as a parent and a grandparent, I only wish my mother could have felt that.

As for myself, psychologists have made famous careers analysing the scars a boy takes from his relationship with his mother. Since I have never found myself on the psychiatrist's couch, I will simply pass on Rae's analysis, which is generally much sharper than mine. She believes my relationship with my mother has warped my judgement about women generally and that I am inclined to be too critical of them in a range of things including driving, responsibility and caring. Reviewing my life with the confidence of hindsight, I have little choice but to plead guilty on all charges.

While I was always conscious of the need to balance a hectic business career with responsibilities as a husband and parent, the long hours and travelling almost inevitably take a toll. If you become a father in your 20s as I did, the years when you are trying to make your professional mark frequently coincide with the crucial early years of fatherhood. Fortunately, I was working for a man who was aware of the stresses that constant travel place on a marriage, and I am forever grateful for the standing offer he made for Rae to fly with me. Yet even so, while I didn't really focus on it at the time, my career was having a cumulative effect on our relationship that, sooner or later, I had to resolve. Frequently it can take a crisis in a family or relationship before these things become clearer in your head, as it did for me several years later.

At the start of 1982, however, as Ronald Regan was beginning his second year in the White House, my goal was to put Barrick Resources firmly on the map by securing exploration rights wherever we could and get our subsidiary Viking Oil pumping at full speed. J. Paul Getty's famous formula for success, "rise early, work late and strike oil," might have been my motto. After the Christmas break the travelling continued. Rae flew back with me to Ankara on 17 January 1982 where I finalised negotiations on the petroleum exploration licence for 9.5 million acres, the whole of the north coast of Turkey on the Black Sea. The potential for the project was mind-boggling. The geological formations were a strong indicator of the carboniferous mineral wealth beneath the surface, but in the oil exploration business you quickly learn not to count your wells before they hatch.

We had other potential exploration opportunities in mind, if not yet in the pipeline. I travelled from Toronto to New York on 9 March 1982 for my first meeting with Bob Foman, chairman of E. F. Hutton, concerning a potential investment in a Viking Petroleum exploration program. This was followed by other meetings, including one with Adnan Khashoggi.

Back in Toronto, it was becoming apparent that our investment in Viking Petroleum was not going as well as we might have hoped. Nelson's nickname Swede seemed a good fit for the president of a company named after a tough breed of ancient Scandinavian warriors. Nelson had previously been president of the international division of Chevron. He was beginning to falter, however, in the much smaller environment of Viking and a decision was made by the directors to terminate his services. Subsequent analysis vindicated the decision, and Viking's founder and chairman Milton McKenzie again took the reins as president.

Two weeks later, I arranged a critical meeting in Houston between Swede Nelson and Essam Khashoggi. The following day we closed the reorganisation of Viking Petroleum, which included the resignation of Nelson. The problems at Viking were absorbing more of my time. I again travelled from Toronto to New York for a series of consultations, principally concerning Barrick Energy, Inc. of which I was chairman, and Viking Petroleum, Inc. These included several meetings and lunches with both Adnan and Essam Khashoggi in their apartments in Olympic Tower.

In late 1982 I met with no less than seven vice presidents of Goldman Sachs, who were assembled at their office in New York City. The purpose was to discuss the possible flotation of Viking Petroleum, of which I was then President. It so happened that the weekend before there had been a massive devaluation of the Mexican Peso, with every newspaper featuring the headline. After the usual pleasantries, one of the Goldman Sachs VPs asked if we had heard that over the weekend President de la Madrid had called in his Prime Minister, Premier Hertzog, and asked him how much the national debt was. Hertzog replied in a flash, "One hundred billion dollars, Your Excellency."

"No, no, Premier, how much in pesos?"

To which the premier replied, "All of them."

In June, Rae and I attended a spectacular private party at Peter and Melanie Munk's house in Toronto to celebrate David and Jill Gilmour's marriage and Peter and David's 25-year partnership. Guests included Essam and Layla Khashoggi. This was an absolutely stunning event with over 100 guests in dinner suits and the most glamorous dresses. We will always remember it as one of the best social evenings we've experienced. The following day we were invited to a barbecue at Peter and Melanie Munk's house at Caledon for Essam Khashoggi.

Yet the company continued to struggle and by mid-1982 it had become clear to me and to Peter that we needed to take action. I volunteered to spend my time in Tulsa, trying to get things right and began the arduous job of commuting each week from Toronto to Tulsa. Peter was very grateful and penned me this note:

I did not want this opportunity to go by without going on record expressing my appreciation for your enthusiastic willingness to assist us with our problems in Viking.

The spirit and the speed with which you accepted this exceptional challenge says it all! I know the almost insurmountable personal problems your move to Viking has caused, both within your family and affecting your personal financial well-being in terms of your two homes being in the middle of the move. The fact that, despite this, you have assumed the responsibility and thrown yourself into the breach causes me to express to you my respect and admiration for your professionalism, your team spirit and above all for the overriding determination in being willing to set corporate priorities ahead of your personal ones.

I know I speak on behalf of all my colleagues when I wish you the best of luck, our total support and our appreciation of your personal sacrifice in filling this major corporate need.

I told Rae I thought I'd be commuting to Tulsa for two or maybe three months while I sorted out the company. As so often occurred in my crowded life, however, things didn't quite turn out as planned.

## CHAPTER 8

# TORNADO ALLEY

STREETS FLOODED. PLEASE ADVISE.

ROBERT BENCHLEY

TELEGRAPH MESSAGE ON ARRIVING IN VENICE

As I flew into Tulsa International Airport on September 27, 1982, a row of private jets parked on the apron bore witness to the unprecedented oil boom that was reaching its peak. Tulsa was known as the "Oil Capital of the World" for most of the 20th century. Many fortunes had been made and many had been broken in the switch-back ride boom to bust to boom again. The riches that flowed from the energy industry had driven a construction boom in the 1920s. This had bequeathed the city some of the best Art Deco buildings in the world, the most conspicuous of which is the Boston Avenue Methodist Church with its 85-metre tower soaring heavenwards with a grandeur I had never previously associated with Charles Wesley's down-to-earth interpretation of Christianity. Beyond oil and architecture, Tulsa's third claim to fame is its weather, particularly its tornados, the severity of which we were later to experience first-hand.

I took a suite at the Excelsior, a swish hotel then just nine months old, built to cater for the oil trade. A vintage Rolls Royce parked conspicuously outside advertised its opulence while the crispness of the Waterford Restaurant's tablecloths promised more than the average hamburger. My plan was to leave a bunch of clothes there and commute back to Toronto on weekends. I could sort out the problems at Viking, clear my suite and be home in good time for Christmas.

The problem at Viking, like 90 per cent of companies in difficulty, was cash flow. It couldn't raise the money to support the ambitious new exploration program it needed to secure its long-term future. Banks were getting nervous and threatened to pull their loans. The oil price had slipped from its historical peak of $38 a barrel two years earlier, and while it was still hovering at around $30, speculation of a glut was rife.

The process of renegotiation with the banks would take months while we simultaneously managed operations, looking for efficiencies to compensate for tightening margins.

I settled into my commuting routine, flying out of Toronto International Airport on Sunday evening, or occasionally Monday morning, hoping that the de-icing of the plane would not unduly delay our departure. A couple of hours later at Chicago, I would connect with another American Airlines flight to Tulsa. I would return by the same route late on Friday afternoon. One of the few consolations to this gruelling schedule was my promotion to the rank of Admiral by American Airlines. In May 1981, AA became the second airline in the world to introduce a frequent flyer program and I had been one of the very first to sign up. With a minimum of four American Airline flights a week, I quickly clocked up the 100,000 miles which elevated me to Gold status, which came with a raft of benefits, including admission to AA's Admirals Club lounge. Welcoming as the lounge might have been on a cold Sunday evening layover in Chicago, the routine quickly became tiring and very unsettling. It was compounded by my extensive other travel commitments (both local and international) and also by occasional mid-week returns to Toronto for family issues. I remember, for example, having to dash back to attend a dinner at St George's when son Scott was awarded the prize for the school's best athlete, the first student to win the prize outright. He had won the Canadian cross-country championship. The following morning, I had to turn around and return to Tulsa.

Strange and unexpected things began to happen as a result of my commuting. The joy of getting back home to my loved ones at the end of the week was wonderful. But leaving again only hours later was painful. Rae rushed to get all my washing done and then packed my bag for my return. She then had to kiss me goodbye for another week. I believe I felt the pain of parting again as much as she did as I jumped in a cab to the airport. Fridays dawned with mixed emotions. I would be looking towards leaving the office around 4 pm to catch my flight to Chicago, although occasionally I had to defer that until Saturday morning, because of work commitments. Yet I found myself, subconsciously, looking for excuses to remain in Tulsa for the weekend. What was causing this? Didn't I desperately want to be back with my family? "Yes", was the answer, but what I did not understand at the time, is that the dread of departing again was nagging deep inside me. The routine continued for the best part of a year until all of us decided we'd had enough.

In March 1983, Rae, Samantha and I flew in the company's Falcon Jet—previously owned by Oral Roberts, the famous televangelist—from Tulsa to Phoenix for the Easter weekend. Scott and Stuart travelled from Toronto to Phoenix. We all stayed at the Registry Resort. In past years, we had always stayed in the private house at the John Gardiner Tennis Ranch in Scottsdale, near Camelback Mountain. The Easter week was a good time to get out of Toronto as it was the "mud month" when the snow was melting and all was messy. It was also great to fly above the clouds and see the blue sky that had been hidden for months during the winter in Toronto.

Whilst in Phoenix, all the family, together with Jenny Hill (with whom we had socialised when we lived in Cairo) and Paul Hazenfus, flew in the Falcon jet over and through the Grand Canyon. It was an amazing experience, deep inside the canyon, bouncing wildly as we climbed over the edge with the difference in air pressures. On our way back to Phoenix, we surveyed from the air the scene of the major meteor crater in northern Arizona, 30 kilometres west of Winslo. The huge crater is 1300 metres long and 174 metres deep. After our adventure, Rae and the children flew back to Toronto, and I took the jet back to Tulsa.

A few months later on 4 July 1983, Independence Day, the whole family, including our cat, boarded the company's jet and flew to Tulsa to begin our time as residents of the United States. We moved into a ground-floor condominium in The

Yorktown at Utica Square, imagining that we would be here for a few years.

By now I had assumed the role of President and began digging into the Company's finances. In May 1983, Peter Munk and I travelled to Madrid to discuss with Hispanoil a possible joint venture with Viking, which was not accepted by the Spanish national oil company. It became clear that we were not performing and would need to restructure our debts with a group of four banks, led by Northern Trust, based in Chicago. This led to protracted negotiations over several months, before I finally executed a comprehensive agreement with all the banks. Because every one of our oil wells formed part of the security for the loans, the documentation was extensive to say the least. When we closed on 3 February 1984, I had to sign 3666 documents, staying back in the office until 9pm to work through the pile and returning early the next morning to complete the task.

We had been living in Tulsa for almost a year when we decided to take the family to Eureka Springs near Beaver Lake for the 1984 Memorial Day weekend. This was a charming town in southwest Arkansas, not far from the Oklahoma border—originally established on the back of the nearby hot springs. We had a very pleasant time and headed back home to Tulsa, after stopping at a friend's blueberry farm in Arkansas. We had no idea of what had happened in Tulsa whilst we were away.

The state of Oklahoma lies within an area of the Great Plains known as Tornado Alley, a region stretching from South Dakota to central Texas. It is the area where warm humid air from the Gulf of Mexico, hot dry air from the deserts of Arizona and New Mexico, and cold air from Canada collide. The warm air funnels through the colder air, causing an updraft which in certain conditions begins to rotate, rapidly building in speed. While we had been enjoying the Spring weather a couple of hundred kilometres to the east, a massive tornado had descended on Tulsa bringing 24 hours of nonstop rain averaging 9.35 inches (240mm), with some areas measuring up to 14 inches (355mm). Intense floods engulfed the city, damaging thousands of homes and businesses, killing 14 people, and ultimately cost between $150–180 million. After the storm subsided, the public outrage grew, and resulted in a $140 million flood prevention project to ensure this flood severity never occurred again.

The first inkling we had of the disaster was the sight of a car in a tree on the outskirts of Tulsa. Quickly we came upon more signs of the disaster that had devastated parts of the town. The closer we got to our apartment, the more the streetscape came to resemble the set of a disaster movie. Our building was situated near the foot of a hill down which a wall of water had descended with the force of a torrent from a broken dam. The water had smashed through the ground floor, filing the lobby to the ceiling. The doorman had nearly drowned. The power was off and the electric doors would not open. He was saved by a log that smashed open one of the plate glass doors.

As we drove in, we could see rubbish everywhere. On entering the ground floor car park there were cars piled up, some on top of the others. We opened our unit fearing the worst, but fortunately the floodwater had only seeped in under the entry door and through the exterior windows. It had reached a depth of about 15 inches (about 40 centimetres), most to it draining away over the weekend. Nevertheless, the damage was expensive. Everything on the floors was ruined. It had reached up to the stereo, to certain bed linens, and, of course, all the carpets were destroyed. A foul smell permeated the place. The basement, where we had stored many items, such as luggage and bicycles, was still full of water and was not pumped out for several days.

We had to make a decision; should we stay and work our way through the sodden mess or should we now move to Houston, where we had planned to go in the coming months? We elected to salvage what we could, pack up and move to Houston. I managed to secure a wonderful hospitality suite in the Four Seasons Hotel, Riverway, Houston, staying there for a few months until we found a very nice large house at 5703 Tecumseh Circle, at Chimney Rock and Woodway. The owner agreed to structure a deal whereby we would purchase the house, which he would finance, and accept an option for us to sell him back the house at the end of the agreed period of three years. The advantage of such an arrangement over a regular lease, is that property owners are allowed to deduct the cost of their mortgage interest from their income for tax purposes: renters have no such advantage.

In Houston I took up a new role as frontman for ACDC, not the Australian rock band but the American Completion and Development Corporation, a Barrick Group company, of which I was made president and chairman. ACDC raised capital in the market to finance the completion of oil and gas. We would help resource companies transition from the exploration phase, when investment was tax-deductible, to the production stage when a well was expected to make profits and a different form of investor was required. ACDC was not performing as it should have done and Peter was keen that I get down and try to figure out what we should do. As with Viking, the challenge boiled down to capital raising. I managed to secure a partnership with Lehndorff Investment Corporation from Germany and a $20 million line of non-recourse credit from Prudential Insurance. The beauty of the arrangement was that our clients bore the risk, not us. So in late 1986, when the oil price fell to as low as $13 a barrel, turning lucrative oil development projects into loss-makers, I was able to return the capital to the lenders and investors.

When I had offered to purchase the company Peter was delighted, since he was keen to remove a potential problem from his books. With the oil industry in a downturn, the decision had been made to turn Barrick's attention to gold. It was a shrewd move that gave Peter and his company the success and financial security they had worked so hard to achieve.

By the end of 1986, however, it became apparent that there was no future for the company with oil prices so depressed. Rae and I started to think about our future. Was this the time for us to return to Australia? Rae was not mad about Houston with its humid, sub-tropical climate and the kids were growing up, and I might have happily returned too. However, the chance to give the boys a US college education was tempting, given the career prospects it might open. We decided to give the US a fresh shot, with the luxury of being able to choose where in that wide country we would like to live.

Making a fresh start in Atlanta and taking up the new job with LJ Hooker brought to an end my business involvement with Peter. Five years later in September 1992 we were able to enjoy a final seminal moment when after being in an out of court for almost 14 years our litigation against the Egyptian Government over the cancellation of the Pyramids Oasis project was finally settled. We had been through an incredible journey together that lasted a dozen years from our first meetings in Sydney when he enticed me to move with my family to Egypt to build a city for 45,000 people. The journey had taken me to London to assist with the development and operation of the company's chain of hotels and resorts, to Tahiti to reinvigorate a unique luxury hotel, to Toronto to open the company's office and become the founding President of Barrick Resources, to Tulsa, Oklahoma to rationalise the group's investments in the oil and gas business and finally Houston, Texas. I wrote to thank Peter for investing his faith in me and for the opportunities that flowed. His reply was another example of his generous spirit:

> Your letter and very impressive enclosures arrived just as I'm leaving for Europe, but I do want you to know before I depart how thrilled all of us here are at your magnificent new undertaking. I have no doubt whatsoever that you will do your usual spectacular job since, of all the senior executives I have ever known, you are without a doubt the most talented, the most resourceful, the most able and the most results-oriented. It is I who should thank you for giving so much of yourself to our company in the many years of our association; I should be the one to thank you for the learning experience!

When I get back in a week or two, I'll spend a bit more time going through the information you sent on Hooker/Barnes. It would indeed be great if at some stage in the not-too-distant future we could do some business together again. I think we know each other well enough by now to pull off something extraordinary – in terms of both scope and profitability!

In the meantime, my very best wishes to you and Rae and all the family. I told George Herscu how lucky he was to get you and I'm sure he's already discovering the magnitude of his good fortune!'

More than 20 years later in Sydney, in the early hours of 29 March 2018, I received an email from Sheila Fennessy, my former personal assistant at Barrick Gold, with the following sad news:

> It is with deep sadness that Barrick Gold Corporation announces the passing of the Company's Founder and Chairman Emeritus, Peter Munk. Munk passed away peacefully in Toronto today, surrounded by his family. He was 90.

The company's formal tribute gave a more complete picture of an entrepreneur who earned his fortune through sheer persistence and, once having made it, demonstrated that same persistence to help others.

One of Canada's most significant philanthropists, Munk donated nearly $300 million to causes and institutions that were close to his heart. With his wife, Melanie, he established the Peter Munk Cardiac Centre at the Toronto General Hospital in 1997. Munk donated more than $175 million to the institution, including a $100 million contribution in 2017 that remains the largest single gift ever made to a Canadian hospital. To his alma mater, the University of Toronto, Munk gave $47 million to create what has become Canada's preeminent degree-granting institution for the research and study of global affairs, the Munk School of Global Affairs. In 2008, he founded The Munk Debates, which quickly became Canada's most important public policy debate series, bringing the world's brightest minds together to debate the biggest issues of our time.

For his leadership as an entrepreneur and philanthropist, Munk received numerous awards and honours, including honorary doctorates from the University of Toronto, Concordia University, Bishop's University, and the Technion-Israel Institute of Technology. In 2008, he was named a Companion of the Order of Canada, the country's highest civilian honour, limited to no more than 165 living Canadians at any one time.

Dr Samuel Chand, a close friend in Atlanta, wrote me a poignant letter after Peter's death that moved me to tears:

> He was a generous man, you are too.
> He was a forward-thinking visionary, you are too.
> He was sensitive to people's contexts, you are too.
> He was a man of honesty and candor, you are too.
> He was authentically appreciative of his team, you are too.
> He invited you on a "let's do something together" journey, you do too.
> He was your mentor. His fruit did not fall far from the tree.'

Honesty and candour are indeed among the qualities I admired most in Peter for whom ethics remained paramount. The extent to which I had absorbed them were to be put to the test the moment I began working for Herscu.

Tony's father Allan Kenneth McLellan.

Rae's Grandparents Alfred Thomas and Viola Hand.

Tony's mother Bonnie about to depart.

Tony's grandparents George and Amy McLellan and family.

Loyal greetings to

*HRH The Prince of Wales
and The Lady Diana Spencer*

on the occasion of their wedding
at St Paul's Cathedral
on 29th July 1981

**British
airways**

MENU

A Concorde menu—Prince
Charles and Lady Diana's
wedding.

Tony's father Allan Kenneth
McLellan and Wendy at Jumble
Plains during flooding.

Tony and Rae's wedding at All
Saints, Parramatta (1961).

Rae Hand—Buxton Queen.

Rae and her father Lennox Hand.

Tony and Rae—Topwoodlands Colts Cricket (1960).

Tony and Rae
ballroom dancing
in Warren.

Tony and Rae at the
Australian Embassy
in Cairo (1976).

Tony and Rae
leaving Cairo.

Tony at Camenae
Capital Corporation.

Tony duck
shooting in
Egypt.

Rae on Farida at the
Great Pyramids.

Tony and Rae's children in upper Egypt.

Rae at the tomb of Tutankhamun.

TOMB OF مقــبرة
Tutankhamun توت عنخ آمون
18 DYN. أسـرة ١٨

Samantha in a sarcophagus at Valley of the Kings.

Off to dinner in our gallabayas.

Tony and Jeff Rawson in Houston—"all hat and no cattle".

Tony and Rae's first matrimonial home in Warren.

Tony with his
Centrepoint project.

Tony's mother Bonnie and new stepfather, Ken Mallett.

Rae and Samantha at Ephesus.

Tony and Rae playing tennis at Gezira Sporting Club.

Leaving Istanbul for London on Khashoggi's jet.

Tony accepts the Prime Minister's award for Habitat for Humanity.

Village at Pyramids Oasis by Francois Spoerry.

George V Hotel at Pyramids Oasis.

Tony with Stan Smith at
Wimbledon.

Tony and Dr James Tickner
launch Chrysos Corporation
office.

The Menzies Research Centre board of directors.

GEORGE W. BUSH

January 15, 2001

Mr. Anthony McLellan
2221 Peachtree Rd NE Ste D428
Atlanta, GA 30309-1148

Dear Mr. McLellan,

Dick Cheney and I want to thank you for all you have done for us.
Your leadership, energy, and generous commitment of time were
crucial to our campaign's success.

I am grateful for your hard work and honored you were on my team.
I look forward to leading our great country.

Sincerely,

George W. Bush

Letter from President George W. Bush.

Tony McLellan at
the Great Pyramids.

Concorde takes off.

Jumble Plains sign.

Tony, Scott and Stuart on top of Cheops Pyramid.

Tony with James
Wallace and
John Howard.

A skyscraping plan in 30 days flat.

## CHAPTER 9

# SHAKE-UP CALL

What good is it for a man to gain the whole world, yet forfeit his soul?

MARK 8:36

Atlanta, Georgia, in early 1987 felt like a city with its engines running, cleared for take-off, much as Sydney had been a quarter of a century earlier when Rae and I moved there from the bush. They called it the capital of the new South, a city that was forging a new destiny after the civil rights reforms. Northerners could be quick to highlight the stain of Jim Crowe that still hung off the Confederate States, but Georgia's enlightened Governor William B. Hartsfield had succeeded in nurturing Atlanta's image as "the city too busy to hate" during the struggles of the 1950s and 1960s.

When we settled in Atlanta in March 1987, the population of the greater metropolitan district was nudging 2 million, around the same size as Sydney in the early 1960s. Atlanta would grow to 3 million over the next ten years, spurred in part by its success in staging the 1996 Summer Olympics, which would carry the baton as the "best Games ever" until handing it to Sydney four years later. Today Atlanta's population has passed the 6 million mark and the roads built for a city half that size are straining under the weight of traffic. Yet Rae and I still recognise its charm, and the special Southern charm of its people, whenever we return to visit the many special friends we made there. Atlanta, for all its growing sophistication, is still the kind of city where taxi drivers will waive drivers into the lane in front of them, rather than sitting with clenched teeth hugging a bumper.

As I looked forward to the next chapter in my business life early in 1987, although the company had its own private jet, the easy access to the William B. Hartsfield Atlanta International Airport, was a definite plus. Atlanta first started to develop as a city when it became the terminus for a major state-sponsored railway line and its importance as a transport hub expanded with the jet age. When you die, I used to say, you'll never know whether you're going to heaven or hell. But you do know that you are going to change planes in Atlanta.

What was more, it seemed a great place to base ourselves while the boys completed university. The city's altitude, higher than 1000 metres, is enough to take the edge off the humid, summer heat making it an outdoor city virtually year-round. It is a city that loves its sport: the Braves, the Falcons and the Hawks.

Back in Houston, we had all but made up our mind to move to Atlanta, when one day in early February 1987, I got a call out of the blue from a head hunter in Sydney from whom I hadn't heard in years. "Would you be interested in becoming president of LJ Hooker in America?" he asked. "They've got a few thousand employees and active investments in residential, industrial and commercial real estate." I told him it sounded a good offer for a year or two. "In that case, we'd very much like to talk with you," the head hunter said. "But there's a catch. You'd have to move to Atlanta." The timing seemed serendipitous, since we had already cast our minds to other options, on the west coast before concluding that Atlanta was the best. Perhaps it was evidence of a greater hand at play, although I wasn't fully conscious of God's role in shaping our lives back then.

I flew to Sydney via Los Angeles for discussions with the Hooker Corporation's chairman, George Herscu. A Jewish refugee from Romania, Herscu had become a flamboyant figure in the Australian property sector of the 1980s, who appeared to be riding high after buying the 60-year-old family-run Hooker property business for $450m in 1985. I'd crossed paths with Herscu in Melbourne where we had done some valuation work for him. He ran his operation out of the trunk of his car, as I recall. He had no office, no nothing. He was just a driven entrepreneur. I didn't know him very well, and probably only met him two or three times. Under Herscu, the Hooker Corporation expanded at a barely believable rate into the development and acquisition of retailers and large-scale shopping complexes in the United States. It was a bold move to say the least since neither Herscu nor the company had any experience of the complexities of retail. Neither had they had the time or expertise to undertake due diligence on the properties they acquired, their location or the businesses that were occupying them.

For much of the 1970s and 1980s, when the only way in which property prices travelled seemed to be up, brash entrepreneurs like Herscu escaped the reckoning. As the 1980s drew to a close, however, with the property market slowing and interest rates at record highs, the pressures were taking their toll. One by one, businessmen who had once been seen as miracle workers became undone, bringing large sectors of the finance sector crashing down with them. The State Bank of Victoria, the State Bank of South Australia, the Teachers Credit Union of Western Australia, the Pyramid Building Society and others were brought to the point of insolvency by bad property debts.

I took the job with no illusions as to the work that had to be done. I had taken on the task of fixing flawed enterprises before, however, and I was excited by the challenge and the prospect of the upside for a company that was making an impact. It wasn't until I got my feet under the desk, however, that I began to appreciate how much needed to be done. There were five divisions each with their own president, no central president, all run as separate fiefdoms, with no one having a clue as to what anyone else was doing. In aggregate it was an enormous operation employing several thousand people building a couple thousand houses a year and developing industrial and commercial centres. Yet it was being run like an anarchist's collective, with everybody making their own unaccountable decisions whether or not they accorded with the company's strategy, if indeed the company had a strategy, which I quickly began to doubt.

In a few months into the job, I discovered fraud in the housing division. A crash in the housing market meant we had a lot of development in the bad markets, cities like San Antonio, Dallas and Houston where the value of property was falling with the oil prices.

Our policy dictated we should never have a new house unsold for more than two months, and our inventory should never be more than about 350 houses. However, I discovered to my horror that we were holding over 900. As I waded through the records, I unearthed what was happening: The key executives in the housing division, who were earning a bonus based on the number of new houses constructed, had not assumed responsibility for ensuring that they were being sold. And then they were lying to the company. As soon as I had satisfied myself on the facts, I wasted no time in firing the president, the executive vice president, and the chief financial officer. Later on, I was approached by the Florida Police who were enquiring into an alleged marital dispute involving the ex-president. This again highlighted a lesson for me: A man who cheats on his wife is capable of cheating on his company.

When Herscu came over, I put the evidence in front of him and explained why a write down was inevitable. He looked at me with absolute horror. "No, no, no," he said, "you can't do that. Our shares would go down and my shares are on margin call. Do you understand what that would do to me?" I told him that at the very least we had a duty to inform the auditors and invite them to assess the value of the assets on our books. Herscu began to plead with me.

"You must keep it a secret from the auditors", he said. I had never come across anything like this in my business career, and I became so concerned that I took the hand-written ledgers to my house wondering whether they might have been manipulated.

Herscu's crude attempts to conceal the problems went against everything in my upbringing managing a rural property and my 25 years as an executive. When problems emerge, you face up to them, assess what needs to be done, and attend to it immediately. Procrastinating or turning a blind eye only makes things worse in the long run. The iron rule of farming is: "If the fence is broke, fix it before you lose your sheep." I had been through times with my previous boss, but if there was one thing Peter Munk liked less than hearing bad news, it was not hearing the bad news because it had been kept from him. Deal with it and move on was always his approach. Procrastination always makes things worse. One should never do what a friend of mine did in the days before the internet by putting everything in the LTBW tray. Larry, the managing partner of a large law firm in Oklahoma, had three trays on his desk, one marked IN, one marked OUT and one marked LTBW. When I asked him what the LTBW meant, he said, "Let the Buggers Wait."

After meeting with Herscu I packed the pile of hand-written ledgers into my car and took them home. It was the days before electronic accounting. When I brought them back the next day, I presented them to Herscu. "George, I can't work like this. You'll have to find another guy. I'll stay until you do." When I reflected on the way his aides sucked up to him, I realised that they were behind him, not me. They would have perceived me as weak and were not prepared to stand up to Herscu on matters of proper corporate governance, let alone a matter of principle.

There is nothing new about white-collar crime, as we like to call it. When Jesus saw the activities of the money changers in the temple, he drove them out.[3] When there is clear, irrefutable evidence of corruption within the organisation, the leader must move immediately to handle it. And he should never try to cover it up. It is important also to make sure that others who may be involved know that their leader can be trusted not to put it off but to take action.

Two years later, my successor at Hooker was fighting off the creditors, pleading for time to make an orderly selloff of properties to raise cash. On July 11, 1989, Herscu resigned as chairman and two weeks later Hooker Corp went into liquidation in Australia owing $1.77 billion to 42 banks. Herscu's career ended in disgrace a year later when he was found guilty of bribing Queensland planning minister Russ Hinze to intervene in a dispute with the Brisbane City Council about a shopping centre, with two $50,000 payments. Herscu was carted off to Brisbane's jail in a paddy wagon to begin a five-year prison sentence. Upon his parole in June 1993, he returned to the United States. After his release, he became embroiled in a court case with his son, Robert, over an alleged fraud. He died in Los Angeles in 2013.

No one succeeds in business unless they are determined to win. What sets men like Herscu apart is a determination to win whatever the cost to your integrity and the damage it might cause to those around you. In business, ends, however noble, never in themselves justify the means. Behaviour doesn't have to be criminal, as Herscu's self-evidently was. I

3    Matthew 21:12-13; Mark 11:15-17; John 2:14-16

have seen corporations focus on keeping within the law, whilst paying scant regard to integrity.

Ethical issues include the rights and duties between a company and its employees, its suppliers, customers and neighbours and its fiduciary responsibility to its shareholders. Other issues include relations between different companies, hostile takeovers and industrial espionage, corporate governance and political contributions. Particular corporate ethical abuses include creative accounting, misleading financial reporting, insider trading, securities fraud, bribery, kickbacks and facilitation payments.

In employment, there are issues such as industrial relations, health and safety, sexual harassment, discrimination, policies for handicapped employees, how to treat whistle blowers, and so on. In sales and marketing, ethical issues include truthfulness and full disclosure in advertising, bait and switch marketing, sales of undesirable products in schools, multi-level marketing etc. In production, companies may be faced with how to deal with products that might cause needless harm, tobacco for example, or the environmental impacts from mining. There are no grey areas in business if you abide by the golden rule of conduct most of us try to observe in our everyday lives: "So in everything, do to others what you would have them do to you" (Matthew 7:12).

This simple precept, drawn from our Judeo-Christian heritage, is the thread that binds our social fabric. It is much more than simple tribal reciprocity. The "others" includes our enemies as well as our friends. In Christian teaching, the golden rule has a deeper, spiritual context in which the love one shares towards one's neighbour is inextricably attached to the love God has shown for us. "Love the Lord your God with all your heart, and with all your soul, and with all your mind, and with all your strength. The second is this: Love your neighbour as yourself. There is no commandment greater than these" (Mark 12:30-31).

Whatever you do, never ignore or condone improper behaviour. Your people are watching you. I was living in Houston, Texas, in 1985 when Kenneth Lay—a well-respected businessman and philanthropist—merged Houston Natural Gas with InterNorth. Most people regarded this as a major coup for Houston and looked forward to the new Enron expanding its operations in the city. The Chief Financial Officer and other executives not only misled Enron's board of directors and audit committee on high-risk accounting practices, but also pressured the auditor, Arthur Andersen, to ignore the issues. The shocking manipulation of Enron's accounts eventually led to Enron filing for bankruptcy—then the biggest in US history.

I feel certain that the CEO, Jeffrey Skilling, knew and understood what was going on. He later faced a 53-count, 65-page indictment covering a broad range of financial crimes including bank fraud, making false statements to banks and auditors, securities fraud, wire fraud, money laundering, conspiracy and insider trading. Skilling was convicted on 19 counts and sentenced to 24 years and four months in prison. That is a long time to be away from home. He was released in 2019 after serving 12 years of his sentence.

Enron's auditor, Arthur Andersen, earned $25 million in audit fees and $27 million in consulting fees in 2000. Over $50 million in revenues for a professional accounting firm proved too enticing, and the firm lost its judgement and committed a series of mistakes. In its accounting work for Enron, Arthur Andersen had been sloppy and weak. But that's how Enron had wanted it. In truth, even as they angrily pointed fingers, the two deserved each other. Arthur Andersen was found guilty of obstruction of justice for shredding thousands of documents and deleting e-mails and company files that tied the firm to Enron. Although the ruling was later overturned by the US Supreme Court, by then the firm had shut down and 85,000 people had lost their jobs.

It is hard to imagine a more egregious example of rampant unethical practices. How did it happen? Surely it was not just by coincidence that so many unethical human beings ended up working for the same company at the same time and the same place? We cannot neglect the role of a company's culture in which bad practices may be tolerated, endorsed or even encouraged. As one commentator said, "The Enron scandal grew out of a steady accumulation of habits and values and actions that began years before and finally spiralled out of control." I saw elements of that dysfunctional corporate culture at LJ Hooker, and responsibility for it stems from the top. At Enron, executives obsessed with short-term earnings to maximise bonuses. The value of director stock ownership was $659 million for the chairman and $174 million for the effective CEO. In 2000 the top 200 highest-paid employees received $1.4 billion (that is with a "B") from salaries, bonuses and stock. That is equivalent to an average of $7 million each.

One good thing to come out of the Enron disaster was the Sarbanes-Oxley Act. This sets standards for the preparation of audit reports; the restriction of public accounting firms from providing any non-auditing services when auditing, provisions for the independence of audit committee members, executives required to sign off on financial reports, relinquishment of certain executives' bonuses in case of financial restatements and expanded financial disclosure of firms' relationships with unconsolidated entities. Regulation, however, is always the second better solution. Far better that individuals obey their consciences and behave in business life as they would do in any other sphere of human activity. In the words of Jesus, once again from the gospel of Mark, "What good is it for a man to gain the whole world, yet forfeit his soul" (Mark 8:36)?

I had the good fortune to be raised by parents for whom honesty and respect for others was paramount and which they instilled into me. We were not regular churchgoers, but when the census collectors arrived every five years, my parents, like 96% per cent of Australians in 1911, would have had no hesitation in marking themselves down as Christians. This has now fallen to a little over 52% at the last census. It was more than lip-service. Back then the Bible was part of the canon, and its stories and teachings were unapologetically taught in schools. The parables of the Prodigal Son or the Good Samaritan, to take just two significant examples, were as familiar to our generation as The Adventures of Harry Potter would be to children today.

While my brush with Herscu prompted me to think about the ethics of business, it was becoming clear that I was not always acting with Christian charity to those closer to me. I might have excused the sharp words with my children or my wife as a consequence of the pressures of business life, and comforted myself with the thought that I was providing for their comfort by earning the kind of money and living the kind of life of which my parents had only dreamed.

A great experience we had in the summer of 1987, not long after we moved to Atlanta, was attending with Gerald and Susan Lancaster the famous Palio bare-back horse race around the town square of Sienna, Italy. It consists of 17 horses, each representing a district or contrada in the walled city of Sienna. The winner, we understood was to become the de-facto mayor of the city for the coming year. The race has been conducted for 1000 years and was all over in a few minutes. Afterwards, I traipsed the city seeking one of each of the 17 capstones used on the front entrance to the houses in each contrada, and managed to collect a complete set, which I had shipped back to Atlanta. They are displayed today in our home and visitors are absolutely fascinated with them—especially those from Italy.

Looking back in that first year in Atlanta in our 27th year of marriage, we seemed to be approaching a pivotal point in our lives. In February our son Scott celebrated his 21st birthday while in April, our youngest, turned 15. They remained close to us, but the days when the incessant demands of caring for our children dominated our home lives were fast disappearing. As I turned 47, I was showing all the symptoms of a man on the edge of what would fashionably be called a mid-life crisis. For me, however, it was just another step on the journey everyone must take if they aspire to be a mature adult, the realisation that despite everything I had done to deny it, Allan Anthony McLellan was not the centre of the universe.

With success in business comes exposure to the risk of pride, one of the seven deadly sins. All men are affected by pride, and I was far from the exception. I can relate to the dry wit of Dame Edith Sitwell who said: "I have often wished I had time to cultivate modesty . . . but I am too busy thinking about myself." The Bible reminds us that "God opposes the proud but gives grace to the humble" (1 Peter 5:5; cf James 4:6).

During the revival of Christian faith known as the First Great Awakening in the US in the 18th Century, Jonathan Edwards was presiding over a massive prayer meeting attended by 800 men.

A woman sent a message into that meeting asking the men to pray for her husband who she said had grown unloving, obstinate and full of pride. Edwards read the note to the 800 men and asked if the husband in question would raise his hand so that the whole assembly could pray for him. Three hundred men put up their hands. I could have been one of them. In 1988 pride nearly cost me my marriage.

Despite all my effort and strain in my career, I was disappointed with my performance as a father and a husband and feelings of bitterness began to creep in. I became insecure in these relationships and began to abuse them. To give an example; when Rae underwent a total hysterectomy in Toronto, I left the next day on a business trip to Madrid rather than remain at her side at the hospital.

While at Hookers, we were doing business with a real estate agent, Bill Bugg of Cushman & Wakefield, who I was beginning to get to know socially. Knowing of our time in Egypt, he offered to introduce me to an Egyptian who had been living in Australia and was now the minister at his church in Atlanta. I readily agreed, so Bill arranged for us to meet the minister, Rev Dr Michael Youssef, over lunch.

Michael had an interesting story. I discovered, to my surprise, that my Arabic was a little better than his. Michael had left Egypt when he was 17 to come to Australia, because it was preferable to being recruited into the Egyptian Army. He later met an Australian girl and studied theology at Moore College. Afterwards, he completed a doctorate in California before getting involved in ministry work. He founded the Church of the Apostles, a new Episcopal Church in Atlanta, which by then had a congregation of around 70 people. He was pleasant company and an interesting, thoughtful guy. So, when he invited me along to his church, I said I would.

I wasn't opposed to going to church. Rae and I attended occasionally if sporadically. With all the hectic activity of settling into a new city and forging a new direction for my career, however, attending church was not exactly top of our "to do" list. As any new minister would, however, Michael called me several times to repeat the invitation. Finally, on Christmas Eve, we went along with our whole family and their three friends who were staying with them. The eight of us sitting in the pew, increased the congregation by 10 per cent. What's more, we absolutely loved it. The music was fantastic, the whole spirit was wonderful, and the place just felt right.

The simple act of turning up at church, however, does not make one a better person. Over Christmas and New Year, Rae and I had one of the biggest rows I could remember. With no Guiding Force, the pressures increased, and I allowed anger to take over our marriage. I became verbally abusive of Rae and the children. To Rae's eternal credit, she stuck by me until she could bear no more. She could not stand my pride, my domination, my insolence. My shameful attitude towards her finally wore her down, and she called it quits. Finally, Rae looked me in the eye and said, "I'm not going to put up with this anymore." I said, "I'll just leave you to calm down" and took off for some time to play tennis in Florida.

It was only on my return that I realised there was nothing idle about Rae's threat. She and Samantha had packed up their things and were about to board a flight via San Francisco for Sydney. I called Qantas and tried to upgrade her flight to first class. I was broken. If Rae had stayed and argued with me, I would have tried to patch things up, but it would only have been a band-aid. Sooner or later, we would have got back to the same point, with Rae feeling she came second to my work life and me too immersed in my business papers to read the signs staring at me on the wall written in letters two metres high.

In hindsight, Rae did the smart thing. She didn't ever contemplate divorcing, but she gave me the jolt I needed, and a taste of what the world would be like without the smart, loving and generous soulmate who entered my life in the dining room of the Tottenham Hotel almost three decades earlier. I cannot recall a moment in my life of such despair and seldom have I felt so broken. Excuse my language, but everything that I busted my arse for, for the last 30 years, was now out the window. What's the point? Why did I move around like a maniac and work so hard for nothing? I lay on the floor in the front of the house crying in front of our two sons. It was wretched. I needed help, but from where?

I tried to call Rae in Sydney to reason with her, as best as my tortured state would allow. But Rae was going through her own private pain and couldn't bring herself to talk to me for more than a week. I can only imagine how she felt, and what had driven her to take such a drastic step. For my part I felt desolate, with no strength to deal with this exhausted me, not knowing to whom I could turn. It was then, at my lowest moment, that Michael Youssef called.

"Apparently, I was coming today to visit you and Rae," he said. "Well Rae's not here," I replied without elaborating. Michael said not to worry, since in any case it was snowing, as it did from time to time in Atlanta with its high altitude. I said, "Michael, I'd really like to see you. I'll send one of the boys to get you in the four-wheel drive."

When Stuart brought Michael over, it didn't require the wisdom of Solomon to see I wasn't in the best of states. "Where's Rae?" he asked in a tone that was more than just conversational. I told him the whole story, choking back the tears. "You're in a mess," said Michael. "You need Jesus." "No," I protested. "I need help. I don't know what the heck is going on." Michael leant forward and took my hand. "Well, let's just start by praying together," he said. So we did.

You don't have to resort to a spiritual explanation to explain the healing power of prayer at a time like that, the comfort it brings to a man whose pride has been broken and is feeling wretched and desperately alone. The very presence of another human being who neither jumps to judgement about your character nor indulges you in self-pity is profoundly comforting in itself. The opportunity to talk openly about things you have been bottling up for years, much of it shameful, in the company of someone who shows no embarrassment, is a form of release. Finally, the appeal to a greater power, a figure who controls your own destiny at a time when you are definitely not, offers the hope of order in a world that appears to have collapsed around you.

The spiritual explanation, however, offers a truth far more profound and, for me, ultimately more believable. The Lord the Shepherd of a sheep who has gone astray, a creature who in his wretchedness recognises his sins, begs for mercy and hopes for redemption, which, thanks to the sacrifice of God's own precious Son, is the gift of all who surrender to his mercy. I responded first with sobs, then with an enormous flood of tears, entirely involuntary, as if under pressure from the tension I could feel in my heart. The two assistants working in the room alongside my office must have wondered what in heaven's name was going on.

Having dealt with the not insubstantial matter of my spiritual salvation, Michael moved on to practical matters. "I think one of the things you might want to do is go and get some psychological counselling. I'll give you the name of a guy I think could help you." My counsellor was a sympathetic Christian man, who had helped many people in my situation before, who helped me realise that many men go through the hell I was experiencing, and most emerge a stronger person. I met him three times a week for a couple of weeks.

Michael asked me what more he could do. I said: "Michael, all I want you to do is call Rae and pray for her." So, he did, and after two weeks of separation, Rae cautiously agreed that I could join her back in Australia.

As luck would have it, there could hardly have been a better time to be in Sydney. I landed at Mascot airport in bright sunshine on January 24, 1988, two days before the celebration of Australia's bicentenary, the 200th anniversary of the arrival of the first settlers aboard the First Fleet. They, like me, had been imperfect human beings, yet many of them found redemption in the enlightened colony of New South Wales, founded by people of high principle who believed the Christian teaching that, thanks to the sacrifice of the Lamb of God, no sin is unpardonable, and that every sinner deserves a second chance.

We stayed with our friends Gerald and Susan Lancaster at their waterfront home in Elizabeth Bay with a dress circle view of the tall ships recreating the arrival of the First Fleet and the fireworks display on the Harbour Bridge. Rae and I went to the Presbyterian Church in Macquarie Street that I'd been to as a young man, and in which my mother had been married twice, but sad to say it was not the experience I once remembered, and there were only a few in the congregation. We flew home via Tahiti, stopping there for two or three days, before arriving back in Atlanta to begin our lives again.

After we settled in, Rae and I decided to give our remaining time to serving Christian ministries. We established The McLellan Foundation and set up a number of ministries for which we provided seed capital.

While in Atlanta, and to kick off my career in the Christian not-for-profit world, I co-founded Citizens for Community Values, of which I served as chairman. I then established We Care America, which we later based in Washington, DC, and of which I was deputy chairman. There, we worked closely with President Bush's faith-based initiative.

When we returned to Australia, I was elected to the board of Opportunity International, on which I served for seven years. This was followed by my appointment as chairman of Habitat for Humanity for five years before I joined the board of Australian Christian Lobby and its affiliates. After ten years at ACL, I stepped down as chairman when I was given the honorific title of Chairman Emeritus.

Gabriel Garcia Marquez, the Columbian author of "One Hundred Years of Solitude" and winner of the Nobel Prize in Literature, once said: "A man has the right to look down on someone only when he is helping him to get up." These prophetic words—which could have come from the mouth of Christ—have inspired Rae and me to try to help lift people up.

Psychologists believe that leaders frequently come from dysfunctional families and that, subconsciously, they spend their lives battling with their insecurity whilst striving to put things right. I think of the shy and afraid young boy from the bush. For sixty-five years, he has accompanied the man I have become on an incredible voyage of discovery. Together, this scared and lonely young boy and I can now look forward to the future with hope, for as Desmond Tutu once said, "People of faith are prisoners of hope."

Eventually, all of us will depart this life, or "cross the bar." But when comes the sound of low music, the scent of sweet flowers, and the crunch of footsteps on the gravel, those of us who have been called by God and made Jesus the Lord of our life can rejoice in the eternal lines of Alfred Lord Tennyson:

Twilight and evening bell,
  And after that the dark!
And may there be no sadness of farewell,
  When I embark;

For tho' from out our bourne of Time and Place
  The flood may bear me far,
I hope to see my Pilot face-to-face
  When I have crost the bar.

—Alfred Lord Tennyson

## CHAPTER 10

# CHASING HOME RUNS

Let us not become weary in doing good, for at the proper
time we will reap a harvest if we do not give up.

PAUL THE APOSTLE[4]

We returned to Atlanta from several months in New Zealand
in March 1990 in time to celebrate my 50th birthday with
a surprise party Rae had worked secretly to organise with a
large group of friends. Those years of constant travel made
the world seem a smaller place, if ever more magnificent.
Technology had transformed our lives since I entered the
world in Tullamore District Hospital half a century earlier.
In my childhood at Jumble Plains the tyranny of distance, as
Geoffrey Blainey called it, had been keenly felt. In 1940 there
were less than 700,000 telephones to serve a population of
7 million. Most communication was by post, with Australia
posting 120 letters per person. By 1990 the world felt pretty
sophisticated by comparison. Jet travel was commonplace and
we had mobile phones in our cars, if not yet in our pockets.

---

4    Galatians 6:9

Time sensitive messages could be sent by telex and increasingly by fax.

These developments were nothing, however, compared to the transforming technology that was just around the corner: the World Wide Web. In 1990 the British computer scientist Tim Berners-Lee came up with a commercial way of linking hypertext documents into an information system accessible from any computer in the world plugged into the network. The first Internet Service Providers began to spring up, introducing the enticing possibility of near-instant communication by electronic mail as well as access to a growing wealth of information on what quickly became known as the World Wide Web.

Atlanta too was becoming a more connected city with one of the fastest growing populations or any city in the country. CNN moved its headquarters there from New York in 1987 helping to put it on the map as a city of international importance. CNN's founder, Ted Turner, was a leading light in the city whose forceful views earned him the nickname the Mouth of the South. I was invited to a party in his office, an experience that confirmed my suspicions about the size of his ego. There were probably fifty pictures of presidents and princes on the wall, all of whom just happened to have been photographed in the company of Ted Turner. There were so many that they overflowed into his PA's office and the waiting room. This is a popular style amongst leaders in America, but I had never seen a collection of selfies quite like Turner's. He also had perhaps ten television screens in his office. He was, of course, in the television business, but this struck me as somewhat excessive.

When I shared my impression with Rae later that evening, she was not entirely surprised. A member of Rae's women's Bible study group was JJ Ebaugh, who was Ted Turner's pilot, and had considered herself his girlfriend before being dumped in favour of Jane Fonda. Turner could be extraordinarily rude in public towards the women in his life. One of his friends once recalled an occasion when Turner introduced Fonda to a table at a social gathering. Someone had said: "You sure have a beautiful woman there," to which Turner replied, "Yup, and if she doesn't stay beautiful, the next one will be even better."[5] Not surprisingly, Turner's marriage with Fonda, like his previous two marriages, ended in divorce.

One day Rae found herself in a lift with Turner in a tall, downtown office building in Atlanta. Turner had turned to the two people accompanying him and enquired quite innocently, "Do I own this building?"

He was the founder of CNN, and when he sold it, he donated $1 billion to the United Nations. He was also owner of the Atlanta Braves, which won the World Series in 1995, setting the city alight with pride. I would occasionally spot Turner at the baseball game, if I were fortunate enough to have secured seats behind home plate in the "grand circle".

Turner had turned the Braves and had turned them into a popular national franchise. As I was standing at a party in his office, not knowing quite who to talk to, I went over to a tall, black man and introduced myself.

"Hello, I am Tony McLellan", I said.

"Hello" the man responded, "I am Hank Aaron."

---

5    Priscilla Painton, 'The Taming of Ted Turner", Time, 6 January 1992.

I was temporarily struck dumb. I was talking to the Hammer himself. Hank Aaron is America's Don Bradman, the greatest baseball player of all time. A monument at the Atlanta Braves stadium celebrates Hammerin' Hank's 715th home run in April 1974 that broke Babe Ruth's record. It was a cathartic moment for America, and the south in particular, less than a decade after the end of Jim Crow.

I had passed by the monument many times and had often wondered what sort of a man Hank Aaron was, and what it must have been like to have been there that night. The son of a poor black family from Alabama, Aaron bore the brunt of racial taunts all his life, but always maintained his dignity.

At the end of the 1973 season, Aaron was only one home run short of Babe Ruth's record of 714. During the winter break, he received death threats and hate mail from people who did not want to see a black man break Ruth's sacrosanct record. The editor of the *Atlanta Journal* reported receiving numerous phone calls from people opposed to Aaron's chase and even secretly had an obituary written, afraid that Aaron might be murdered.

Aaron also received much support. Charles Schulz did a series of Peanuts cartoons satirising his bigoted opponents. Babe Ruth's widow denounced the racism and declared that her late husband would have enthusiastically cheered Aaron's attempt at the record. A record crowd of 53,775 showed up at the Fulton County Stadium for the Braves' first home game of the 1974 season. In the fourth inning, Aaron hit career home run number 715 off the Los Angeles Dodgers pitcher. As cannon were fired in celebration, and as the fans cheered wildly, Aaron's parents ran onto the field. The Dodgers broadcaster Vin Scully famous call of the match captured a cathartic moment: "What a marvellous moment for baseball; what a marvellous moment for Atlanta and the state of Georgia; what a marvellous moment for the country and the world. A black man is getting a standing ovation in the Deep South for breaking a record of an all-time baseball idol."

Aaron was never flashy or flamboyant. He simply set out to make the best at whatever was thrown at him, an approach to life that is especially applicable in baseball. "I concentrated on the pitchers," he wrote in his memoir, "*I Had a Hammer* published in 1991. I didn't stay up nights worrying about my weight distribution, or the location of my hands, or the turn of my hips: I stayed up thinking about the pitcher I was going to face the next day. I used to play every pitcher in my mind before I went to the ballpark."

Aaron hit his 755th and final home run in 1976 shortly before his retirement. "My motto was always to keep swinging. Whether I was in a slump or feeling badly or having trouble off the field, the only thing to do was keep swinging."

So, what did I learn from the late, great Hank Aaron beyond the importance of persevering? I learned that, in spite of his extraordinary achievements, his fame and his fortune, he remained a simple black man from Alabama—without a trace of guile. Hank Aaron taught me the beauty of modesty. Thirty-three years after his record was set it was finally beaten by Barry Bonds of the San Francisco Giants. Aaron was among the first to congratulate the new record holder. "My hope today, as it was on that April evening in 1974, is that the achievement of this record will inspire others to chase their own dreams," he said.

The opportunity to chase dreams, as well as our growing connection with new friends, was what brought us back to Atlanta, after a far from unpleasant interlude in New Zealand. Always on the hunt for business opportunities, I decided to get into the software business using the profit we had made from the deal in New Zealand as working capital. I set up The McLellan Software Center after being introduced to some developers of software from Brazil then living in Atlanta who were trying to get the product launched in America. These were very early days for the IT industry, as you can tell from my business card, which had a fax number but no email address. The potential excited me, and in January 1991 I signed a licensing deal for their software. Called Icon-Hide-It, it offered a way of providing security on personal computers by authorising a user to only use certain applications or get to certain folders.

Later I came up with the idea of using the same core technology to protect families from internet pornography with a software product called ClickChoice. Conceptually, it was a revolutionary idea for its time giving a parent the power to decide the appropriate level of access for each family member. The first challenge was to keep track of what was available on the web at a time when search engines were primitive and inefficient. I struck up a joint venture with a company in Calgary which had compiled a database of every known website and then categorised it according to the type of content. Pornographic or other undesirable material could be placed well out of reach of children.

The beauty of our business model was that the software would be available for free. It would be funded by targeted advertising, then a revolutionary concept. All we needed to know from the customer was a zip code. Armed with that information, we planned on companies such as Delta Airlines putting a free copy of our software in the back of their seats. We could gauge the size and composition of the family when the product was installed. Delta could then send a message through our mechanism to the customer, such as an offer for a family package on flights to Orlando, which is where Disney World is situated. Targeted advertisements in the days before Google seemed pretty clever to us at the time. What we hadn't anticipated, however, was the exponential increase in the size of the internet. It quickly became apparent that it would be all but impossible to keep track of every new site. In the early 1990s there were just a few thousand sites. By 1998, when Google arrived, there were more than two million. Today there are estimated to be around 1.5 billion registered websites, 200 million of them active.

The second hurdle, as I quickly learned, is that the path of software development is never smooth. It turned out to be a much bigger, more complex job than anybody thought, for me especially, because I was fresh to it. I could see our capital whittling away and set a deadline after which I would refuse to fund it anymore. When the Brazilian company responded by suing me, I sued them back. We had a massive arbitration, which I won. It was a Pyrrhic victory, however, because I didn't have any money. Instead, the arbitrators awarded me the source code and I scrambled trying to raise some money to keep the thing going. I made 140 presentations with no luck. Not only was I new to the sector, but I was dealing with financiers who struggled to understand the concept, even though with hindsight, the software was ahead of its day.

Slowly it ate up every penny of capital that we had and our financial situation went from bad to worse. Our life savings were gone. The banks foreclosed on our beautiful $1.3 million home in Buckhead, Atlanta. We had to sell our two Mercedes to raise cash to survive and then some of our furniture. Several times we were down to less than $20 between us, with no liquid assets and no credit cards.

We were sometimes so depressed that we even found it difficult to pray. Each evening Rae and I knelt together beside our bed, but we found the words would not come and all we could do was groan in the Spirit. Our Minister gave us some good advice: he told us to spend our time praising God and giving him thanks for all we did have. This wisdom was transforming and proved a great help in opening up our hearts.

For two years we lived on the gifts and support of our friends, plus tiny amounts of investment capital I was able to raise. One day we returned from church to the house a friend had provided and found pinned on the front door a $100 bill, with the simple message, "We love you."

Our daughter Samantha was married in 1996, but we could not afford to travel to her wedding in Geneva, Switzerland. A business colleague offered to cover our airfares, but a week before the wedding we managed to close a small financing deal that enabled us to pay our own way.

Samantha was to marry Alexi Vrontamitis whom she had met at the Swiss Hotel Management School at Bluche. Alexi was born in Kenya of Greek parents who were living there. Following their graduation, both Alexi and Samantha were then appointed general managers of small hotels in Geneva. One of the most interesting aspects was that they were married in Holy Trinity Anglican church in downtown Geneva. The city was originally a place of refuge from the horror of Bloody Mary who was terrorising protestants. The church's early head was John Knox. He sat at the feet of Calvin, who was then living in Geneva and he took his philosophy back to Scotland, where he founded the modern Presbyterian church. This had a profound effect on Scotland—particularly its education system, including the development of its world-leading universities in Edinburgh and Glasgow.

One time when we were seriously worried about how we would be able to eat in the coming week, a member of our home Bible study group that I led, came into the office unexpectedly. I had helped him to secure the exclusive rights to sell ice-cream at the 1996 Olympic Games in Atlanta. Our friend had done very well with this concession and unexpectedly brought us a thank-you gift of $550. On another occasion I was invited to breakfast by Joe Spence, who attended our church and was a head-hunter with a large firm. We met at the famous OK Café in Atlanta. When we had eaten, Joe invited me to his car where he wrote me out a cheque for $5,000. His only condition: "When you are able, I want you to pass on the funds to someone else."

There were many moments over that testing four years when we were tempted to despair. We were sustained, however, by our deepening Christian faith and the fellowship of others. We had been supporters of a ministry called Walk-thru-the-Bible, founded by Dr Bruce Wilkinson, where we learned an invaluable lesson that helped us understand God's purpose in the ordeal we were going through. John 15—Jesus's well-known discussion about the vine—says that, "every branch that does bear fruit the Father prunes so that it will be even more fruitful." In other words, God prunes those that are abiding in him so that they can bear more fruit. Those who have been pruned, or cut back, know how painful it can be. It comes with the promise, however, that you will emerge enriched.

While I was desperately short of capital, I did at least own what I still believed was valuable software. Once again, perseverance was the key. I dug deep into my inner reserves, praying for strength, as I made hundreds of presentations, fighting the temptation to give up. As Thomas Edison once said, 'The most certain way to succeed is always to try just one more time.'

Finally, after struggling for years and after losing virtually all of our possessions, the breakthrough came. In June 1988, I was introduced to Jan Baan, a Christian man in The Netherlands, who was looking to invest in a product like the one we had developed. After speaking on the telephone, he sent his man to Atlanta to investigate further. After a long day of demonstrating and testing, we had a quiet dinner. The following morning, I met Baan's man at his hotel for coffee. He took one sip then blurted out "Will $10 million do?" To which I replied "YES!"

I arranged to travel to The Netherlands to begin discussions on the proposed new company, ClickChoice.com, in which Baan had agreed to invest. I was not in the best of shape. I had recently had an operation to remove a melanoma from my forehead, which I had expected to be straightforward. A few days later I went back to the doctor complaining about pain along the back of my head and learned from the doctor she had had to scalp me in order to be able to close the wound. Rae travelled with me to help dress the wound a couple of times each day, but even so I was a sorry mess as I boarded the flight, looking like an extra from a B-grade war movie. The deal was cemented, however, and after six months of legal due diligence and innumerable meetings, ClickChoice.com Inc, moved into new offices and grew from a team of four to 50 people. This time my business card included an email address.

Baan's initial investment of $10 million was later followed with a further $15 million. I owe much more to him, however, than capital. Baan became an inspiration to me and a spiritual friend. He had been raised the son of a carpenter in a middle-class family of eight children. When his father died of cancer Jan became profoundly aware of God's calling on his own life and became a member of the conservative Dutch Reformed church.

Baan became convicted of God's calling on his own life, dedicating himself to serving him and becoming committed through engagement. He built a giant software company with 6,000 employees and operations in more than 70 countries. At its peak, it had a market capitalization of over $10 billion. When it ran into financial difficulties, Baan set out on a new beginning, retiring from the company he had founded to operate a $1 billion Christian foundation, the Vanenburg Group. On a visit to Atlanta, Jan Baan dined at our home with our minister, Rev Dr Michael Youssef. Afterwards, I asked Michael his opinion of Jan and Michael's reply was profound. He said, "He is so Calvinistic, but boy does he love God." If someone said that about me, I would feel immense pride.

I learned from Jan Baan that when failure strikes, we must look for a new start. Faced with a similar situation many of us would fear that our life was about to come to an end: what should really concern us is that it may never have a new beginning.

We took the company public in March 2000 and nested it in Canada. Rae and I were able to recover the substantial investment we had made in the company, giving us the capital to purchase a house in Sydney as a bolt-hole should we decide to return. More importantly, recovering our financial security also allowed me to keep the promise I had made to Joe Spence on the day he wrote me a cheque from the seat of his car. Our friend Julie Hunter was suffering badly because of the disappearance of her husband, Alex, who was bi-polar. I had been trying to help him get well again and on the guidance of his psychologist, we had been playing strenuous games of tennis. I wrote Julie a cheque telling her the same thing Joe had told me. "First, when you are able, I want you to pass the money on to someone else. And, second, I want you to call Joe who gave me the $5,000 and thank him." Joe was very appreciative to know that his gift had paid off twice.

Throughout the four long years of struggling in my business dealings, our involvement with Christian ministry continued and indeed helped sustain us. For years I had led a number of weekly Bible studies, in our home, in our church, and at restaurants. I had been asked by our church to recruit and train all our new-Bible study leaders and had written an extensive manual on how to lead these groups. None of the groups I led were aware of our prior financial predicament but when the news became known all the members celebrated with us. They complimented us for refraining from burdening the group with our difficulties and they rejoiced at the news that we could now enjoy some financial security.

Why am I sharing this? Because it is important to remember that whatever your circumstances, there is always someone suffering more than you. Someone who has lost a loved one, who is experiencing ill health, or is having trouble with his family. Or even worse, someone who does not have the understanding that comes through faith that suffering has a purpose, that God who is the one putting them through the refining process and that he will never allow us to suffer more than we can bear.

People who struggle with faith often put forward the existence of suffering in the world as reason to doubt God's omnipotence, if not His very existence. Our troubles in the mid-nineties taught us firmly that the opposite is true. God is firmly in control of his world, and on this, the Bible is clear: Nothing occurs outside of his sovereignty. He is King every day, every hour, everywhere. What's more, suffering and evil are not exceptions to this. God says: "I form the light and create darkness, I bring prosperity and create disaster" (Isaiah 45:7). And even in the midst of agony Job understood this reality with faith: "The Lord gave and the Lord has taken away; may the name of the Lord be praised" (Job 1:21).

I am conscious that the spiritual explanation for suffering may not convince everyone who reads this book of the reason why we should accept life's difficulties with magnanimity rather than rail against them as we are frequently tempted to do. So let me instead offer a practical explanation as to why I prefer the Bible's teaching to the alternative. If we can conclude that God is not in control and that our suffering does not have a greater purpose, we resign ourselves to living in a world of random chaos, in which anything could happen to us with no-one to stop it. We surrender control of our own destiny and succumb to the status of the victim. Victimhood has become fashionable today and even comes with rewards. Personally, however, I am convinced that the assurance that God is at work in "all things" for the good of those who love him (Romans 8:28) is ultimately far more empowering, even when we can't see how.

Staying on a practical note, a community of people who see a greater purpose in suffering will be a stronger community. Its members will be inclined to be far less judgemental of others and far more willing to offer a hand of support. They will understand that when bad things happen to people, we should not assume that they especially deserve it. The Bible rejects the idea that suffering is always connected to people's sins or mistakes.

The second practical consequence is that people in such a community are far more likely to reflect on their own conduct and will strive to become better citizens. They will understand the message that God relents when we pray to him. God's great prophet Jeremiah relayed God's advice about this: "Now reform your ways and your actions and obey the Lord your God. Then the Lord will relent and not bring the disaster he has pronounced against you" (Jeremiah 26:13-14).

Rae and I heard the lesson of the vine as supporters of the Walk-thru-the-Bible ministry , and were invited to a President's Council at Peachtree City on the outskirts of Atlanta. It was a life-changing revelation to learn that Jesus has said that every branch will be affected: that everyone who is in Christ will either be cut off (if he bears no fruit) or pruned so that he can bear much fruit. Then at the end of John 15:5 Jesus says: " . . . apart from me you can do nothing."

We suddenly realised that God was not punishing us but rather was pruning us. We made a special effort to confess all known and unknown sins and to thereby free ourselves up to bear much fruit for the Kingdom. It was enormously comforting to us at that difficult time and I believe helped change our approach to life for the better.

As an aside, some years later, I was helping Bruce Wilkinson develop new on-line training, and he came to our meeting bearing a copy of his new book, "The Secrets of the Vine". He had no idea how much his teaching some years before had impacted us. Bruce signed a copy of the book, which he had just received from the printers, and gave it to me. Rae and I devoured it, although the lessons we had previously well understood. I later purchased cartons of the book and gave copies away to anyone who expressed the slightest interest. I knew personally the power in the message. I mistakenly gave away the signed copy Bruce had given to me, which made me sad because I treasured it. I later learned that over ten million copies of the book were sold.

The refining process is painful, but we all should be grateful for it. In Hebrews 12 we learn that, "No discipline seems pleasant at the time, but painful. Later on, however, it produces a harvest of righteousness and peace for those who have been trained by it." We can therefore rejoice that God has chosen to discipline us to produce a "harvest of righteousness."

For helping me understand these inalienable truths—and for continuing to support me as we passed together through the fire—I want to pay a special tribute to my beloved wife, Rae.

Twenty years later, on 19 January 2011, Rae and I celebrated our 50th wedding anniversary with a special service at St Thomas' Anglican Church, North Sydney, which was attended by many of our close friends. In arranging the service, we asked the Minister, Rev Canon Simon Manchester, if he would preach on the Vine from John 15. Simon gave an extraordinary talk, opening up the passage from another angle. We and our guests really appreciated it, although probably no-one understood it as much as Rae and I did.

So, what are the lessons we learned?

First, we must accept God's discipline and yield to his correction. "God disciplines us for own good," the writer of the letter to the Hebrews reminds us: "That we may share in his holiness. No discipline seems pleasant at the time, but painful. Later on, however, it produces a harvest of righteousness and peace for those who have been trained by it" (Hebrews 10b-11).

Second, we must set our goal. We should never lose sight of that glorious passage: "Let us fix our eyes on Jesus, the author and perfecter of our faith" (Hebrews 12:2).

Finally, we must persevere, knowing that "when we have done the will of God, we will receive what he has promised" (Hebrews 10:36). No matter how hard the going was in those four lean years in Atlanta, the only way of improving our lot was to keep working at it. Or, as Hank Aaron might have put it, just keep swinging, remembering that every ball with which you connect could be your next home run.

## CHAPTER 11

# THE SERVICE BUSINESS

> In the quiet hours, when we are alone and there is nobody
> to tell us what fine fellows we are, we come sometimes upon
> a moment in which we wonder, not how much money we
> are earning, nor how famous we have become, but what
> good we are doing.
>
> A.A. MILNE

The character Gordon Gecko in Oliver Stone's 1987 movie *Wall Street* hit a nerve in our collective psyches. After a decade of expanding prosperity, Gecko's catch cry, "greed is good", reminded us that success is not measured by the width of one's wallet. Hard work, enterprise and the desire to prosper are noble human characteristics. Gecko, however, reminded us that true success requires a deeper purpose, and that prosperity should be shared, not hoarded. Ambition is a virtue, but avarice is a vice. In the words of Henry Edward Manning, greed "plunges a man deep into the mire of this world, so that he makes it to be his god".

My appreciation of this lesson was sharpened by the four lean years we had spent scraping together the cash to pay for the necessities of life while trying to get our business operating. Despite all the deprivations and the near-constant anxiety, we experienced some of the richest days of our lives and came to appreciate the things that really matter: family, fellowship and the abiding love of God. Looking back, it was a turning point in our lives. My desire to be successful in business did not change, but it was driven by a deeper purpose.

In 2001, I had the honour of introducing Adolph Coors IV, the heir to the great brewing dynasty, as our guest speaker at the Buckhead Businessmen's Prayer Breakfast in Atlanta, of which I was chairman. Coors learned early in life that wealth is no protection against misfortune. His father, Adolph Coors III, was kidnapped and killed by an escaped murderer in 1960. The tragedy set Coors on a journey to find a deeper meaning in his life that ended with his conversion to Christianity and a visit to a prison to express his forgiveness to the man who had brutally cut short his father's life.

Before becoming a Christian, Coors' motto had been: "Make all you can, can all you make, and then sit on the can." As a Christian, however, he came to learn one of the great paradoxes of life; that the more you seek, the less you gain. Or, to put it another way, "it is more blessed to give than to receive" (Acts 20:35b). He discovered how to measure success not by improvements to his business or the strength of his share portfolio but by the difference he could make in the lives of others.

Changing one's approach in business for the benefit of others demands more than mere philanthropy, however good the cause. It demands a generosity of spirit that is reflected in the way we interact with those around us and how we behave as citizens. It means treating everyone we meet in the course of the day with respect and avoiding getting so caught up in our own affairs that we forget about the needs of those around us, especially those closest to us. When I was a senior executive my life was frantic and there was little time for anything else. I couldn't even spend proper time with my wife and young family. Just because your life is full of meetings, however, does not mean you are living a full life, which leads to a second paradox. A full life is very different from a fulfilling life. On the contrary, it is frequently born of a fear that we are wasting our lives.

As I started to look for examples of how other people of faith approached their work, I discovered many inspiring examples of what might be called the Christian business model. For someone like me who had been wedded to spread sheets for their entire career, it requires a considerable degree of trust, since it often requires decisions that would be counterintuitive in a pure business sense. If you were running a chain of fast-food restaurants, like Chick-fil-A outlets in the United States, for example, it might seem odd not to open on Sundays. Yet the chains' founder, the late Samuel Truett Cathy, believed that no amount of lost revenue could justify breaking the fourth commandment: "Remember the sabbath day by keeping it holy". If God could create the world in six days and rest on the seventh, he reasoned, there was no reason why he could not run a profitable business on the same principle.

Truett Cathy opened his first restaurant in the Atlanta suburb of Hapeville in 1946, soon after returning from serving in the US Army in World War II. Among those he hired was Eddie J. White, a 12-year-old African American, a contentious choice during a time of segregation. Truett Cathy understood the fundamental principle of egalitarianism which is a foundation of the Christian faith. "There is neither Jew nor Gentile, neither slave nor free, nor is there male and female, for you are all one in Christ Jesus" (Galatians 3:28). He also took on the duty of mentoring an orphan, Woody Faulk, from the age of 13. Faulk later became vice president of product development at Chick-fil-A. Thanks to Truett Cathy's commitment and example, a life was fulfilled.

I had the good fortune to spend a whole morning with Truett Cathy at his office in Atlanta with the Rev Dr Jerry Kirk, to seek his endorsement and possible financial support of Citizens for Community Values. I was chairman of this new organisation, formed to fight pornography and sexual abuse in Atlanta. Truett Cathy declined to help financially, not because he wasn't supportive, but because of his total commitment to his program for young people. One of Truett Cathy's favourite truisms was that it is easier to build boys and girls than to mend men and women. He developed a successful foster home system called WinShape Homes. When I met him there were eleven homes in the U.S. and one in Brazil. His Camp WinShape and the WinShape Foundation provide scholarships for kids and college students.

Chick-fil-A Kids Meals don't come with promotional toys from the latest popular movie. Instead, he offers VeggieTales books, audiocassettes of Focus on the Family's "Adventures in Odyssey," and other character-building materials. Woody Faulk offers a good summary of the "man's character." A lot of people look on Truett as Santa Claus, but he's not. He'll meet you halfway so that you can learn a lesson from the process. He's the personification of the well-known passage "Do not merely listen to the word, and so deceive yourselves. Do what it says'." (James 1:22).

As Rae and I pondered how to translate our rejuvenated faith into action in our business lives we were drawn towards the world of Christian not-for-profit organisations. We established The McLellan Foundation and set up a number of Christian ministries for which we provided seed capital. The first was Citizens for Community Values, which I co-founded with Rev Dr Jerry Kirk in April 1998 and served as chairman for three and a half years until we left the USA to return to Australia.

The purpose of not-for-profit organisations, as the name suggests, is not to line the owners' pockets, unlike commercial business, where the first duty of a chief executive is to safeguard the interests of the company's shareholders. The benefits that flow from a not-for-profit organisation are public, rather than private. They are the means by which we could follow the commandment to serve others rather than ourselves. Successful not-for-profits are anchored by a strong purpose, in our case, our duty as disciples of Christ. Accountability, trustworthiness, honesty, and openness are essential. Not-for-profits should be accountable to the donors, founders, volunteers and the community. Most of all, however, they must remain accountable to God.

One of my guides in avoiding the pitfalls of running not-for-profit organisations has been the principles that have become known as the Modesto Manifesto. In 1948 towards the start of his career as an evangelist, Billy Graham gathered with his team including Cliff Barrows, Grady Wilson and Bev Shea for a prayer retreat in a hotel room in Modesto, California. They focused on the temptations that lay ahead as their ministry grew and the allegations that had plagued other evangelists: immorality, greed, misuse of donations, lies by overstatements and a proud, critical spirit. They drew up a compact in four parts:

- We will never criticize, condemn, or speak negatively about other pastors, churches, or other Christian workers.
- We will be accountable, particularly in handling finances, with integrity according to the highest business standards.
- We will tell the truth and be thoroughly honest, especially in reporting statistics.
- We will be exemplary in morals—clear, clean and careful to avoid the very appearance of any impropriety.

Coincidentally, in the same year the manifesto was formed, the polling company Gallup began compiling an annual list of America's ten most-admired people. Graham's name appeared on the list 61 times. When he left this earth in February 2018, nine months shy of his 100th birthday, newspaper obituaries noted his "controversial" views on issues like women and homosexuality but could find nothing in his conduct in life that was remotely controversial. The Modesto Manifesto stood him in good stead.

During my career in the Christian not-for-profit world, I have incorporated these very principles in the corporate charters of three organisations of which I was chairman, and also in the governance protocols of several public companies which

I chaired. The Modesto principles provide another reason for me to be thankful for this mighty man of God whose ministry transformed the lives of millions.

An important aspect of leadership, which is often overlooked, is the need first to be a servant. The supreme example of humility and service was set by Jesus on the night his disciples gathered for the Last Supper. In those times it was a mark of honour and a sign of hospitality for a host to provide a servant to wash a guest's feet prior; indeed, it was a breach of etiquette if the host failed to do so. On this special night, however, because of the apparent need for privacy, there were no servants present and all the disciples took their places at the table with unwashed feet. The Gospel of John chronicles what happened next: "So he (that is, Jesus) got up from the meal, took off his outer clothing, and wrapped a towel around his waist. After that, he poured water into a basin and began to wash his disciples' feet, drying them with the towel that was wrapped around him." (John 13:4). When he gets to Peter, Peter strongly objects, saying that this is too demeaning for Jesus, but Peter finally relents. Jesus even washes the feet of Judas.

The power of this image has never ceased to inspire me: God himself, arising from his throne in Heaven and stepping down to become a servant, kneeling at each of his disciples' feet in order to wash them. If ever there was a supreme example of humility and service, this was it. Like the woman who showed her love for Jesus by washing his feet with her tears, wiping them with her hair and then pouring perfume on them (Luke 7:38), Jesus demonstrates his love for his disciples.

That this would have been regarded at the time as a menial task is imbibed with meaning through the stature of the man who performs it. Richard J. Foster captured that defining moment in his book Celebration of Discipline, with these words: "As the cross is the sign of submission, so the towel is the sign of service."

After finishing his work, Jesus put on his clothes and returned to his place, before explaining. "Do you understand what I have done for you?" he asked them . . . "Now that I, your Lord and Teacher, have washed your feet, you also should wash one another's feet. I have set you an example (says Jesus) that you should do as I have done for you" (John 13:12). Or, as a rough McLellan translation, "I have shown you how you should be willing to humble yourself and serve your fellow man, not in the narrow sense of literally washing their feet, but by sacrificing your pride and doing something practical for them. It is not enough just to think good thoughts; we must put them into practice. As the Apostle James writes, "the blessing comes not in the hearing of the Word, but in the doing of it" (James 1:22-25).

This profound illustration of a master who becomes a servant, a person who in other circumstances we would regard not as a leader but someone who is led, is a hard act to follow. We need to be clear on the distinction between the righteousness of service and the vanity of self-righteous service. We should regard our own egotistical impulses with suspicion. Godly service is characterised by humility: seeking to serve others, which in turn tempers the desires of the flesh.

A leader lacking in humility is inclined to blame failure on others. Good leaders, on the other hand, draw out the best in those around them, and compensate for their weaknesses through acts of service. William Law's book, *A Serious Call to a Devout and Holy Life*, counsels us to: "... condescend to all the weaknesses and infirmities of your fellow-creatures, cover their frailties, love their excellencies, encourage their virtues, relieve their wants, rejoice in their prosperities, be compassionate in their distress, receive their friendship, overlook their unkindness, forgive their malice, be a servant of servants, and condescend to do the lowest offices to the lowest of mankind."

One of the great paradoxes of taking on the role of servant is that it leads to freedom. A common fear many of us have about offering ourselves for service is that, "people will take advantage of me ... they will walk all over me". This highlights the difference between choosing to serve and choosing to be a servant. Choosing to be a servant puts us on the high road to freedom, liberating us from the tyranny of others. Because we choose to serve, we are still in charge. We decide who we will serve and when and how we will serve.

At the same time, we abdicate the demand to be in charge; we surrender our right to decide who and when we will serve. This gives us a wonderful freedom. Voluntary servitude brings great joy because once we choose to offer ourselves freely in service we can't be manipulated anymore, so we find total freedom.

During my time with Opportunity International, I once approached a Christian man who worked for a firm which provides HR consulting to ask if he would be prepared to work with the CEO in developing some HR policies for us. Before the words were out of my mouth he said, "Of course I will, Tony. Tell me what you want me to do." He could so easily have pleaded that he was time poor and said he'd get back to me when he had time to spare. David reacted that way not because he had chosen to serve, but rather because he had chosen to be a servant. His warm response has remained with me as a godly example to follow.

Notwithstanding the temptation to become absorbed in our own affairs, we should constantly remind ourselves of the bigger picture and the virtue of obedience. God has a plan and he carries out his work through us. If we don't serve where God has asked us to serve, God will achieve his plan through someone else. A priest I once knew told me he had been called by God to write a book and had got as far as developing the outline and the chapter headings. Like so many would-be authors, however, more pressing, everyday demands of life pushed the book onto an unheated back-burner, "too busy". Two years later, he realised the price of disobedience when he attended a Christian bookseller's convention and saw his book with the same title and similar chapter headings published under the name of another author. God's gifts are not our property to use as we please; they have been given to us to hold in trust for others and are to be used as he directs.

The gifts of the Spirit are not meant for fame or recognition or self-fulfilment. They are not merit badges or rewards. It takes hard work and time to learn how to use the gifts given to us. To paraphrase Dallas Willard, we do not develop our gifts through inspiration or information, but through engagement. It is much like dancing; it doesn't matter how inspired you are or how much information you have, you must practice before you can become an accomplished dancer. The parable of the talents reminds of us what happens if we don't:

"Even what he has will be taken from him," Jesus warned (Matthew 25:29).

One of the hardest things to do as a leader is to discipline oneself for service. But that is critical for those who are in positions of influence and power. To act as a servant while fulfilling a socially important role is one of the greatest challenges a leader can face, and I think is one of the most difficult spiritual attainments. We need to set our goals high. As Professor Ian Frazer, a former Australian of the Year, says about service: "Each of us should do more than is reasonably expected."

Frequently, service does not require a physical task. We can serve simply by listening to someone with tenderness and compassion. One can serve by waiting in silence as John Milton so beautifully wrote, when musing about the limitations of his own blindness: "They also serve who only stand and wait."[6]

Acts of service to our communities are the thread that helps bind the social fabric. Having witnessed the planning and execution of the 1996 Atlanta Olympics, I am convinced that the key to success was the recruitment of an army of volunteers, ordinary citizens largely unknown by name, who offered their service because they loved their community and wanted the Games to succeed. Their example was taken up with even greater enthusiasm at the Sydney Olympics four years later when more than 40,000 citizens enlisted to serve as drivers, parking attendants, stewards and much more.

Strong societies based on Christian principles are notable for the amount of work that is performed by volunteers. In

6    On His Blindness, Sonnet 19: When I consider how my light is spent. John Milton.

Atlanta, we had great friends who lived in a large house in the best part of town. Every Saturday morning, Carl and Elaine got up and made hundreds of sandwiches. They then loaded their kids in the car and took them downtown where they fed the homeless. And they did this to show their young children, Jackie and Zac, that living in Buckhead was a privilege that not all of God's people enjoyed, and that we all need to serve in humility those less fortunate than ourselves. The big question we will face when we get to Heaven is: "What did you do with what I gave you?"

In his book, *The Servant: A Simple Story About the True Essence of Leadership*, James C. Hunter makes an important distinction between power and authority. Power is dominion; the capacity to hire and fire, for example. Authority is the capacity to influence. These are two separate realms. Aleksandr Solzhenitsyn had no power inside the USSR, but his authority was so great the powers-that-be were forced to exile him lest he undo their power, which eventually he did. A person with authority has great influence. Often those in power have little authority. How much power did Mother Teresa have? And how much authority did she have?

At the coronation of an English monarch, he is given a sword. Elizabeth II took it last, and as she held it before the altar, she heard these words:

> Receive this kingly Sword, brought now from
> the altar of God and delivered to you by us, the
> bishops and servants of God, though unworthy.
> With this Sword do justice, stop the growth of
> iniquity, protect the holy Church of God, help and

defend widows and orphans, restore the things
that are gone to decay, maintain the things that
are restored, punish and reform what is amiss, and
confirm what is in good order; that doing these
things you may be glorious in all virtue; and so
faithfully serve our Lord.

Our incredible Queen has now served us with honour and
dignity for nigh on 70 years.

Would that we all come once again to understand that
leadership is not the appetite for power, but a holy calling for
self-abnegation and self-sacrifice.

**CHAPTER 12**

# CHURCH LEADERSHIP

The ultimate measure of a man is not where he stands in
moments of comfort and convenience, but where he stands
at times of challenge and controversy.

MARTIN LUTHER KING

The Church of the Apostles was Atlanta, Georgia's youngest
church when Rae and I first joined the congregation on
Christmas Eve 1987. The first service had been conducted
seven months earlier on Mothers' Day when 38 parishioners
gathered in temporary accommodation under the ministry
of its founder, Rev Dr Michael Youssef. Yet it was firmly
anchored in sacred text almost 2,000 years old. Its founder,
Dr Michael Youssef, was uncompromising in his commitment
to the Bible and that meant all of it, not just the passages a
modern audience might find acceptable. He wasn't looking
for an audience, he wanted to build a community of disciples,
and he succeeded. The earliest ceremonies Rae and I attended
were held in a school hall where 70 or 80 of us would
gather. Today, Michael addresses a congregation of 3000

in a purpose-built auditorium. He speaks to millions more through his TV and radio ministry, notably in his homeland of Egypt, where believers face enormous pressures. "There is no pop psychology or pat on the back that is going to make disciples," he said recently, "only the unadulterated Word of God can do that."

In a little more than three years, the Church of the Apostles had grown from a few dozen members to more than 1000 and was the fastest growing congregation in the Episcopal Church, the denomination to which it was attached. Popularly regarded as the church of the "landed gentry", the Episcopal denomination was often associated with people of influence. It had been established by the wealthy land-owning families who settled on the East Coast of the USA, especially in the deep South where many planted cotton. Rooted in the Anglican Communion, it was envied by some. The Episcopal Church was in decline, however, and its congregations were shrinking; shrinking rapidly. Today there are fewer Episcopalians in America than Muslims. In 30 years, it has lost one-third of its members—well over one million worshippers.

The Church hierarchy had responded to this precipitous decline in membership by seeking to "modernise" its theology and practices in the hope of raising its relevance to the modern world. Inevitably, it began to embrace social liberalism, downplaying or reinterpreting some of the Bible's more challenging passages. Predictably, this only accelerated the decline. The consistent pattern of liberalising movements in Christianity from the 1960s onwards is that the modernisers make churches less relevant, not more. It shouldn't come as any surprise. After all the Gospel of Jesus has been at odds with the fashions of a sinful world for 2000 years.

In October 1990, our rector Rev Dr Youssef, took me to lunch and asked if I would consider, and then pray about, becoming the Senior Warden of the Church of the Apostles. I shall never forget that moment as long as I live. It was the greatest honour ever bestowed upon me. I looked out the window of Café Chanterelle and caught a glimpse of God's beauty with the sun shining on the gorgeous Fall leaves and I burst into tears. Only God knew why Michael had selected me at that time. The reason did not become clear for almost two years.

Just prior to my assuming the role of Senior Warden, on 6 December 1990, I was given the honour of introducing the guest speaker at our annual dinner. Our speaker was Cal Thomas, a well-known syndicated columnist who is published in hundreds of newspapers and magazines, the author of several books and a radio commentator. Thomas brought the house down when he told the audience that he reads the New York Times and the Bible every morning, so that he can get both sides of the story.

The Senior Warden serves for a year and I was invited to take up the reins in January 1991. One of the first things I did was lead the entire vestry, together with their wives, on a weekend retreat out of town on 8–10 February 1991. This proved to be a great time of bonding which helped us through a difficult year ahead—although none of us was then aware of the issues we were about to face.

In the fall of 1991, we were then the fastest growing Episcopal Church in all of America, and were faced with a major decision concerning our affiliation with the denomination. The Episcopal Church in America is a part of the world-wide Anglican Church. In America the Senior Warden is the President of the church, and I thus had an enormous personal responsibility for the large and rapidly-growing congregation.

Prior to the Triennial Convention of the denomination in July, I recommended to the vestry that we sponsor a resolution at the next Diocesan Council, which stated quite simply: "That this Diocese affirms the Word of God revealed through the Holy Scriptures that sexual relations are to be conducted only within holy matrimony." It was hardly earth shattering; hardly radical; and was only likely to offend those who either wanted to practice homosexuality or were adulterers. But the North West Convocation, to whom we submitted the resolution, declined to endorse it. Furthermore, the Bishop had stated to our Rector and members of the Vestry that it would never pass at the Diocesan Council. The message from the Bishops to the vestry could be summed up in the words of Cole Porter's famous song: "from now on, anything goes".

Our discomfort with the direction in which the Episcopal Church was heading was crystallised during the Triennial Conference of July 1991 which erupted into bitter arguments over what we would now recognise as identity politics. The church had become absorbed with claims of institutional racism, sexism and homophobia, forgetting the Gospel's message that the path to redemption starts when each of us examine our own hearts and seek forgiveness through Jesus Christ, not through applying quotas for "Episcopalians of Colour," as one motion proposed or resolutions condemning discrimination against women. More than 20 years after the end of segregation in the South, it seemed to me that the famous words of Martin Luther King Jnr were closer to the message of the Gospel. We should not judge a person by the colour of their skin, but by the content of their character. Four decades on and the advent of the Black Lives Matter movement, King's message has been turned on its head by the rise of identity politics.

At the conference, the denomination took some aberrant un-biblical stands on a number of issues. For example, a number of bishops stated their intention to ordain openly practicing homosexuals, in direct contradiction of the Word of God. The House of Deputies defeated a proposed new canon seeking to affirm that all clergy should abstain from sexual relations outside of holy matrimony. And the House of Bishops subsequently defeated an almost identical amendment which called upon its "bishops, priests and deacons to abstain from sexual relations outside of marriage".

The Convention also approved the continued development of liturgies that use feminine and neutered images of God—in direct contradiction of His revealed nature from Scripture.

On 16 August 1991, I expressed my concerns in a letter to the entire congregation, highlighting a number of issues, including the proposal to ordain practicing homosexuals, the development of liturgies which use feminine or neutered images of God and the determination to hire openly gay and lesbian teachers to serve as role models. A copy of the letter may be found on the website:

www.agloriousride.com.au

As the leader, I believed our church should resign from the denomination. But, at a meeting called to discuss the issue, most of the fifteen members of our vestry appeared to want to stand and fight, rather than resign. Many of the vestry came from families who had been Episcopalians for generations.

I knew it was critical to avoid, at all costs, a schism that so often befalls churches at a time such as this. Rather than allow our discussion held on Monday 9 September 1991 to devolve into a hostile debate, I proposed that we adjourn the meeting. In the meantime, we pledged that none of us would discuss the issue, even with our spouses. We also all agreed that we would dedicate a day—Friday 20 September 1991—in which we would fast and pray for God's guidance.

As senior warden, it was my responsibility to lead us all through this dilemma. I therefore arranged to meet privately with several of the key vestry members during the next few days to encourage them to support the idea of leaving the denomination.

We all gathered again on Saturday morning, 21 September 1991, and began by singing praise songs, before breaking our fast, followed by earnest prayer. In the most Spirit-filled meeting I have ever attended, I could feel the hairs standing up on my arms when I asked:

"Gentlemen, have you come to a decision?"

With one accord they said, "We need to do God's will and leave the Episcopal Church." One man said, "As for me and my house, we will serve the Lord," paraphrasing the immortal words of Joshua. (Choose for yourselves this day whom you will serve . . . But as for me and my household, we will serve the Lord—Joshua 24:15b).

Everyone immediately gathered around to thank God for the unanimity.

In anticipation, but with no-one's prior knowledge, I had drafted a letter to our diocesan bishop announcing that we had decided to leave the denomination, providing a line for the signature of every member of the fifteen-man vestry. A copy is available online at:

www.agloriousride.com.au

Every vestry member immediately signed it.

Can you imagine the power of that letter when I presented it to the bishop the following Monday? And can you imagine the power of our unity, when I announced to the congregation that their vestry had made a unanimous decision to leave the denomination?

A special general meeting of the entire congregation was called for 13 October 1991. I had deliberately left unsaid the purpose of the meeting, lest it foment dissent. In my address to the congregation, I said the rejection of our resolution that simply sought to affirm that all clergy should abstain from sexual relations outside holy matrimony showed that the church was being led astray. I raised my concerns about the development of liturgies which use feminine and neutered images of God, in direct contradiction of Scripture. Further, the vote by the House of Deputies ordering Episcopal schools "to hire openly gay and lesbian teachers to serve as role models..." was nothing short of outrageous.

By way of confirmation, the congregation voted approximately 1000 to eight to support the leaders and to leave the denomination. If ever there was a demonstration of unity, this was it. St. Augustine, the famous thinker and writer of the early part of the first millennium said that:

> The only thing that genuinely unites people is a common desire for the same ends.

I believe the world—our businesses, our not-for-profit organisations, our churches—want to unite behind committed leaders in whom they believe and trust, with a common desire for the same ends. The lesson is to first build unity in your inner group, and then, like a stone dropped in a pond, build collaboration in a series of ripples throughout your entire field of influence.

Agreeing on the terms of separation was like our own version of Brexit. We had incorporated a foundation into which was deposited a $1 million donation by an older man who was saved in our church and we had previously informed the Bishop that the foundation was seeking to acquire a property to be leased to The Church of The Apostles. Tension on that issue rose to a new level, however. In a letter dated 28 March 1991, the Bishop informed us that "no Church or Chapel shall be consecrated until the Bishop shall have been sufficiently satisfied that the building and the ground on which it is erected are secured for ownership and use by a Parish, Mission, or Congregation affiliated with this Church and subject to its Constitutions and Canons."

"I cannot and will not give my consent to the establishment of an Episcopal congregation in any location where the title to the permanent building is not held by the parish in trust for the Episcopal Diocese of Atlanta."

It was clear, therefore, that if we were to continue as a member of the Episcopal Church, we would not be able to lease a property owned by the foundation.

The Bishop agreed that the fundamental issue was simply our conviction that the hierarchy of the Episcopal Church did not accept the Scriptures as the inerrant Word of God. When our Rector took a stand on the ordination of women, our Bishop summoned him to his office and berated him for two and a half hours. By now, it was impossible to imagine how we could remain under the authority of the bishop while remaining true to the Gospel. As I told our congregation, we would continue to follow the example of the Apostle Paul who told the church elders from Ephesus, "For I have not shunned to declare to you the whole counsel of God" (Acts 20:27).

As I describe these events 30 years later, it still remains a mystery why a man as new in the Christian faith as me was given such a heavy responsibility.

The bishop was hardly surprised when the Rector and I presented the formal resignation from the denomination. He asked me why I thought we were having this difficulty. I pointed to a Bible on the arm of the Bishop's chair and said, "I believe, Bishop, it is because we consider the Bible contains all things necessary for faith and life. And I don't think you do"

The Bishop was quick to respond. "You are right, Mr McLellan. The Bible is part of a three-legged stool. On one hand you have the Word of God, on another you have tradition and the third leg is the experience of man." I found his statement shocking. In his letter to the Thessalonians,

Paul spells out that we must respond to the scriptures not as a human word, but as it actually is, the Word of God, which is indeed at work in you who believe (1 Thessalonians 2:13). Yet the hierarchy of the Church had openly adopted a belief system that allowed it to make up the rules as it went along. My sadness was relieved in part by the liberating feeling that we would no longer have to answer to such an organisation.

As Rev John Stott says, the Bible is to "regulate the beliefs and practices of the church of every generation. This is why the Bible is over the church and not vice versa." Stott goes on, "I am emphatically not saying that Scripture, reason and tradition are a threefold authority of equal importance by which we come to know God's truth. No. Scripture alone is God's Word written, and the Holy Spirit its ultimate interpreter."

As the year drew to a close, on 12 December 1991, Rae and I had a celebration dinner as the guests of Rev Dr Michael and Elizabeth Youssef in their home. The following night, Rae and I hosted in our home a black-tie dinner for all the vestry, their wives and all the staff. It was a wonderful way in which to close out what had been a fairly traumatic year. We had been—by a New York mile—the biggest church to leave the Episcopal denomination and our move attracted a lot of media attention, with which I had to deal.

At the final Sunday service of the year, Michael Youssef made a presentation to me in front of the entire congregation to thank me for my role as senior warden, accompanied by a very nice affirming speech. In doing so he burst into tears. With our exit from the Episcopal Church behind us, I expect that Michael then appreciated why God had laid my name on his heart to lead our church out of the denomination and down the new path.

My response ended with a well-known Arabic proverb I had learned when we lived in Cairo, that only Michael (an Egyptian) would have understood: "eid ala eid tesakhaf." As I explained to the congregation, "it takes two hands to clap." In other words, we did this together.

What an experience for a boy from the bush!

Three decades later, I am in no doubt that we made the correct and godly decision. The Church of the Apostles has thrived while, I am sorry to say, the Episcopal Church USA is today in a shambles. It is proof, if proof were needed, that the Word of God is a firmer foundation on which to build a stool than the Bishop's three-legged concept. It testifies to the faithfulness of the congregation's founder and spiritual leader Rev Dr Michael Youssef whose wise counsel helped guide us through the challenging period of separation.

The wisdom of hindsight has also given me greater appreciation of our role as individuals in executing a greater plan. When we are put under pressure, it is only natural to think that everything comes down to us and our plans. The Bible, however, repeatedly reminds us of the bigger picture: "Humans plan their course, but the Lord establishes their steps" (Proverbs 16:9).

When the late Archbishop of Sydney, Donald Robinson, welcomed a young Egyptian immigrant into his theology class at Moore College half a century ago, he would not have imagined that he was playing a crucial role in God's plan to establish a fruitful ministry 15,000 km away in Atlanta, Georgia. Yet his role as mentor and teacher encouraged

Michael Youssef to set out for the USA to begin his important work. I came to know Don Robinson and his wife Marie when they were guests in our home in Atlanta for a week in April 1991. The Archbishop's primary mission was to encourage and counsel Michael as Rector of our Church as he wrestled with the decision to leave the denomination. Don's wisdom showed me the importance of biblical truth, and helped me to see clearly how the Episcopal denomination had lost its way.

The following year, in November 1992, Rae and I travelled from Atlanta to Sydney, where we stayed with Don and Marie at Bishopscourt in Greenoaks Avenue, Darling Point, a magnificent Victorian gothic building that was then the Archbishop's official residence. On the Sunday, after Rae had returned to the USA, Don and I strolled down the hill to worship at St Mark's church, Darling Point. When we entered, Don was appalled to see the church with vases of flowers, apparently left over from a wedding the day before. The Archbishop was a real stickler for tradition. On a later visit, Don and I swapped horror stories about the removal of melanomas. I told Don that the doctor had been unable to close the incision after he removed a cancerous growth from my forehead. Don countered with the story of his dropping jaw syndrome which developed after he had a similar operation. He claimed that after the surgeon had closed the wound his face was so tight, every time he sat down his mouth came open!

Don was so much more than an amusing raconteur, however. As an Arts undergraduate at Sydney University he excelled at Greek, so much so that when he was called-up for service in World War II, his professor suggested to the Central Bureau of Military Intelligence that he should be employed as a code-breaker. He described his job as a traffic analyst as "studying everything about the message without being able to read it." Rory Shiner, who studied theology at Moore and wrote his PhD on Don's life and work, said his code-breaking skills were critical to his approach to the New Testament.

Don was acutely aware of the dangers of theological liberalism, which seems seductive at first, but quickly subverts those who are insufficiently grounded in scripture, those nursing past hurts and resentments or those who want desperately to be seen as smart so that they can make a name for themselves. Don described the typical pattern of how secular crusades for "social justice" work their way into the church. It begins with a small group of revisionist activists who embrace an unbiblical but culturally popular idea such as gay marriage. They win over Christians who style themselves "moderate" but don't often grasp the theological issues at stake. They appeal for unity and patience. They might re-cast the conflict as a dispute over non-essential issues or argue for tolerance by using Jesus' command not to judge.

The theological liberals congratulate and fawn over the moderates for their open-mindedness, feeding the moderates' need to be liked and admired. At some point the secular media (perhaps alerted by the revisionist activists) is attracted to the conflict and reports on the "growing controversy". The media portrays orthodox leaders as stodgy reactionaries. Theological liberals are showcased as cutting-edge enlightened thinkers, courageously challenging the powers-that-be on behalf of the downtrodden. Moderates who hold traditional views, but counsel dialogue, are featured as the voices of reason.

What had been a tiny group of relatively harmless revisionists now begins to gain steam as those unprepared for the controversy are exposed to revisionist arguments for the first time via the media alongside gentle calls for moderation, patience and open-mindedness. Well-meaning, conflict-averse orthodox leaders hope to shield their group by focusing on mission and avoiding the topic. Having leveraged the moderates and the press, the tiny group of revisionist activists now has the political clout to influence the direction of the entire denomination. They then initiate legislative action. Many otherwise-orthodox leaders do not speak forcefully against these measures because those who have already done so have been successfully characterized as "zealots", "fundamentalists" and "bigots".

Disputes over human sexuality, the truthfulness of scripture, the uniqueness of Christ, marriage, euthanasia, the relationship between social justice and evangelism, tend to follow the same destructive cycle. What can we do to stop things happening? I wish I had definitive answers to that question. I don't, but I do have a few thoughts. Based on my experience, I believe we must work to establish biblically-literate, theologically-orthodox, and discerning organisations that understand the need both for prayer and political involvement and are prepared to endure both scorn and loss for the sake of biblical fidelity.

We should promote and support politically-astute, strategically-minded leaders prepared to use the media, and foster legislative action to defend and implement orthodoxy. And, we should contend zealously for the faith, publicly identify, name, and critique and criticise ideas and leaders who challenge orthodoxy. Errors in biblical understanding should be identified early and often from the pulpit, in print and online.

By making a practice of ignoring calls for "patience" and "moderation" we can prevent those making such calls setting the tone of the debate. Further, we should eschew the spiritual sounding advice from well-meaning allies who suggest political involvement and action is unworthy of the Christian.

The over-arching key, however, is belief in, and commitment to, the Word of the Lord through scripture and the sacraments. The Bible teaches that all scripture is God-breathed and is useful for teaching, rebuking, correcting and training in righteousness, so that the man of God may be thoroughly equipped for every good work (2 Timothy 3:16-17). But it also has many other purposes, including being a source of life, for man does not live by bread alone but on every word that comes from the mouth of the Lord (Deuteronomy 8:3b and Matthew 4:4).

Critically, the Bible teaches us that the way to salvation does not come from good works alone, and certainly not from pursuing causes that stem from an aggressively secular agenda for social justice. Salvation comes through accepting Christ and hearing the Word of truth, the gospel of your salvation (Ephesians 1:13). We are sanctified by the truth, for which we must be bold and stand up (John 17:17). A Christian must hold firmly to the trustworthy message as it has been taught, so that he can encourage others by sound doctrine and refute those who oppose it (Titus 1:9).

The third leg of the Bishop's three-legged stool, the experience of man, is a fickle guide at the best of times. It leaves us hostage to activists, the media and their secular agenda. As a source of authority, the Word of God is infinitely better. It is perfect[7]; it is true[8]; it judges[9]; it offers peace[110]; it promises hope[11]; it is eternal[12]. To disavow the Word of God is to do so at your peril[13]; we should listen to what it says, take it to heart, and obey[14]. Finally, we must not modify it[15].

Archbishop Dr Foley Beach whom I first met more than 30 years ago, recently gave an outstanding address as Chairman of GAFCON on the drifting of the Anglican

7     As for God, his way is perfect; the Word of the Lord is flawless. He is a shield for all who take refuge in him (Psalm 18:30); For the Word of the Lord is right and true; he is faithful in all he does (Psalm 33:4); Every Word of God is flawless; he is a shield to those that take refuge in him (Proverbs 30:5).

8     If you hold to my teaching, you are really my disciples. Then you will know the truth, and the truth will set you free (John 8:31-32); Sanctify them by the truth; your word is truth (John 17:17).

9     For the Word of God is living and active. Sharper than any two-edged sword, it penetrates even to dividing soul and spirit, joints and marrow; it judges the thoughts and attitudes of the heart (Hebrews 4:12).

10     Great peace have they who love your law, and nothing can make them stumble (Psalm 119:165).

11     I wait for the Lord, my soul waits, and in his word I put my hope (Psalm 130:5).

12     All your words are true; all your righteous laws are eternal (Psalm 119:60); The grass withers and the flowers fall, but the Word of our God stands forever (Isaiah 40:8, 1 Peter 1:24b-25); Heaven and earth will pass away, but my words will never pass away (Matthew 24:35, Mark 13:31).

13     Because you have rejected the Word of the Lord, he has rejected you as king (Samuel 15:23b); Saul died because he was unfaithful to the Lord; he did not keep the Word of the Lord and even consulted a medium for guidance and did not enquire of the Lord. So the Lord put him to death and turned the kingdom over to David son of Jesse (1 Chronicles 10:13-14); If anyone is ashamed of me and my words in this adulterous and sinful generation, the Son of Man will be ashamed of him when he comes in his Father's glory with the holy angels (Mark 8:38).

14     Blessed rather are those who hear the Word of God and obey it (Luke 11:28), (Revelation 1:3); Do not merely listen to the word, and so deceive yourselves. Do what it says (James 1:22); Let the Word of Christ dwell in you richly as you teach and admonish one another with all wisdom, and as you sing psalms, hymns, and spiritual songs with gratitude in your hearts to God (Colossians 3:16).

15     Do not add to what I command you and do not subtract from it, but keep the commands of the Lord your God that I give you (Deuteronomy 4:2); Do not add to his words, or he will rebuke you and prove you a liar (Proverbs 30:6); I warn everyone who hears the words of the prophecy of this book: If anyone adds anything to them, God will add to that person the plagues described in this book (Revelation 22:18-19).

Communion from the Word of the Lord. Entitled Sexuality, Secularity and Syncretism, his speech pointed to numerous examples of churches rejecting the integrity of the Bible. Liberal innovations in theology and sexual ethics are pushing the Christian church towards embracing an understanding of God, gender and sexuality that has much more in common with pagan theology and ethics than with orthodox Christianity. The liberal tactic has often been to change substantively the theological content of belief while maintaining the façade of orthodoxy. The house looks alright, until you open the door and step inside.

The Episcopal Church claims that the Bible *contains* the Word of God rather than it *being* the Word of God. We are also told that Jesus is *a* way to the Father, not *the* way to the Father. Jesus is *a* son of God, not *the* Son of God. They believe that Jews or Muslims or Hindus have their own way to God. This is not the gospel of Jesus Christ and the message of the Bible. England's most senior female bishop recently said the Church should stop calling God "He" because it turns off young people. Bishop Rachael Treweek is quoted in the Daily Mail as saying: "I don't want young girls and boys to hear us constantly refer to God as "he." She went on to say that non-Christians feel alienated from the Church if the image of God is depicted as male only. Meanwhile, the Diocese of Washington D.C. in the USA Episcopal Church voted to limit the use of masculine pronouns referring to God in its liturgy in order to be more inclusive in their approach. Linda Calkins of St. Bartholomew's Episcopal Church in Laytonville, Maryland, who supported this proposal, wants it included in the new Episcopal Prayer Book.

These new "progressive" ideas are often just re-packaged old pagan theology; it's not Christian. God has revealed to us his preferred pronouns. In the Gospels, God has been revealed to us as Father over 160 times. When Jesus taught us to pray he taught us to begin with "Our Father". Jesus said that He and the Father are one (John 10:30) and that when you have seen him, you have seen the Father (John 14:9).

On three occasions, the Greek text transcribes the Aramaic word Abba, or Father, leaving no question that it could have been misconstrued in translation. Yet in the Fredericksburg, Virginia, Episcopal Church, the priest changed the words in the Lord's Prayer from "Our Father who art in Heaven" to reflect Mother Earth and the Creative Being of the Universe. And the priest at the Episcopal Church in Clayton, Georgia, changed the Lord's Prayer from "Our Father in Heaven," to "Our Mother in Heaven." In the Episcopal Church of St John the Divine in New York City, there is a chapel which now has a female Jesus on the Cross— Christa is her name. These pagan conceptions of God are now accepted in various parts of the Christian church.

It is not just pagan theology which has invaded the Church however; it is also the pagan morality, that was practiced by the pagan societies that existed everywhere during the establishment of the early Church. The development of describing God with interchangeable gender pronouns has been paralleled by an attempt to treat gender in sexual relationships as equally interchangeable.

In the name of "marriage equality," the USA Episcopal Church, the Anglican Church of Canada, The Scottish Episcopal Church, The Episcopal Church of Brazil, The

Anglican Church of Aotearoa, New Zealand and Polynesia, and, more recently, the Anglican Church in Wales, have all taken steps to override the words of Jesus that marriage is between a man and a woman, in order to normalise same-sex marriage (see Matthew 19:11).

Sadly, it is not hard to discover examples of pagan morality that is now being accepted as Christian practice. In 2003 the House of Bishops of the Episcopal Church tore the fabric of the Anglican Communion when it confirmed and consecrated Gene Robinson, a priest living in a same-sex relationship as the Bishop of New Hampshire. In 2010 Mary Glasspool, a non-celibate lesbian woman, was consecrated a bishop in the Episcopal Diocese of Los Angeles. The diocese of Maine in the USA Episcopal Church has elected the Rev. Thomas Brown as their bishop. He is in a same-sex marriage with another Episcopal priest. The Cathedral in Brisbane, Australia, held a "Pride Evensong" celebrating the practice of homosexuality. As part of the liturgy, they even had a prayer to the erotic Christ: "Orange is for sexuality, the fire of spirit. Erotic Christ, you are our Fire, the Word made flesh." Churches in the UK and the USA have had Muslim services in their churches, even inviting some Muslim clerics to preach and pray during Eucharistic services. And there are several churches in the Episcopal Church which celebrate Hindu and Buddhist practices.

These examples are just a small sampling of the syncretism which has now become commonplace and is being normalised within the life of the Church.

After our Church of the Apostles left the Episcopal denomination, we formed a new group of like-minded ex-Episcopal churches. I was asked by the ministers of all these churches to draft the articles of faith and articles of governance for what was, in effect, a new denomination. I was gobsmacked as I had no formal training in theology.

But I prayed and I researched, and over several weeks drafted a 3000-word document that I believe captured the essential elements of the Christian faith, and also outlined a comprehensive system of governance for the new organisation. I forwarded this document to all the participants, including ministers and bishops, and they all met in Atlanta to consider it formally. I was nervous. After plenty of discussion the entire document was adopted unanimously with just one word to be changed.

Only years later, did I pause to look back and try to discern the primary influences on my Christian faith. God had raised me up to be Senior Warden of The Church of the Apostles; to be charged later with the responsibility of writing the articles of faith and articles of governance of the Fellowship of Free Anglican Congregations. Subsequently, I had the honour of serving as chairman of several Christian organisations in both America and Australia, including Habitat for Humanity and Australian Christian Lobby—the latter now with over 200,000 supporters.

These opportunities were planned by God before the beginning of time and, through Archbishop Donald Robinson's early mentoring in belief in the truth of the Word of the Lord, I was encouraged to seize the opportunities as they arose. I now know why God raised me up. He wanted to prune me so that, in the words of John 15, I would seek to be his disciple and become more fruitful.

## CHAPTER 13

# HOME SWEET HOME

No one is useless in this world who lightens the burdens
of another.

CHARLES DICKENS

On Boxing Day morning, 2004, a huge undersea earthquake
erupted off the coast of northern Sumatra, Indonesia sending
a series of tsunami waves up to 30 metres high surging across
the ocean. It was the third most powerful earthquake ever
recorded. It lasted from eight to ten minutes and, according
to scientists, the force it produced caused the entire planet to
vibrate by up to 10mm.

As the news reached us on a hot summer afternoon in
Sydney, fears began to mount for the people that lay in the
Tsunami's path. The picture grew worse by the hour. The
tsunami was to kill more than 220,000 people in 14 countries,
making it one of the deadliest natural disasters in recorded
history. As we watched the television pictures of devastated
coasts with barely a building left standing, it was clear that
there was a role in the recovery for Habitat for Humanity
Australia, a not-for-profit, Christian housing organisation of

which I was then chairman. Our expertise in building afford-able homes in partnership with low-income families might easily be adapted to help ease the massive humanitarian crisis that was unfolding in front of our eyes. As the world leader in providing homes for the working poor, and with its experience and infrastructure, Habitat for Humanity International led in the efforts to provide the housing component of the massive relief and development programs in several disasters.

The disaster response program we established had three objectives. First, our response would be effective and timely. Our second goal was to implement social and community benefits. The Habitat for Humanity community model helped restore the dignity of homeowner families and create community by providing a hand-up, rather than a hand-out. It had been shown to improve income generation, health, education levels and the stability of the homeowner families. Not only did these changes affect the lives of families, they also improved the way in which families interacted with their communities. Finally, we would leave a sustainable operation in place, capable of building more homes with no further financial support, for the benefit of the people of the region.

Working with Habitat was hugely rewarding. We saw thousands of poor families, both in Australia and over-seas, take possession of new homes. We were able to assist hundreds of families in places such as East Timor, The Philippines, Vietnam and Cambodia. We led the way after the Indonesian tsunami, building the first homes in Aceh, ultimately completing 25,000 in the region.

My association with Habit for Humanity began shortly after we returned to Australia, while I was serving as a director of Opportunity International. I was appointed chairman of Habitat for Humanity Australia in February 2003, a role I served in for over five years. It was a hugely effective organisation at that time, completing a home somewhere in the world every 26 minutes. The organisation has now constructed more than 300,000 homes in 100 countries.

Through donations of money and materials, and the use of volunteer labour under trained supervision, Habitat for Humanity Australia built and renovated simple, decent houses with the help of homeowner families. The completed homes were sold to the partner families at less than market value, financed with affordable, no-interest loans. The partner family gave us a nominal deposit of $500 and then spent 500 hours working on the building of their house. That is equivalent to 10 hours every Saturday for 50 weeks, which is no small commitment. The husband and the wife usually worked on the house together, which we found was a critical element in ensuring the long-term bonding of the family.

The interest-free loan repayments, which were never more than 25% of the family's income, were then used to build still more Habitat for Humanity homes. When a property was transferred, I designed a program which required the new homeowner to sign two mortgages. The first was for the sales price less the $500 deposit, reducing each month as the interest-free loan was repaid. The second, which was only triggered if the homeowner sold the property, was for the difference between the original sales price of the home and the market value at the time the homeowner sold. And this amount reduced on a sliding scale to zero over the life of the loan. At Habitat for Humanity Australia, we were all volunteers and sometimes the job could become tiresome. But it was always worth it when we handed the key to the family and listened to the children tell us about the room they would have and where they would hang their posters.

The challenge was far more complex in the tsunami-ravaged areas we felt moved to help. Almost all the civil infrastructure we take for granted in a country like Australia had been badly damaged or destroyed. When the wall of water hit Banda Aceh, 10,000 out of a total of 50,000 local civil servants were killed. Hundreds of offices were destroyed or damaged, and survivors were finding that an otherwise simple bureaucratic task could stretch on for weeks, delaying their plans to start rebuilding. Gone were many of the government offices that held deeds and survey documents. Property boundaries that people once easily recognised were erased by the waves, covered over by anonymous piles of bricks, mud and tree trunks.

Further complications could arise if the government followed through on plans to relocate tens of thousands of families from vulnerable coastal villages, raising questions about compensation. The Government was advising residents to delay buying or selling tsunami-damaged land before the establishment of a system to document ownership. Compounding the problem was a deep distrust of government and government officials. Even in good times, the local government in Aceh was considered corrupt and merely the tool of an abusive military and police. The province of Aceh had also suffered from a decades-long separatist insurgency. It is not easy building 25,000 new houses in conditions like this. But our donors expected us to ensure that their funds were employed for the purposes for which they were intended; to build simple decent houses for the poor. The obligation we felt to them drove us to overcome obstacles and finish the job.

The first secret to Habitat for Humanity's growth during my tenure was securing substantial corporate support. Indirectly, however, this caused some anguish to some of the volunteers because it became necessary to be much more accountable to donors, and meant we had to implement a raft of new governance measures. When a company matches its mission with the values of its workers, morale is transformed. Becoming passionate about the organisation for which they work, employees create a culture which brings out the best in people. Working with values they have internalised, employees feel the immense power of these values in their own lives. And performance and profit are automatically improved. As Levi Strauss & Co chairman Robert Haas once said, "A Company's values—what it stands for, what its people believe in—are crucial to its competitive success."

As chairman, I also developed a set of corporate values which we proudly referenced when dealing with our partners. We made no secret of being a Christian, ecumenical, grass-roots organisation that encourages people to work together towards a common goal. The focus of our ministry was not the construction of homes for its own sake alone but as a means to empower individuals and communities. The organisation's by-line is: "Building homes; building communities; building hope." The importance of home ownership was second nature to me, having grown up in post-war Australia under Robert Menzies, a prime minister who considered the increase of home ownership from 50 per cent to 70 per cent during his 16 unbroken years in office as one of his finest achievements. I was too young to have heard his famous Forgotten People radio broadcast on 22 May 1942, but when I attended a Menzies Research Centre gala 75th anniversary dinner in which the broadcast was re-enacted by actor Peter Cousins, I was struck with the emphasis Menzies put on homebuilding in his vision of post-war Australia.

"The home is the foundation of sanity and sobriety; it is the indispensable condition of continuity; its health determines the health of society as a whole… The material home represents the concrete expression of the habits of frugality and saving 'for a home of our own.' Your advanced socialist may rave against private property even while he acquires it; but one of the best instincts in us is that which induces us to have one little piece of earth with a house and a garden which is ours; to which we can withdraw, in which we can be among our friends, into which no stranger may come against our will."

As a Christian who believes in the importance of the family as a building block for a healthy society, Menzies's words rang true. A home is far more than a building. "My home is where my wife and children are," said Menzies. "The instinct to be with them is the great instinct of civilised man; the instinct to give them a chance in life—to make them not leaners but lifters—is a noble instinct."

At Habitat, homeowner families are chosen according to their need, their ability to repay the loan and their willingness to work in partnership with Habitat for Humanity Australia. We follow a non-discriminatory policy of family selection. Neither race nor religion is a factor in choosing the families who receive Habitat for Humanity Australia homes. It was a people-to-people partnership, which puts into action our belief in the equality and dignity of each person, without discrimination. All board members and volunteers agree to serve without pay.

The most important factor in Habitat's success was the commitment to our biblical faith which calls us to do the right thing for the right reasons, whether or not anyone will know. It means that we were committed to a biblical stewardship of all God has entrusted to us, by integrating actively what we believe with what we do. We are accountable, particularly in handling finances with integrity, according to the highest biblical standards. We told the truth and were scrupulously honest and accurate at all times. We honoured and respected our employees, their families, and all our volunteers and were committed to exemplary moral behaviour, clear, clean and careful to avoid even the appearance of impropriety. And we did not criticise, condemn or speak negatively about similar organisations.

With such large sums raised in this country, I believed it was likely that a spotlight would be shone on not-for-profit agencies as we sought to carry out work in the tsunami affected areas. And to avoid adverse publicity with respect to our stewardship of donated funds, it was critical that we all adopted good governance procedures.

Far from being a barrier in our approaches for support from the commercial world, Habitat's transparent declaration of Christian faith offered reassurance to prospective large donors that we could be trusted to do the right thing. As an example, I made a submission to ANZ Bank at the highest level and received a wonderful commitment to donate

$250,000 per year towards the construction of new homes. The former managing director described the Bank's involvement this way:

> Our association with Habitat for Humanity Australia has enabled our staff, through their generosity of spirit, to help with the projects and to touch the lives of those families in need—often in small ways, but making a huge difference to those families. It has also helped us to build upon the sustainability of our business...
>
> We have found that working with Habitat for Humanity Australia has been a sincere two-way relationship. And the organisation's tenacious pursuit of its goals is totally aligned with our company motto, "tenacity of spirit"...
>
> By combining our strength and experience, we can surpass anything we could achieve as separate organisations ... it's about putting people into homes and being relevant and committed to the communities in which we operate.
>
> Volunteers loved the experience of actually assisting to build a home for a deserving family. Not only did they often learn a new skill and see the tangible results of their efforts, but the shared "hardship" of a day's work on a building site created bonds between the team members that is hard to replicate in an office environment. And employees enjoyed a "feel good" experience that lasted for a long time.'

The tsunami was not just a physical challenge but a spiritual challenge as well. In the wake of the disaster, I spoke to staff and volunteers at Habitat's Parramatta headquarters, reflecting on discussion in the media about how we should "understand" the disaster. It had prompted questions like: Is God responsible? Is God judging the world? Did victims deserve their fate? Is it just a freak of nature? I said to the assembled team:

> The first question all of us ask ourselves is: Is God in control of the world? On this question the Bible is clear. God is in control of the world. Nothing occurs outside of his sovereignty. He is King— every day, every hour, everywhere. What's more, suffering and evil are not exceptions to this. God says: 'I form the light and create darkness, I bring prosperity and create disaster' (Isaiah 45:7)…
>
> When we can't see the 'good' that some tragedy brings, we find it harder to accept that God is in control. But I prefer the teaching of the Bible to the alternative. If there are things in this world which are exceptions—things in which God has no control or good purpose—then we are left with random chaos in which anything could happen to us and there may be no-one to stop it.
>
> Instead, we have the assurance that God is at work in all things for the good of those who love him (Romans 8:28), even when we can't see how.
>
> Secondly, we begin to wonder why does God let it happen? Is it his judgement? Or is it a warning?

A revealing passage to consider is Luke 13:1-5:

"Now there were some present at that time who told Jesus about the Galileans whose blood Pilate had mixed with their sacrifices. Jesus answered, "Do you think that these Galileans were worse sinners than all the other Galileans because they suffered this way? I tell you, no! But unless you repent, you too will all perish. Or those eighteen who died when the tower in Siloam fell on them — do you think they were more guilty than all the others living in Jerusalem? I tell you, no! But unless you repent, you too will all perish."

So, what does this teach us? The first message is that, when disaster strikes, we must not assume that the people who suffer especially deserve it. The Bible rejects the idea that suffering is always connected to people's sins or mistakes. The second message is, every deadly calamity is a merciful call from God for the living to repent. "Weep with those who weep," the Bible says. Yes, but let us also weep for our own rebellion against the living God. Finally, the third message is that God relents when we pray to him.

Having lived abroad for so many years, I felt proud to be back in Australia and to see the outpouring from so many in response to the crisis. Their compassion, I believe, reflected the heart of God.

The tsunami was a test for our organisation from which we emerged stronger. In 2005, Habitat for Humanity and PMI Mortgage Insurance Limited won the nation-wide Prime Minister's Award for Excellence in Community Business Partnerships, in the medium business category. The Award recognised our ongoing and successful partnership with PMI, which was assisting needy Australian families to realise their dreams of owning a simple decent home. As Prime Minister John Howard said when we won the award, "Working in partnership has the potential to enrich people's lives but can also deliver tangible results for all Australians. Community and business partnerships are a driver to accomplish better outcomes than any group acting alone could achieve."

Arising out of Habitat for Humanity's relationship with a number of corporate partners, I was invited by Senator Grant Chapman, the chairman of the Senate Enquiry into Corporate Responsibility, to make a submission and give evidence to the committee, which I gladly did:

> Corporate social investment is not about guilt or self-congratulation. Corporate social investment is about building bridges while building brands; empowering communities while creating a corporate ethic of which staff and shareholders can be proud. It is not about writing cheques, but a way to benefit their communities, and at the same time a powerful marketing opportunity...
>
> Apart from globalisation which has greatly increased awareness of corporate social investment, it is clear that as the old "bricks and mortar"

companies fade, and knowledge-based corporations emerge as the powerhouses of the economy,
the value of a company's intangible assets becomes
much more important. Many businesses have
become like their competitors, offering virtually
the same product or service in the same way at the
same price.

Intangible assets, such as employee commitment, reputation, and the emotional aspects of the
brand become vital and can represent the great
bulk of a company's total value. Corporate social
investment then becomes a valuable tool through
which a corporation can protect and enhance these
assets.

Despite our successes at Habitat, I came to realise that not all
problems associated with housing are easily solved. A number
of the homes we built in Australia were for Aboriginal families and I was keen for us to do more to help close the gap
between the welfare of Indigenous and non-Indigenous
Australians. In June 2008, I met with the Cape York Institute
for Policy and Leadership, based in Cairns. The meeting had
been organised by Ian McCauley, who had recently retired
as chairman of Felix Resources Limited, of which I was a
director, and who had made a substantial donation to the
Institute.

At that time, the Cape York Institute was chaired by the
well-known Aboriginal leader Noel Pearson. The executive
director, whom I grew to respect enormously, was Alan Tudge.
Tudge later became the Federal Member for Aston and an

outstanding minister in the Coalition government. Following meetings at the Cairns headquarters, we flew to Cooktown and then toured Hopevale. We then drove further north to where Noel Pearson had a beachside retreat for a meeting in one of the most beautiful settings on earth. Noel was kind enough to drive me back to Hopevale and on to Cooktown for our return flight to Cairns.

Felix Resources had extensive coal mines in the Bowen Basin in Queensland. There was a significant shortage of labour in the region and the employment of even unskilled and untrained Aboriginal workers would have been guaranteed. As a way of assisting the community, Ian McCauley believed the local council would provide us land on which to build houses for the new workers.

The feedback we received from Aboriginal leaders was that not a single aboriginal family would wish to take up our offer of a new home, financed with an interest-free loan and a highly-paid job in a booming sector. I was very disappointed that people were prepared to continue living in squalid circumstances in an isolated community, unemployed and relying on government handouts. In many ways it had been easier to achieve results overseas than it proved to be closer to home.

Habitat played an important role in the establishment of East Timor as the world's newest independent state. In the savage counter-insurgency campaign that followed independence, 100,000 East Timorese were killed and tens of thousands of homes destroyed. One night, Rae and I were invited to dinner at a friend's home in Mosman where the guest of honour was Kirsty Sword Gusmão, the Australian wife of the President of Timor Leste, Xanana Gusmão. Kirsty was a passionate lady, concerned about the plight of the people in East Timor. As chairman of Habitat for Humanity, I saw a great opportunity for us to rebuild many houses throughout the newly-formed nation. I was inspired and, after some investigation, set out to raise the funds that would allow Habitat for Humanity to play a role in building new homes there.

Many families still owned their land, albeit with their homes in ashes, which made it a much easier task for us. We were able to secure donations of materials to rebuild a very simple house (shelter may be a better word) for $1,125. In one of the most heart-warming experiences I had had during many years of fundraising as chairman of Habitat for Humanity Australia, I approached a comfortable professional man and made a proposition that he and his wife fund a total of five houses at a cost of $5,500. I handed him a formal proposal. As we sat on his front balcony overlooking the water in Drummoyne, he was quick to answer. "Yes," he said, "we would be delighted to do that."

"Well, thank you, but don't you want to first discuss it with your wife?" I ventured. But he assured me she would be supportive. A week later the man called me and said that after speaking with his wife they had decided to fund one house a week.

I was overjoyed and later toured a number of villages in East Timor with the generous couple, inspecting several of the houses then being built. It was a very happy few days, with many tears of joy from the new owners. The donor's wife told me she was a palliative care nurse. She told me story after story of her experience of people dying. I promised myself there and then, on a mountain track in the backwoods of East Timor, that I would never allow myself to die angry.

Sometime later, in March 2003, I took Rob and Julie Owen (managing director of a large foundation which had also funded many houses through Habitat for Humanity in East Timor), and the then managing director of Habitat for Humanity Australia, Michael Pailthorpe, to an Asian Society luncheon. There we all met the guest of honour, HE Kay Rala Xanana Gusmão, President of East Timor. As I told him of our work in East Timor, tears welled in the President's eyes as he expressed deep appreciation for the construction of approximately 400 houses by Habitat for Humanity. It was a deeply touching moment and made me grateful for the opportunity given to me to play a small part in this recovery project in his war-ravaged country.

My time at Habitat for Humanity was very rewarding and I felt that the work was a great witness to the broader community, including the companies and their employees who supported us, many of whom would not call themselves Christian. I was succeeded as chairman by my colleague David Benn who wrote a very nice note:

> The key was your Christian commitment and ded-
> ication to HFHA. You persevered; you went the
> extra mile. The draining toll on you was enormous
> but you "kept the faith" and by so doing bolstered
> me and a lot of others in a team effort.

The task of keeping a not-for-profit organisation focused requires strong commitment to its founding principles and tough resolve. It is never easy, but during my time at Habitat, I believe we achieved the task better than most. Not all of my experiences were so fruitful. My first involvement in the not-for-profit world after we returned to Australia was my appointment as a director of Opportunity International Australia on 24 May 2002, where I served for over seven years.

Opportunity International did wonderful work in many countries, providing loans to poor people to help them build businesses. Regrettably, Opportunity International was challenged and in my view lost its way as a Christian organisation. My experience working with Christian organisations is that, inevitably, they lose their focus and their Christian purpose. A wise man, who saw this happen before his eyes once told me, "No organisation has ever been known to become more spiritual." He was saying that there is an almost inexorable drift away from an organisations' Christian beginnings and beliefs into something more secular.

This drift usually begins subtly, imperceptibly and remains undetected. If an organisation's mission is to head due north towards its goal, an ever-so-slight change in direction of one degree will rarely be noticed. Then, on its new bearing, a subsequent change of one degree will likewise be undetected. With 180 of these tiny, cumulative changes, the organisation will ultimately find itself heading due south. I have seen it myself in a number of different Christian not-for-profits.

In my view, the decline of Opportunity International began when an anonymous donor, an extremely generous person, gave $25 million to OIA. Understandably, the gift came with some conditions. Indeed, if I were a non-Christian donor, I might well have done the same. The donor asked that the funds be applied in a particular way that was outside our normal modus operandi. It cut across our usual practice and did not allow us to fulfil our mission. In a paper to the board of directors, I argued that we should only partner with Christian organisations, as we had done up to then, to ensure our mission to transform lives was fulfilled, and which would "adhere to the common mission, motivation, and core values that bind us together". Our by-laws stated that in following Jesus' example and teaching, "we seek to serve those in poverty; offering a glimpse of hope to those whose hope had been lost." We offer friendship, respecting the diversity and pride of those whom we serve. And we celebrate, rejoicing with those whose lives have been changed. We were motivated by Jesus Christ's call to serve the poor and believed that we should always be ready to give the "reason for the hope that is in us", and that we must make certain our clients are exposed to the Gospel as the ultimate source of their hope.

In conclusion, I argued, if we cannot do that, we should invest our God-given resources somewhere else. Only one other board member supported my views, which is always a bit embarrassing. But, in my humble opinion, this resulted in a setback to Opportunity International in Australia. Some years later, Rae and I took the founder, David Bussau and his wife Carol for a lunch in Moore Park to celebrate David's 70th birthday. Sadly, it was apparent that David had checked out mentally from OIA and no longer attended board meetings. In his words, "The organisation has lost its way."

The lesson from my time at Opportunity International is one I sought to implement in my future work for not-for-profit organisations. For some, the quest for funding becomes all-absorbing. Difficult as fund-raising can sometimes be, however, it is in some ways the easy part. The challenge is to spend the funds raised wisely. The act of giving to a not-for-profit is a donor's means to an end. It is how the organisation uses those resources to give back to the community that really counts and either honours or dishonours the donor's intent. In the words of the Apostle Paul, "we must help the weak, remembering the words the Lord Jesus himself: 'It is more blessed to give than to receive'" (Acts 20: 35).

My experience with a number of Christian organisations, strengthened my belief in the need to take affirmative action in order to protect an organisation's Christian ethos. As a result, as Chairman, I developed a detailed plan and policy for Australian Christian Lobby, which was formally adopted by both the board of directors and the trustees. A copy can be found at www.agloriousride.net.

CHAPTER 14

# ONWARD CHRISTIAN SOLDIERS

The chief danger that confronts the coming century will
be religion without the Holy Ghost, Christianity without
Christ, forgiveness without repentance, salvation without
regeneration, politics without God, heaven without hell.

WILLIAM BOOTH

Of the many things in which I have been involved in the
last 65 years, my relationship with Australian Christian
Lobby has been the most rewarding. It began with an introduction to Jim Wallace in 2003 by Jason Briant, the then
executive director of the Menzies Research Centre of which
I had recently become a director. Jim came to our home in
Waverton where we met fairly briefly as I had to take a flight
to Brisbane for a commercial board meeting.

Jim and I immediately struck up a good relationship
and I became fascinated with his work at ACL. While I
had plenty of other board responsibilities at the time, when
Jim asked me to become involved, I could hardly say no.

The predecessor to ACL had been founded in 1996 as the Australian Christian Coalition under the leadership of John Gagliardi, a former newspaper editor and member of the Christian Outreach Centre in Brisbane. Jim had taken over as executive chairman in 2000 after 32 years of distinguished service in the Australian Army, including three years in command of the Special Air Service Regiment. The organisation later changed its name to the Australian Christian Lobby.

ACL's mission was to secure a place for Christianity in the public square. We wanted to see Christian principles and ethics accepted and influencing the way we are governed, do business and relate to each other as a community. I shared Jim's concern about the effects of the rapid loss of Christian influence in our community. The numbers clearly demonstrate it, and the dramatic changes in our culture are nothing less than frightening. When you get to Rae's and my age, you will see it even more clearly. Sadly, we cannot claim to be leaving this a better world for our grandchildren than the one in which we were raised. Now each of us must all play our part in rebuilding God's Kingdom here on earth. I was formally appointed a director of ACL on 1 March 2006 and elected chairman on 12 June 2009.

My experience in the corporate and not-for-profit world had taught me that if the ACL was to thrive it must stay true to its founding purpose. Its longevity depended on its ability to develop a raft of policies and protocols and I was happy to help. I put in place a set of Board Protocols and a Code of Ethics and Conduct. We embraced a whole range of policies to ensure we did not lose our way, as many Christian organisations do, entitled Maintaining our Christian Ethos. These documents may be accessed at www.agloriousride.com.au.

I also worked closely with Jim Wallace in adopting a new Constitution for the organisation and a host of other policies.

The issue of same-sex marriage which was to dominate the agenda over the next decade was not yet a mainstream political issue. John Howard's amendment to the Marriage Act defining marriage as a "voluntarily entered-into union of a man and a woman to the exclusion of all others" had passed without opposition from the Labor Party in 2004, due chiefly to ACL campaigning and meeting directly with the shadow attorney general to get the ALP's commitment. This on the back of a huge joint Christian event in the Great Hall of Parliament, carried the day. Nonetheless, a number of Labor parliamentarians, including Anthony Albanese, had voiced objections. Kevin Rudd, who had been elected as Prime Minister in 2007, was a church goer who firmly supported the biblical definition of marriage at that time, although he later changed his mind and came out in favour of same-sex marriage. Julia Gillard was also a supporter of traditional marriage despite publicly declaring herself an atheist. When a private members bill to introduce same-sex marriage was introduced to Parliament in 2012, Gillard and most of her Labor colleagues voted against it. This was in no small part due to the pressure exerted by ACL and particularly through annual meetings it organised between the majority of denominational leaders with the Prime Minister and Opposition Leader.

Even so, many of us were beginning to sense a new hostility towards Christians and their beliefs. Richard Dawkins' book *The God Delusion*, published in 2006, had become a *New*

*York Times* bestseller and Dawkins was eagerly welcomed as a guest on the ABC whenever he happened to be in town. Christopher Hitchens' 2007 book *God is Not Great: How Religion Poisons Everything* was also given extensive coverage in the media. As the years went by, Christians who stood up for time-honoured values, like Jim Wallace and Cardinal George Pell, would find themselves branded as extremists. It became harder than ever for Christians to get a fair hearing and the threats to religious freedom were becoming apparent.

An address by the Prime Minister had become something of a tradition at the ACL's annual conference. In 2012, Prime Minister Gillard had accepted an invitation to speak and I was looking forward to introducing her. In contrast to her sometimes abrasive political style, Ms Gillard could be warm and personable in private. A month before she was due to speak, Jim made some remarks in a speech about the health risks associated with homosexuality that the press chose to misinterpret as a statement "smoking healthier than gay marriage". In one of the gay activists earliest uses of cancel culture, social media whipped up a storm and Ms Gillard buckled to the pressure and announced she would boycott our conference.

So it was that I found myself in the unusual position of speaking in place of the Prime Minister as I rose to give the opening address on 6 October, laying out the challenges we faced. I warned of the threats to religious freedom that lurked behind the campaign for gay rights. "Religious institutions of all kinds will find that their freedom to practice, and even to say, what they believe about sexuality and marriage will be challenged and restricted." I said. "This is already happening around the world where gay marriage has been legalised, or civil unions are held to be the same as marriage." I recounted a conversation with one gay rights activist who had openly admitted that same-sex marriage was just a step along the way to abolish religion itself. There was a lot more at stake than many were prepared to recognise.

Against overwhelming odds, we fought back against same-sex marriage and a fiercely partisan media. Indeed, we had been described in the press as the biggest single obstacle to same-sex marriage, an epithet we wore with pride. We were spoken of as punching above our weight, a claim that revealed how little some journalists knew of the weight of support for upholding the traditional definition of marriage. While we ultimately lost the battle, I remain immensely proud of the courage and commitment of ACL and its supporters who stayed true to the Gospel's teachings throughout. Disingenuous as many of the proponents' arguments may have been, we respected the Parliamentary process, understanding the truth of Winston Churchill's words that 'democracy is the worst form of Government except for all those other forms that have been tried from time to time.'

The important thing was not to dwell upon the past but to look to the future, focusing on what we could do to build strength within the Christian community in Australia. With membership growing and the ACL's finances strengthening, we were in a position to purchase our own office building in Canberra. Ownership of a permanent headquarters for the ACL was crucial to ensuring that the organisation endured. It seemed fitting that the building we eventually found in the

Canberra suburb of Deakin had been named Eternity House by its then owner, Christian businessman Dennis Barnes. In 2015, we set up a company, Eternity House Limited, to purchase the building. The acquisition was financed by two loans, totalling $1.25 million, the second of which we were able to pay off.

I will digress for a moment to explain the inspiration for the building's name. Eternity was the legacy of Arthur Stace, a former misfit in Sydney society who got a new start in life in 1930 when introduced to the teachings of Jesus. Stace, who served as a stretcher-bearer in World War One, returned to Sydney in 1919 as a sick and shattered man. He became an alcoholic and fell into crime, at one stage working for his sister's brothel. On a bleak winter's evening in August 1930, he took himself along to St Barnabas' Anglican church on Broadway where the minister, Rev. R.B.S. Hammond, promised everyone who came a cup of tea and a rock cake. But first they had to listen to a sermon. We do not know exactly what Hammond preached that night. But we do know the effect his words had on Arthur. Straight after the service Arthur left the church, crossed over into nearby Victoria Park, and got down on his knees. He prayed: "God, God be merciful to me a sinner".

Stace spent the next 37 years wandering the streets of Sydney at night chalking an anonymous one-word sermon on the pavement. The word was Eternity and he wrote it more than half a million times in his distinctive handwriting. It intrigued Sydneysiders who pondered its meaning whilst trying to identify its mysterious author. On New Year's Eve 1999, an estimated 2 billion television viewers

around the world watched Sydney's spectacular millennium celebrations. Sydney was to host the Olympic Games
in 2000 and the city was the centre of national and global
attention. At the climax of the celebrations, just after midnight on 1 January 2000, the Sydney Harbour Bridge was
lit up with the word Eternity. The huge crowds clustered
around the harbour foreshores applauded as one. Somewhere
in their inner being they recognised the significance of this
single mighty word.[16]

During my time as chairman, we set about establishing the
Lachlan Macquarie Institute, a centre to train wise Christian
leaders. Conceived by Jim Wallace, based on a vision from
God, the Lachlan Macquarie Institute was dedicated to
improving the quality of leadership in Australia. The Institute
opened its doors in 2011 and is now located at the Lachlan
Macquarie Homestead close to Canberra which we had
raised funds to purchase. It was a serious investment in future
leadership that only ten years after its foundation is already
yielding rich dividends. The programs are led by Australian
experts including leading academics from Australia's top
universities, elite public policy analysts, media specialists, and
church and business leaders. Regular guest speakers include
former and serving parliamentarians, among them former and
current cabinet members.

The Institute's flagship, 14-week program, places a strong
emphasis on future leaders in politics and public service,
promotes intellectual rigour and discernment, character
formation, and involves work-experience in key areas of

16   © Roy Williams, author (with Elizabeth Meyers) of *Mr Eternity: The story of Arthur Stace* (Acorn
Press, 2017) Used with the author's permission.

government. A twelve-week summer program targets potential leaders in the arts, media, politics, public service, law, académia, and education. LMI also offers other programs, including a two-day one designed for church leaders. This covers questions such as: What is the separation of church and state? Where has secularism come from and how does it affect our culture? Why is religious freedom so important? What threatens Christian leaders' right to speak biblically and freely? How should churches lead in a secular society?

Another week-long program enables participants to navigate their way through the landscape of ideas and ideologies that universities promote. Designed for people aged 18–25, it addresses questions such as: Where did our secular age come from? Where is it going? How can Christians respond? What is the relationship between science and religion, reason and faith? How does Christianity address the complexities of our secular age—of human identity, sexuality, technology, justice, the problem of evil, and world religions? Delegates fellowship and dialogue on these questions with Australia's top Christian thinkers.

The Human Rights Law Alliance is another ACL initiative that pushes back against the progressive tide. It focuses on the freedoms neglected by the Australian Human Rights Commission, such as: "freedom of speech, freedom of religion, freedom of conscience and freedom of association". Led by its outstanding Managing Director, John Steenhof, HRLA has developed a highly-skilled legal capacity to act in strategic legal cases to reinforce, protect and advance fundamental freedoms for Christians. Building on his predecessor Martyn Iles' work, John has built an alliance of Christian lawyers in the States and Territories that are increasingly equipped and skilled at defending Christian freedoms. HRLA has also sought to raise the visibility of religious freedom issues in the Christian community and to carry out public advocacy for religious freedom rights to build momentum to change the social environment of public apathy that is turning to hostility. Through legally effective representation and advocacy, HRLA is advancing within Australian legal precedent, public policy and culture, promoting increased protection of Christian freedom and the freedom of belief, thought, speech and conscience.

Australian society is an increasingly hostile environment for Christians and other people of faith. Religion, especially traditional Christianity, is increasingly being seen as bigoted, backward and a threat to the flourishing of Australian society. The West is becoming increasingly less tolerant of Christian values and truth more generally. This opposition, often coalescing around the LGBTQI+ agenda, is aggressively assertive and increasingly intolerant, seizing any opportunity to demean faith. Where Christians speak up for Biblical truth, they are not just shouted down, but are specifically targeted. Christians are being fired from their jobs, stripped of their qualifications, sued for discrimination and vilification and prevented from living out their beliefs. Christian teachings are not just the subject of derision, but they are now grounds for making Christians the victims of cancel culture in an attempt to remove the Christian voice from the culture. A civil society requires strong protection of freedom of thought, speech, conscience and association, so that robust discussion and debate of ideas are protected and so that Christian thought and practice are not extinguished in the public square. Good and true ideas should be allowed to be expressed. Speech should be met with speech. Ideas should be contested with ideas.

Under our new constitution which I helped compose, the chairman's term in office was limited. I stepped down as a director and chairman on 20 November 2015. I was then honoured with the title Chairman Emeritus. By August 2010 when the ACL celebrated its 10th anniversary, its finances had strengthened enormously. Our supporters had grown from 3,850 to 50,000 (it is over 200,000 today).

In my final speech as chairman, I told the story of a great fire that swept through a cathedral southwest of Paris on June 10, 1194. Its loss threatened to devastate the people and the towns for miles around. There must have been plenty of villagers living then who wanted to give up, declare disaster the existential winner, and go elsewhere. What happened instead was something extraordinary by any standard. Those people and their leaders persevered and they resolved to not have their lives disrupted by the disaster. In a remarkably short time, a cathedral bigger and even more magnificent was raised up in its place.

Today Chartres Cathedral is one of the outstanding examples of Gothic architecture on God's earth. And it was built by men and women who had witnessed the signature disaster of their times and who refused to resign themselves to it. 'Having witnessed the waning Christian influence in our society, we must rebuild the equivalent of Chartres Cathedral in our world of politics,' I told the audience. 'And I cannot imagine a finer group of people to undertake the task, led by the inestimable Jim Wallace.'

Stepping down from the chairmanship of ACL was never going to be easy, but I kept reminding myself that in God's scheme of things, every day is a new beginning; every sunset is merely the latest milestone on a voyage that never ends.

I concluded by referring to my proud Scottish father who would turn in the grave in which he had lain for sixty years if anyone thought I was Irish. But the Irish are romantic, poetic people, and when they are about to depart, they have a lovely prayer, which I offered as my closing remarks:

> May the road rise up to meet you,
> May the wind be ever at your back.
> May the sun shine warm upon your face
>   and the rain fall softly on your fields.
> And until we meet again,
> May God hold you in the hollow of his hand.

When I stepped down as chairman, Jim Wallace assumed the role and, under his leadership, we have experienced exponential growth. We had appointed Lyle Shelton as Jim's successor as executive director and it proved to be a wise choice. Lyle truly blossomed in the role, showing great courage and leadership in his readiness to argue for principles of faith in a world that was frequently hostile. I had the great pleasure as his chairman of working very closely with him for many years. By his example we all learned what it takes to represent God in a world that little understood Christian teaching. I think, in particular, of Lyle leading the battle to retain traditional marriage against a fierce LGBTQI+ seeking to adopt same-sex marriage.

One of the more memorable times with Lyle was having him to stay with us in Bowral on a Friday night before his talk at the nearby St Stephens church at Mittagong the following morning. On his drive up from Canberra, I received a confidential telephone call informing me that Lyle had just won the International 2016 Daniel of the Year Award. I was thrilled for him and wondered how I could honour him at the dinner party Rae and I were hosting in our home that evening. We had a wonderful array of guests, including Rev Dr Vic Roberts and his wife Delle, former Senator Ross Lightfoot, and Peter Thomas, the principal of Capernwray Bible School. I did not mention the secret to anyone— including Lyle.

During dinner I read a few selected passages from Daniel, highlighting his courage and his commitment. I then told those gathered around the table that we had amongst us a person who had just been awarded the international Daniel of the Year Award. Lyle is so humble, he was embarrassed, but I was so proud and everyone around the table rejoiced. They knew well what he had been through, leading the fight to maintain traditional marriage.

One of the most traumatic days in ACL's history was getting a call at 6am on 22 December 2016 that our building, Eternity House, had been firebombed. I jumped into my car and raced down to Canberra just as Lyle arrived from his holiday in Queensland. It was very distressing. Apart from the physical damage, the emotional toll, when we realised that someone had wanted to destroy our building and presumably us, was enormous. What compounded the problem was the apparent indifference of the police who did not appear to accept that this was a deliberate act by someone bent on destroying us or disrupting what we were doing.

Sometime later, we established that the man who did the act, and who later committed suicide, had a history as an activist for same-sex marriage, including internationally. It traumatised some members of the staff—all fine Christian men and women—and forced us to really step up our security of the building.

Lyle was very brave, but I know he was also disturbed by this event and it must have weighed on his mind when he thought about his future with ACL. Later, he chose a political career and I am pleased to say I have managed to stay in close touch. Lyle also wrote a book, "I Kid You Not," that has been a best seller, and includes his experiences at ACL.

When Lyle resigned from ACL, he was succeeded by the brilliant Martyn Iles. Martyn has done a spectacular job and refocused the organisation on younger people and developed an activist/campaign group. Martyn's latest report shows a 36% increase in donations, a growth in supporters to over 200,000, and a social media reach of reliably over five million a month.

The Australian Christian Lobby is the work of many committed people with whom I feel fortunate to have worked. The person I came to admire most is Jim Wallace whose leadership, courage and clear-sightedness have inspired and motivated many others to play their part, including me.

Jim was the commander of Australia's famous SAS Regiment and later a brigadier commanding our mechanised forces. Jim was placed first in the list for promotion to major general, a ranking that would have guaranteed him the most senior appointments in the Army. He was top of a very select group. But Jim felt called by God to launch the Australian Christian Lobby, following the founding of its predecessor the ACC by John Gagliardi. Jim sacrificed his career in the services to take on this daunting task, for which innumerable people are deeply grateful.

In August 2010, we celebrated ten years of ACL when a number of prominent Australians wrote letters to Jim affirming his incredible work. Let me quote from just three:

> Jim Wallace is one of the finest men with whom I have had the privilege of being associated and part of his attraction besides his strong Christian ethical beliefs, lies in his wonderful sense of humour, his ready smile and charming personality. He is also a devoted husband and father. If the world was full of Jim Wallaces, it would be a much happier and better place in which to live.'
>
> —MICHAEL JEFFERY
> FORMER GOVERNOR GENERAL

> As Prime Minister of Australia for some three-quarters of the time that you have been advocating the values of the Australian Christian Lobby, I can only say that you have been most influential, always articulate, never over-zealous but persistent in arguing the essence of issues that go to Christian influence in our national life. I thank you warmly for such selfless and dedicated service.
>
> —JOHN HOWARD
> FORMER PRIME MINISTER

It has always been humbling for me to know a man who, on stepping away from a stellar military career chose not to enrich himself but to enrich the community…

There is deep integrity about you.

Once drawn into the vortex of politics, it is easy to be caught in the verbal trickery of point-scoring and deal-making. No matter how pure the intention, that process has a way of sullying the participants. You, more than most, manage to avoid this. Congratulations, Jim, on your contribution to things of the spirit in our national life. Thank you for your sacrifice, commitment and conviction.

—KIM BEAZLEY

FORMER LABOR LEADER AND FORMER AMBASSADOR
TO THE USA

Afterwards, when Jim stepped down as managing director of Australian Christian Lobby, a Testimonial Dinner was held at the Hyatt Hotel in Canberra in his honour. The turnout was immense. Supporters, donors, politicians all flocked to farewell Jim. I was given the honour of hosting the evening, beginning with a definition of a hero as a person of distinguished courage or ability, admired for his or her noble qualities and person who, in the opinion of others, has heroic qualities or has performed a heroic act and is regarded as a model or ideal.

I went on to list some of my heroes and what made them so. George Washington was endowed with great presence, he had charisma, and energy. He was charming and had an even temperament. As a leader he seized the opportunity to change things for the better, evicting the British so that America could be independent.

John Flynn was a Presbyterian pastor who spent his whole life in selfless service ministering to the people in the bush. He travelled from station to station in his old "flivver"—baptising infants, burying the dead and preaching the Word of the Lord. He created the Royal Flying Doctor Service, which I have visited many times in Broken Hill. He pioneered the pedal radio, so that people in distress could call in. He founded the Bush Nurses organisation. He also created the School of the Air, through which I learned to read and write.

William Wilberforce laboured for twenty years before bringing an end to Britain's involvement in the slave trade. A great strategist, Wilberforce was an early practitioner of the marketing concept of "touch points"—using facts and data to support his political and social reform arguments. These techniques are all used today by the Australian Christian Lobby.

In one of the most oft-quoted speeches of all time, delivered at the foot of the Lincoln Memorial, Martin Luther King didn't outline a plan. He simply said: "I have a dream". That is how all my heroes operated. They didn't command so much as they convicted.

Our Lord Jesus Christ practiced this to perfection. He didn't rely on his unlimited power or his authority. He simply convicted others of his beliefs, and they all (or nearly all) became his followers—not because they were commanded to, but because they believed in him.

The common thread that linked these heroes was that they had been called by God to perform their extraordinary acts.

To paraphrase the words of Samuel E. Roberts, when a man is called by God, what can stop him? Cripple him and you have a Sir Walter Scott. Put him in a prison cell and you have a John Bunyan. Have him born in abject poverty and you have Abraham Lincoln. Make him second fiddle in an obscure South African orchestra and you have an Arturo Toscanini. Bury him in the snows of Valley Forge and you have a George Washington.

I continued: "Roberts might have gone on to say: Take him out of the leadership of the SAS, call him to fight for Christian principles and ethics, and you have a Jim Wallace. In Jim Wallace, we have George Washington's courage, John Flynn's commitment to service, William Wilberforce's strategic thinking, and Martin Luther King's gift for inspiring others. Others tonight will describe Jim's accomplishments. I would just like to say that Jim is the finest, most decent, man I know."

"People often say that as you get older, you get more emotional. 'The kind oblation of a falling tear,' as the poet, John Dryden, said. And I feel very emotional now, thinking of what Jim Wallace has meant to me—to my wife, Rae—and to every single Australian who longs to see Christian principles and ethics accepted and influencing the way we are governed, do business and relate to each other as a community.

"I'm a Calvinist and I believe that we did not get here by accident. God had a plan for each of us from before the beginning of time, which he has executed through people like James John Arundel Wallace.

"He is one of my heroes."

## CHAPTER 15

# LEADERSHIP LESSONS

The job of a football coach is to make men do what they don't want to do, in order to achieve what they've always wanted to be.

TOM LANDRY

Inspiring others to follow your lead demands tough calls and tough love. It means encouraging people to make the sacrifices in order to achieve their goals. Jesus' call to his disciples in Matthew's Gospel serves as the ultimate example: "If anyone would come after me, let him deny himself and take up his cross and follow me" (Matthew 16:24).

Winston Churchill's promise to the British people after becoming prime minister in May 1940 was also a call for sacrifice. "I have nothing to offer but blood, toil, tears and sweat."[17]

The best way to generate the commitment of subordinates is not to rely on your power or authority, but to inspire them. As George Washington once said, "Impress upon the mind of every man, from the first to the lowest."[18]

17  Winston Churchill, *Hansard*, 13 May 1940

18  George Washington, letter to Colonel William Woodford, 10 Nov 1775

It begins with **courage,** "the ladder on which all other virtues mount," as Clair Booth Luce describes it. For C. S. Lewis, the English literary scholar, courage was not simply one of the virtues "but the form of every virtue at the testing point."[19]

During the Second World War, a Filipino college president was ordered by the Japanese to take down the American flag. When he refused to do it, the Japanese shot and wounded him. As he lay there, his secretary came running to him, asking "Why, why did you refuse to lower the flag?"

In response, the president made one of the most powerful statements of personal courage I have ever heard: "There comes a time in every person's life when they must certify and seal by their behaviour that which they say they believe."

The great US president with a military background, Theodore Roosevelt, once said something that captures that sentiment exactly:

> The credit belongs to the man who is actually
> in the arena, whose face is marred by dust and
> sweat and blood, who strives valiantly, who errs
> and comes short again and again, who knows the
> great enthusiasms, the great devotions, and spends
> himself in a worthy cause, who at best knows
> achievement and who at the worst if he fails at
> least fails while daring greatly, so that his place
> shall never be with those cold and timid souls who
> know neither victory nor defeat.

19   C.S. Lewis, in Cyril Connolly, *The Unquiet Grave.*

Tony Blair, the former British prime minister, understood well the need for courage, especially when you do not have all the information:

> Courage in leadership is not simply about having the nerve to tackle difficult decisions, or even in doing the right thing, since oftentimes God alone knows what the right thing is. It is to be in our natural state—which is one of nagging doubt, imperfect knowledge, and uncertain prediction— and to be prepared, nonetheless, to put on the mantle of responsibility and to stand in full view of the world—to step out when others step back, and to assume the loneliness of the final decision maker.

At the 1936 Berlin Olympic Games, Jesse Owens—the black athlete who was born in Alabama near where we lived in Atlanta—seemed sure to win the long jump. Just the year before, he had set the world record that would stand for 25 years.

As he walked to the long-jump pit, however, Owens saw a tall, blue-eyed, blond German taking practice jumps well within range of his record. Owens was nervous. He was aware of the tension created with his presence. He knew the Nazis' desire was to prove Aryan "superiority," especially over the blacks. The pressure was overwhelming, and on his first jump Owens inadvertently leaped from several centimetres beyond the take-off board. Rattled, he over-shot on the second attempt, too. He was only one foul away from being eliminated.

At this point, the tall German approached Owens and introduced himself as Luz Long. The white model of Nazi manhood and the black son of a sharecropper chatted in view of the entire stadium. What could they be talking about?

Since the qualifying distance was well short of Owens' record, Long suggested making a mark several centimetres before the take-off board and jumping from there, just to play it safe. Amazing! At the beginning of World War II, this model of Germany's strength was providing technical assistance and words of encouragement to a foe both on and off the field.

Owens qualified easily. In the finals, he set an Olympic record and earned the second of four gold medals during the 1936 Olympics. The first person to congratulate Owens was Luz Long—in full view of Adolf Hitler.

Owens never saw Long again, for Long was killed in World War II. "You could melt down all the medals and cups I have," Owens later wrote," and they wouldn't be plating on the 24-carat friendship I felt for Luz Long." Long's courage in the face of his Fuhrer was extraordinary, and Jesse Owens never forgot it.

Second, all great leaders have a noble and incorruptible **character**.

George Washington, one of my heroes, said, "I hope I shall always possess firmness and virtue enough to maintain what I consider the most enviable of all titles, the character of an honest man."[20]

20  George Washingon, letter to Alexander Hamilton, 28 August 1788

Leaders must act with honesty, integrity, decency, and responsibility at all times—irrespective of who may be watching.

Third, successful leaders must also have **constancy** or perseverance.

One of the world's most inspirational leaders, Winston Churchill, once said: "Sometimes doing your best is not enough; you must do what is required." Leaders must be prepared to persevere. We desperately need men and women who will do what it takes when the chips are down. As a leader, I have learned that, when times are tough, there are few who will do what is necessary. We must constantly remind ourselves that the hardships of life are not sent by an unkind destiny to crush us, but to challenge us. We must persist.

Martin Luther King was the African-American pastor of Ebenezer Baptist church in Atlanta, where we lived for fifteen years. Think for a moment about how a simple black preacher from a small southern church could attract 250,000 people to come to the National Monument in Washington on a summer's day in 1963. No invitations were sent. There was no Internet site. Yet this enormous crowd arrived at precisely the right time on the right day.

Did these people come because Martin Luther King used power and authority to command that they be there? No. They came because they believed what Martin Luther King believed. They came because they wanted to follow Martin Luther King—not because of his power or authority, but because they believed what he believed. They wanted to follow him for their own sake, for King's passion had become their passion.

In one of the greatest orations of all time, King didn't outline a plan, but a dream. That is what leaders need to convey to their followers: their dreams; their aspirations; their hopes for them. I have learned that effective leaders really believe in their cause, and are able to convey those beliefs to others. We must not command so much as we convict.

Once again, we turn to the example of Jesus as one who practiced this to perfection. He didn't rely on his unlimited power or his authority. He simply convicted others of his beliefs, and many became his followers—not because they were commanded to, but because they wanted to.

Great leaders are also great communicators. They know how to connect with their followers and instil into them a belief in their cause. And they do this by communicating with their followers' spirit.

A former commander of our SAS regiment, there are few in my life experience who know more about leading men than Jim Wallace. It was he who taught me the three keys to convicting a person's spirit.

First, we must communicate through the eyes. We must sit down with our people, and share with them our vision for them, telling them what we expect from them. We cannot do this by email; we cannot do this by letter; we cannot do this over the telephone. Some refer to it as MBWA, or management by wandering around. We need to sit on their desk, look them in the eyes and share with them our vision for them and our organisation.

Second, we, ourselves, must be committed. Passion is critical, and it, or the absence of it, will be spotted at once by any follower. We must commit to our cause with every fibre of our being. As someone once said, great leaders leave their footprints in their areas of passion.

Third, we must love our followers, and be prepared to sacrifice ourselves for them.

During the Second World War, a company of Australian soldiers entered a swamp at Buna, to attack the Japanese there. A machine gun burst into fire, halting the advance. Corporal Connell was ordered to flank the machine gun emplacement and take it out.

Now, Corporal Connell is not mentioned in our war dispatches, and his name does not appear in the annals of bravery and this story would be unrecorded if it weren't for the battalion chaplain. But Connell was a man who understood the principles of leadership. He knew that leadership is of the spirit; that leaders need to be passionate; and that they must love their followers.

Connell took his captain's orders and headed off with his six men to get around the gun. The jungle was thick and the Japanese positions well concealed and the knee-deep swamp gave a false impression of distance covered. Thinking he was on the gun's flank, Connell stood up to signal for his men to attack, but was met by a fusillade from the machine gun which was actually in front of him. He was badly wounded.

The corporal's men all rushed to recover him, but he waved them back. "Down", he ordered. But his men were insistent and kept moving forward to save him.

Connell, realising that his troops were putting themselves in danger in an attempt to save him, stood up and bravely walked straight towards the machine gun.

His men never forgot that, as their leader, he had told them he loved them.

As we all know, in periods when there is no leadership, society stands still. Progress only occurs when leaders seize the opportunity to change things for the better.

Who among us is going to lead our beloved country out of the hands of the deconstructionists? Who is going to ensure that our children and our grandchildren will see Christian principles and ethics influencing the way we are governed, do business, and relate to each other as a community?

You may not understand how gifted you are. I am convinced that there are people now reading this who have the belief, the courage, the character, and the perseverance to become great leaders. And I trust that some will feel called to take up their cross and lead us through the narrow gate and down the path of justice and righteousness. Now I know that none of us is likely to become a Moses, or a Washington or a Churchill, but whether as a leader or a follower, we must all play our part.

As Helen Keller wrote:

> I long to accomplish a great and noble task, but
> it is my chief duty to accomplish humble tasks as
> though they were great and noble. The world is
> moved along, not only by the mighty shoves of the
> heroes, but also by the aggregate of the tiny pushes
> of each honest worker.[21]

This is the model Christ gave us. He recruited ordinary people, just like you and me. Then, after instilling in them a

---

21 Helen Keller (1880-1968)

belief in the Kingdom, he set them free to change the world. The world is crying out for great leaders; for statesmen instead of politicians; for men and women who have the faith, the belief, and the courage to change things for the better. And whether we lead or follow, we must all give a tiny push.

Christ apart, no leader who has walked this earth has ever come close to perfection. What distinguishes them is not their human failings, but the courage to strive to do what they know is right whatever the personal cost.

Easy Eddie was the nickname of a Chicago lawyer in the days of Prohibition whose professional reputation was built on his ability to keep the gangster Al Capone out of jail. To show his appreciation, Capone paid "Easy Eddie" very well. His estate was so large that it filled an entire Chicago city block.

Eddie turned a blind eye to the mob violence around him, but he did have one soft spot: a son who he loved dearly. He wanted his son to be a better man than he was and gave him a good education and every material benefit. The two things he couldn't give his son, however, were a good name and a good example.

One day, Easy Eddie reached a difficult decision. He wanted to rectify the wrongs he had done. He decided he would go to the authorities and tell the truth about Al "Scarface" Capone, clean up his tarnished name and offer his son some semblance of integrity. To do this, he would have to testify against the mob and he knew that the cost would be great.

Within the year, Easy Eddie's life ended in a blaze of gunfire on a lonely Chicago Street. But he had given his son the greatest gift he had to offer, at the greatest price he could ever pay. Police found in his pockets a rosary, a crucifix, a religious medallion and a poem clipped from a magazine.

The poem read:

The clock of life is wound but once,
    and no man has the power to tell just when the hands
    will stop,
    at a late or an early hour.
Now is the only time you own.

Live, love, toil with a will.
Place no faith in time,
    for the clock may soon be still."

World War II produced many heroes, such as Lieutenant Commander Butch O'Hare. He was a fighter pilot assigned to the aircraft carrier Lexington in the South Pacific.

One day O'Hare's entire squadron was sent on a mission. After he was airborne, he looked at his fuel gauge and realised that someone had forgotten to top up his fuel tank. He would not have enough fuel to complete his mission and get back to his ship. His flight leader told him to return to the carrier. Reluctantly, O'Hare dropped out of formation and headed back to the fleet.

As he was returning to the mother ship, O'Hare saw something that turned his blood cold; a squadron of Japanese aircraft was speeding its way toward the American fleet. The American fighters were gone on a sortie and the fleet was all but defenceless. He couldn't reach his squadron and bring them back in time to save the fleet. Nor could he warn the fleet of the approaching danger. There was only one thing to do. He must somehow divert them from the fleet.

Laying aside all thoughts of personal safety, Butch O'Hare dove into the formation of Japanese planes. Wing-mounted 50 calibre's blazed as he charged in, attacking one surprised enemy plane and then another. Butch wove in and out of the now broken formation and fired at as many planes as possible until all his ammunition was spent. Undaunted, he continued the assault. He dove at the planes, trying to clip a wing or tail in hopes of damaging as many enemy planes as possible. Finally, the exasperated Japanese squadron took off in another direction.

Relieved, O'Hare and his tattered fighter limped back to the carrier. Upon arrival, he reported in and related the event surrounding his return. The film from the gun-camera mounted on his plane told the tale. It showed the extent of Butch's daring attempt to protect his fleet. He had, in fact, destroyed five enemy aircraft.

This took place on 20 February 1942, and for that action Butch became the US Navy's first Ace of World War II, and the first naval aviator to win the Medal of Honour.

A year later Butch was killed in aerial combat at the age of 29. His hometown would not allow the memory of this WWII hero to fade, and today, the all-too-familiar O'Hare Airport in Chicago is named in tribute to the courage of this great man.

Twice a week for more than a year while commuting from Toronto, Canada to Tulsa, Oklahoma, I passed by Butch's memorial at O'Hare International Airport in Chicago, with his statue and Medal of Honour. It's located between Terminals 1 and 2.

So, what is the connection between Easy Eddie and Butch O'Hare? Butch O'Hare was Easy Eddie's son.

This inspiring account was sent to me by Butch O'Hare's daughter, through an old friend of mine then living in London. I shall never forget it.

During our time in the United States, Rae and I witnessed the leadership of President George H W Bush as he made the courageous decision to send forces to the Middle East to push Saddam Hussein's Iraqi invaders out of Kuwait.

President Bush Snr was a top-down, no-nonsense, decisive leader who set his eye on the far horizon and didn't "go wobbly" getting there. David Gergen described him as a big-picture fellow who focused on only two or three goals at a time and pursued them fiercely. To lead, in President Bush's book, was to decide.

This brand of leadership runs against the grain of current leadership studies. Most academics in the field believe that the person at the top should engage in consensual, collaborative leadership. But I don't agree with this and think to a large extent it is driven by the "soft thinking" I often found in America.

Over the years, a number of people have accused me of having an autocratic style. But in my defence, I want to quote you what Sir John Monash, one of Australia's proudest sons, once said about the characteristics of a good leader.

A successful leader must have determination and steadfastness of purpose of a very high order. He must have an exalted confidence in himself and in the correctness of his judgement, amounting to an intellectual arrogance.

Leading organisations through periods of great change calls for different leadership qualities from those needed during periods of stability. In challenging times, decisiveness and the courage to think and act quickly are essential attributes in making unpleasant decisions without wasting precious time.

Successful turnaround or change leaders are able to analyse at speed—often based on incomplete data—and have the strength and determination to drive through such drastic changes as are necessary . . . and even in the face of strong resistance. Such times call for a leader with real toughness, who will often become unpopular in the process.

What President H W Bush showed me is that, as Paul Keating once said: "Leadership is not about being nice. It's about being strong."

For many years I was chairman of Habitat for Humanity Australia. This volunteer-based Christian not-for-profit was a perfect example of a collaborative organisation. Unfortunately, however, without strong leadership it was going nowhere. When I became chairman, I changed the leadership to a more autocratic style. The net result was that instead of building three or four houses a year, we increased that to over 1000 per year.

The changes we made required a completely different level of corporate governance; of systems and controls and accountability. And implementing these changes, with thousands of volunteers who were committed to the original way of doing things, proved to be an extremely challenging task, and caused much anguish and many sleepless nights.

Participatory decision making may be used in certain circumstances, but it is critical to know where the buck stops in your organisation. As a leader, it is important to be aware of the extent of your authority and be ready always to exercise it. Playwright George Bernard Shaw captured this idea when he once said: "Reasonable men adapt themselves to their environment; unreasonable men try to adapt their environment to themselves. Thus, all progress is the result of the efforts of unreasonable men."

During our time in America, we got to know the Rev Dr Jerry Kirk, who had been a Presbyterian minister for 34 years before forming a Christian ministry in the USA to fight pornography and sexual abuse. At Jerry's invitation, I later joined the board of his organisation, which was headquartered in Cincinnati, Ohio. We became good friends, and Jerry always stayed with us when he was in Atlanta. On one occasion, we had a wonderful few days in his holiday home high in the Colorado mountains. Later, Jerry and his wife Patti came to Sydney and stayed with us as our guests for the 2000 Olympic Games.

One of the things Jerry practiced was never to criticise anyone behind his back. That way you can face anyone without shame or embarrassment. I have tried, somewhat, to follow Jerry's example, but I often fall into the trap of lashing out about someone who has irritated or frustrated me. But not criticising your people behind their back must surely be one of the keys to building unity in any organisation. As a leader, it is vital to be able to look across the table at your colleagues and have nothing to conceal.

US President Lincoln, one of my all-time heroes, was a master at this. He was also a master at the way in which he always affirmed his subordinates before taking them to task. In January 1863, the President dismissed General Ambrose Burnside and appointed General Joseph Hooker in his place. Lincoln then summoned Hooker to the White House where the two men discussed the sweeping strategies for pursuing the war effort. During the course of the meeting, Lincoln told Hooker what he expected. To help the general ponder the issues more deeply, Lincoln handed him a letter on Executive Mansion stationery dated January 26, 1863:

> I believe you to be a brave and skilful soldier, which, of course, I like. I also believe you do not mix politics with your profession, in which you are right. You have confidence in yourself, which is valuable, if not an indispensable quality. You are ambitious, which within reasonable bounds, does good rather than harm.
>
> But I think that during Gen Burnside's command of the Army, you have taken counsel of your ambition, and thwarted him as much as you could, in which you did a great wrong to the country, and to a most meritorious and honourable brother officer.
>
> The Government will support you to the utmost of its ability ... And now, beware of rashness. Beware of rashness, but with energy, and sleepless vigilance, go forward, and give us victories.
>
> Yours very truly<br>A. Lincoln

Notice the way in which President Lincoln first affirms General Hooker, then takes him to task for Hooker's dreadful undermining of his predecessor, General Burnside. Finally, Lincoln confirms his total support for Hooker and then challenges him to go on to victory. Hooker was deeply impressed. Several months later he remarked that this communiqué was "just such a letter as a father might write to his son."

In a similar way, I have had the experience of having to terminate the services of very senior people. It is never pleasant, but I always try to remember the advice of Jim Slater, the former chairman of the conglomerate, Slater Walker, who I first met as president of Barrick Gold. When faced with a termination, said Slater, one needs to be "ruthless in the decision and considerate in the execution." Warren Buffet offers similar advice: "Be fair, be swift, be decisive—and be prepared to fire people."

Slater's advice proved sound and I have often thought of it when I have had the unpleasant task of letting go a senior employee. One must always be prepared to make the ruthless decision—unpleasant as it may be—and not delay it. Indeed, in my experience, when you sit down with the employee, they often know in their heart long before you have the conversation that they are not fitting in or not performing. On one occasion, the employee was relieved that he no longer needed to be concerned about his inadequacies and that he could now get on with the rest of his life.

As a leader, it is important to understand not only when to use power but when to give it up. Many leaders find it difficult. The very thing that inspires them to assume control can create a blind spot, making it hard for them to see when they are no longer needed. It has happened to me in my own career and there are many examples of politicians who failed to recognise that their time was over. Sir Robert Menzies, who left the office of Prime Minister of his own volition on Australia Day 1966, is one of the few examples of a political leader wise enough to choose the time of his departure. Sir Robert had the courage and foresight to put his people first after more than 16 years in office.

"One becomes tired, one becomes not quite 100 per cent in efficiency," he told a press conference on the day he announced his departure. "And I have an old-fashioned belief that the Prime Minister of this country ought to be 100 per cent efficient at all times." This noble act is just one more reason why Sir Robert deserves the title of Australia's greatest prime minister.

## CHAPTER 16

# PERSONAL ENCOUNTERS WITH NINE GREAT LEADERS

Lives of great men all remind us
We can make our lives sublime,
And, departing, leave behind us
Footprints on the sands of time.

HENRY WADSWORTH LONGFELLOW[22]

## Dr Billy Graham

Billy Graham held his second last major campaign, before his retirement, in Atlanta in October 1994. As leaders in our church, Rae and I were invited to participate in the campaign and to work with the people who came forward in answer to Billy Graham's altar call. Billy Graham himself attended one of the training sessions over lunch in Atlanta on 19 August 1992 where he gave an inspiring talk on the four keys to leadership. The first was integrity, being the same on the inside as

22   Henry Wadsworth Longfellow, 'A Psalm of Life', 1838.

the outside. He went on to discuss personal security, the need to diversify our emotional portfolio. His third key was priority, separating the important from the unimportant according to life's plan. Finally, he spoke of vision, the determination to do God's will in our world.

We attended the Billy Graham crusade most nights during the crusade. I'll never forget the pleasure of seeing one of our favourite artists, Johnny Cash and his wife June, on the platform with Dr Graham singing spiritual songs. The highlight, however, was to listen to Dr Graham's powerful addresses and to witness its ability to change lives. A confidant of Dr Billy Graham, Dr John Woodbridge, gave some insights into Dr Graham at a Christian convention in Sydney of over 2,000 men at which I also spoke. Dr Woodbridge said:

> When St. Paul indicated in Romans 1:16, that he was not ashamed of the Gospel of Christ for it is the power [Greek word used for dynamite] of God unto salvation, he provided a model that Billy Graham has followed. Whatever the circumstances, Graham is ready to preach the Gospel of Jesus Christ in a courageous and winsome manner. He believes that the Gospel of Jesus Christ genuinely changes people and brings to them the Lord's salvation.

Dr Woodbridge talked of how Billy Graham emphasised "believing prayer" rather than pro forma prayer. Graham was known to have stressed "believing prayer" to members of prayer groups prior to the 1959 Australian crusade, which was an enormous success. Archbishop Peter Jensen was one of thousands saved during that incredible summer.

On 12 May 1989, Rev Leighton Ford, who was Dr Billy Graham's brother-in-law, and who worked with Graham for many years, conducted a seminar in our church for pastors in the district. I was called and asked if I could come and give my testimony. It was a tremendous honour. Afterwards, I was sent a lovely note by my assistant minister Rev Maurice Lee:

> Just a note to say how very impressed I was with your contribution to Leighton Ford's seminar. You articulated your experience with clarity and sincerity. I'm sure the folk there were blessed by it.
>
> You really have a gift as a communicator of ideas and experience.

I told Leighton Ford that a dream of mine was to have a quiet time with Billy Graham. His response was that Graham is such a humble man he would sit me on a log and focus everything on me.

When Dr Graham retired in January 2000, leaders in Charlotte NC, where one of our sons lives with his family, invited him to a luncheon in his honour. Dr. Graham, then in the early stages of Parkinson's Disease, stepped to the rostrum, looked at the crowd and said: "I am reminded today of Albert Einstein, the great physicist who this month has been honoured by *Time* magazine as the Man of the Century. Einstein was once traveling from Princeton on a train when the conductor came down the aisle, punching the tickets of every passenger. When he came to Einstein, Einstein reached in his vest pocket. He couldn't find his ticket, so he reached in his trouser pockets. It wasn't there, so he looked in his briefcase but still couldn't find it.

"The conductor said, 'Dr. Einstein, I know who you are. I'm sure you bought a ticket.' Einstein nodded appreciatively. As the conductor was about to move to the next car, he turned and saw the great physicist down on his hands and knees looking under his seat.

"The conductor rushed back and said, 'Dr. Einstein, don't worry, I know who you are.' Einstein looked up and said, 'Young man, I too, know who I am. What I don't know is where I am going.'"

Billy Graham told the audience he had bought a new suit for the luncheon. "This is the suit in which I'll be buried. But when you hear I'm dead, I don't want you to immediately remember the suit I'm wearing. I want you to remember this. 'I not only know who I am. I also know where I'm going.'"

## President George W. Bush

I have had the good fortune to spend time with President George W. Bush and came to admire him greatly. One of my most prized possessions is a cheque he signed. It was a cheque I originally sent to him as a donation but it had been returned to me by his fundraising team because they realised I was not an American citizen. US electoral laws prevent candidates from receiving funds from foreigners. When I next met President Bush at a function, I asked if he would sign it on the back, which he did. Five days prior to his inauguration on 20 January 2001, the President Elect wrote me a personal letter of thanks:

Dick Cheney and I want to thank you for all you have done for us. Your leadership, energy, and generous commitment of time were crucial to our campaign's success.

I am grateful for your hard work and honoured you were on my team. I look forward to leading our great country.

Sincerely,
George W. Bush

We had received an invitation to President Bush's inauguration but were unable to attend. We did, however, obtain a special Washington registration tag for our car, which I still have in my office: AAM 000.

One of President Bush's first initiatives upon taking office was to support Christian charities that were serving the community including food banks, drug rehabilitation and a myriad of other services. I had founded and was deputy chairman of We Care America, whose mission was to strengthen faith-based and community organisations that serve people in need by supporting and leveraging public, corporate and private resources. We had established a large network of Christian leaders throughout the country and were asked to invite a number of these leaders to a meeting in the White House to learn of the President's initiative. We managed to round up over 120 key Christian leaders throughout the country.

Following our regular board meeting in Washington, we hosted a reception for the leaders. The following day we all met in the White House for a briefing on President Bush's plans.

Not long after We Care America got started on this, Rae and I left America and returned to Australia. I returned for one more board meeting and then resigned as a director. It was only a few years later that We Care America lost its way and folded its tent.

## Dr Sam Chand

I first met Sam Chand when I asked him to become a director of Citizens for Community Values, of which I was chairman. Sam was the President of Beulah Heights Bible College in Atlanta, said to be the largest Bible college in America. Approximately half of the Atlanta population belonged to the Southern Baptist denomination, and because it has a system of congregational governance, new Baptist churches were springing up, led by committed but often uneducated pastors. These people needed theological training and Beulah Heights was there to provide that schooling.

Sam decided to withdraw from full-time work at Beulah Heights and to begin a ministry throughout the country working with John Maxwell. Rae and I attended the ceremony when Sam Chand bestowed a doctoral degree on John Maxwell at Bishop Eddie Long's church, New Life Baptist Church.

After we left Atlanta in 2001 Sam decided to break out on his own, offering counselling and advice to pastors throughout the country on a wide range of issues, including leadership and church growth. He wrote several books. In a review of one of his recent books, I said:

> As iron sharpens iron, Sam sharpens me. A friend
> for 25 years, I admire the extraordinary wisdom in

one who is honourable, perceptive and grounded. In all the time I have been leading I had never thought about the fact that the challenges of leadership inevitably cause us pain.

This book is another example of the great mind with which God has blessed Sam Chand.

Later he began a speaking career—particularly with Pentecostal churches. He is an electrifying presenter, and appears from time to time in Australia. One time, Sam and Brenda stopped in Sydney on their way to Adelaide for a speaking engagement and called from their overnight hotel. "Where is a nice restaurant?", they asked. We suggested our favourite, the Spice Temple. "Good," they said, "Now we know where to take you for your Golden Wedding anniversary dinner."

The last time I was in the USA I flew from Charlotte NC to visit Sam for lunch in Atlanta. Later, Sam sent me a very nice note:

> In your journey from the bush to the boardroom, you met a lot of people and affected their lives for good and forever—Sam Chand being one of them. I am indeed the major beneficiary of this friendship. You are indeed blessed of the Lord and you do not hoard—you share.
>
> Your exuberant love and gracious attitude coupled with hard-knock wisdom bathed in godly reflection is a life changer for those who are graced by your presence.

Sam Chand knows how to give encouragement. He is, without doubt, a master of this underappreciated art. Sam corrects, rebukes and encourages daily. As Paul told his young minister, Timothy, "Preach the Word; be prepared in season and out of season; correct, rebuke and encourage—with great patience and careful instruction" (2 Timothy 4:2).

## The Hon John Winston Howard AC OM

Successful politicians require equanimity, a quality John Howard has in spades. In my lifetime, only Sir Robert Menzies would be in the same league. A quarter of a century since he was first elected as Prime Minister, most people would agree that he is the finest leader of the modern era.

After we returned to Australia, we had the great honour of meeting John Howard on many occasions. It began in 2004 when, as chairman of Habitat for Humanity Australia, I was asked to give a presentation to Mr. Howard on housing for the poor. I sought to encourage the Government to approach the problem by offering a hand-up, rather than a hand-out. The meeting was chaired by Malcolm Turnbull, who was then chairman of the Menzies Research Centre which I was later to join as a director.

Not long after, I was asked to thank the Prime Minister for attending a function in Sydney on 3 May 2005. "Mr. Prime Minister", I said, "in my opinion, your incredible leadership has helped us to identify who we were, and what it is we aspire to be. You have helped make our country great. Thank you for that; it means a lot to a couple of wandering Aussies."

I was formally elected to The Menzies Research Centre board on 19 October 2005, and my appointment was renewed every year for 12 years—making me the longest serving director. As such, commonly in company with the then chairman Tom Harley and the then executive director Julian Leeser, I met with Mr. Howard in the Prime Minister's parliamentary office about every quarter. I remember being mightily impressed by Mr. Howard's grasp of the political realities.

Mr. Howard, a Christian man, and huge admirer of Jim Wallace, the founder of the Australian Christian Lobby (ACL), was keen to support the organisation. After he retired from politics, Mr. Howard was always ready to speak at ACL's annual Draw the Line fund-raising events, which attracted large crowds when he attended. He spoke in Sydney, Melbourne, Brisbane and Perth, each time to great effect. And to illustrate his heart to help, he offered to speak in other cities as well.

More than anyone I have known, Mr. Howard has an extraordinary memory for names. I have personally seen it time and again and have been told by several politicians that they also have been amazed at his ability to remember people. By way of example, following a board meeting of The Menzies Research Centre in 2012 in Melbourne, I made a dash by taxi to attend the annual lecture at Kooyong in honour of Sir Robert Menzies. Mr. Howard was delivering the oration that night, and I got there just in time. The event was held in a school gymnasium and it was packed. I was standing shoulder-to-shoulder about three rows back from the front and as Mr. Howard was about to mount the platform, he spotted me in the crowd. He came off the steps and forced his way through the crowd to me, put his arm around my shoulder and escorted me to the window, turning his back to the people who were flocking around trying to get his attention.

He looked me in the eye and said, "How is Jim?" I was incredibly touched. Mr. Howard was asking about Jim Wallace, the Managing Director of ACL, and one of my closest friends. Jim had recently suffered vitriolic attacks by the malicious press concerning a comment he is purported to have made comparing the risks of smoking to homosexual sex. Mr. Howard was obviously concerned for Jim and no doubt could relate to the campaign of hate which Jim was enduring. But what touched me most was that I was out of my territory—at an event in Melbourne—and yet he recognised me and then immediately related me to Jim for whom he had great concern. I shall never forget that as long as I live.

The Menzies Research Centre hosted the launch of Mr. Howard's magnificent biography of Sir Robert Menzies, and we held a dinner for several hundred people at the Pier One Hotel on 14 October 2014. There was a fierce storm during the evening that resulted in extensive damage in some parts of Sydney. Amongst the ten guests at our table were Rick Dunham of Dunham + Company from Dallas. We also had Peter Prentice and his wife Margaret. Peter brought along his famous painting of Sir Robert Menzies by the Archibald Prize winner William Dobell and several people had pictures taken in front of the painting.

There were hundreds of people milling around when Mr. Howard arrived. As he entered, he saw Rae some distance away in the middle of the room speaking with some of her friends. I was off somewhere else. Mr. Howard made his way through the crowd and gave Rae a kiss, calling her by name.

Yet another example of his extraordinary ability to remember people and to take an interest in them as individuals.

Mr Howard's legacy as Prime Minister is extensive. He pioneered broad-based taxation, paid off debt leaving our country with money in the bank and he dismantled the central wage-fixing system. He saw us through the East Timor crisis, the 9/11 attack, the Boxing Day Tsunami, and the 2002 Bali bombing. When Rae and I returned to Australia after 30 years living abroad towards the end of Mr Howard's second term, we were struck by how the country had matured under his leadership and developed a strong sense of national pride.

One of the things I admired most was his commitment to charitable organisations, some of which I was involved with including Opportunity International, Anglicare, and Australian Christian Lobby. His commitment stemmed from his strong Christian faith. On issues like same sex marriage, Mr Howard had the courage to stand up for Christian principles. Under his leadership, marriage was defined by law as: "The union of a man and a woman to the exclusion of all others, voluntarily entered into for life."

When former Prime Minister Tony Abbott's book on his defining speeches was launched early in 2020, Rae and I were invited to a private dinner at the Australian Club where we sat alongside Mr. Howard and Tony Abbott. I was struck again by the class of Mr. Howard, sincerely self-deprecating as he is, in spite of his greatness.

### The Hon John Anderson AO

John Anderson served as Deputy Prime Minister to Mr Howard for more than six years. It is hard to imagine a finer pair.

I came to know Mr Anderson as chairman of Bemax Resources Limited, the second-biggest mineral sands miner and processor in Australia. Mr Anderson was Minister for Regional Development, and I arranged to meet him in Parliament House, Canberra, to discuss our plans to build a new plant in Broken Hill to service its enormous mine near Pooncarie, on the Darling River, halfway between Broken Hill and Mildura.

Later, at my request, Mr Anderson agreed to host board meetings for both Opportunity International Australia (of which I was a director) and Habitat for Humanity Australia (of which I was chairman), held on the same day in Parliament House, Canberra. The meetings were followed by a cocktail party, which was attended by a number of prominent politicians from both sides of the aisle. Later, Anderson agreed to be the guest of honour at our Habitat for Humanity annual dinner in Sydney.

When John Anderson later retired from politics, our relationship had been extended. His in-laws lived at Mosman, and he sometimes attended our home church, St Thomas' at North Sydney. Later, Rae and I were invited to stay at John and Julie Anderson's property near Gunnedah.

John's grasp of world economics was and is daunting. A history major, he has strong views on a nation's responsibility to its future generations and often speaks on this topic at public meetings. I have attended various functions, including the Bible Society, the Brisbane Lord Mayor's breakfast and the Katoomba Men's Christian Convention at which he has addressed this topic.

When John Anderson left politics, he received unprecedented praise from both sides of the House, with perhaps the
strongest universal commendation being his integrity. That is
exactly my impression of him. It is a great honour to be able
to call this extraordinary man a friend.

John Anderson continues with his prolific public speaking
program. It is no wonder he is so keenly sought after; he
is such a gifted orator. This has been complemented by a
series of interviews he has recorded with some of the world's
pre-eminent thinkers, entitled "Conversations". Never
miss one of these which can be found online at https://
johnanderson.net.au/conversations/

John has shown me the power of decency and how it affords
one the respect to be heard. When you combine that with his
extraordinary intellect and his experience as our deputy prime
minister you have a person who can wield significant influence
and who uses that influence to encourage others to consider
the Christian perspective on a whole range of issues.

## Archbishop Peter Jensen

Peter Jensen is one of the humblest men I know. And
humility is a peculiarly Christian virtue. It does not figure
among the classic virtues of prudence, temperance, fortitude
and justice. It is not even found in the so-called theological
virtues of faith, hope and charity. Peter has been a fantastic
supporter of Australian Christian Lobby, while in office and
just as much since he retired as Archbishop. I have two particularly fond memories of him.

Peter was scheduled to be the guest speaker at ACL's
annual Draw the Line fundraising dinner in Sydney on 18

March 2013. A couple of days before the dinner, one of the Archbishop's colleagues, Bishop Peter Hayward, was a guest in our home with his wife Julie. I asked Bishop Hayward for an insight into this extraordinary man in preparation for my introduction. This is what I said:

> Ladies and Gentlemen, our guest this evening is someone very special. He holds the post of our Archbishop and Metropolitan.
>
> Have you any idea what a Metropolitan is? I didn't until I looked it up. It is the head of an ecclesiastic province. Begun at the Council of Nicaea in 325, provinces included such areas as Antioch, and Ephesus, and Alexandria and Rome.
>
> A few weeks before the infamous 9/11, our guest was consecrated. And in one of his first acts, he challenged churches in the Sydney diocese to aim to reach 10% of their communities by 2012. He called for an increase in church planting, launching scores of new congregations, and oversaw an unprecedented increase in candidates for the ministry.
>
> We had just returned to Sydney after living 20 years in America, where I led our church out of the Episcopal denomination because of its abandonment of its biblical roots. It was a thrill to begin worshipping in Sydney where we "preach Christ crucified". I attribute much of this to our guest of honour's relentless pursuit of truth.

The Archbishop has been a wonderful supporter of the work of Australian Christian Lobby
and of Jim Wallace. We are all extremely grateful
for that, Sir. It is tough out there—as you know—
and receiving encouragement from church leaders
like you is very meaningful indeed.

I don't know whether you saw our guest on
Q&A a little while ago. I thought he was brilliant
and strongly supported the issues we have been
actively pursuing—our opposition to same-sex
marriage, for example, which he once described as
not for the "moral good."

In 1959, the inestimable Billy Graham pro-
claimed, "The Bible says . . ." and as many as
143,000 in one single audience listened intently.
Sadly, today, many would respond by calling him
a bigot, or challenge him by saying that that is
simply his interpretation. But 54 years ago, in
response to Billy Graham's call, thousands upon
thousands came forward to dedicate their lives to
Christ. Many had tears in their eyes. I was one of
them, and so was our honoured guest.

Out of this simple call to repentance and commitment—and thanks to the mighty work of
God—there grew one of Australia's most famous
churchmen.

Sir, last year I had the honour of introducing
John Howard to this platform. He gave a rousing
talk for which we remain very grateful. And I am
sure much of that is due to your advice to him in

2001 when you told him publicly to "read your Bible!".

Two nights ago we had to dinner one of your bishops to celebrate the blessing of our new home. He told us that in spite of your daunting intellect and powerful position you are one of the most congenial people he knows. Humble: like someone else I know whose death and resurrection we again remember especially this coming week.

The Archbishop stepped up to the microphone. "That is the floweriest introduction I have every received, and it is full of lies!" he said. The crowd roared with laughter.

In 2008 Archbishop Peter Jensen led the effort to launch GAFCON, which can now claim 70% of the world's Anglicans as supporters of its mission to stand together to retain and restore the Bible to the heart of the Anglican Communion. Its mission is to guard the unchanging, transforming Gospel of Jesus Christ and to proclaim Him to the world. Jensen stepped down as General Secretary in 2018, but his work endures.

## David Bussau

I first met David in 2001 when we returned to Australia. I had been invited to join the board of Opportunity International Australia and Opportunity International USA. David was looked up to as the founder and guiding force of the organisation, as he well should have been. David is an outstanding human being who was Senior Australian of the Year in 2008.

It was his idea to provide micro loans to the poor to assist them in starting a business, and to provide an opportunity to witness the Gospel to these people. David began with one small loan to one poor person in Bali.

A humble, self-effacing man, David was an orphan boy from New Zealand, who had done well in the construction business in Australia, before dedicating his whole life to serving others. His first mission was aiding people who had been devastated by Cyclone Tracy, which hit Darwin on Christmas Eve 1974. David packed up his family and moved to Darwin to offer his skills as a builder.

From there, he began operations making micro loans in Bali which later expanded into dozens of countries.

Sometime after I resigned from the board of Opportunity International Australia, David Bussau, wrote me a very nice letter acknowledging the support I had given him and the organisation:

> As founder of Opportunity International Australia, it was my privilege to invite and welcome Anthony McLellan on to the board of directors of Opportunity International Australia on May 24th, 2002.
>
> For seven years, Tony served faithfully and diligently as a director. He brought a new, fresh and dynamic dimension to our governance style and practice. He raised our performance to an international level and injected an exciting and vibrant perspective to our global network (26 countries). His wide international experience and acclaimed

business success positioned him to be greatly respected and valued as a director. He excelled in drafting a revised constitution for our organization, which endeared him to his fellow directors. His eminent and dynamic leadership style was infectious and helped to restructure our global network.

I am greatly indebted to Tony for his persistent insistence that we stay faithful to our Christian heritage and biblical moorings as our anchor and compass.

Thank you, Tony (and Rae).

David Bussau
Opportunity International Australia Founder

## Cardinal George Pell

I first met the then Archbishop of Sydney, George Pell, at the National Prayer Breakfast in Parliament House, Canberra. He was seated at a table immediately behind me, and the person with me asked if I had met the Archbishop. "No", I said, "I have not." With that my friend caught the Archbishop's attention and said that he wanted to introduce me.

The Archbishop stood up and towered over me. He seemed to be about seven feet tall. "Mr. McLellan", he said warmly, "I have always wanted to meet you." I was blown away by the Archbishop's graciousness.

Born into a humble family in the Victorian goldfields, he became one of the most prominent ecclesiastical dignitaries in Australia. He is extraordinarily well educated. He was named Archbishop of Melbourne in 1996 and appointed eighth Archbishop of Sydney in 2001. In 2003, John Paul II announced that he would nominate Archbishop Pell to the College of Cardinals.

Cardinal Pell worked with leaders of other churches in his efforts to strengthen the faith of Christians and their contribution to Australian life. In doing so, he has been a wonderful supporter of Australian Christian Lobby. In defending the importance of religious belief in building a just society, Cardinal Pell has adopted a conservative position on social issues. Upon becoming Archbishop of Sydney, he said, "Any genuine religion has two important moral tasks; firstly, to present norms and ideals, goals for our striving; and secondly, to offer aids for our weakness, forgiveness and healing for every wrong doer and sinner who repents and seeks forgiveness."

As an example of his wisdom and willingness to speak out, Cardinal Pell once had this to say about the hysteria surrounding climate change:

> I am certainly skeptical about extravagant claims of impending man-made climatic catastrophes. Uncertainties on climate change abound ... my task as a Christian leader is to engage with reality, to contribute to debate on important issues, to open people's minds, and to point out when the emperor is wearing few or no clothes.

Perhaps the highlight of Pell's career was Sydney's hosting of the 2008 World Youth Day, one of the largest regular international gatherings of young people in the world, often attracting crowds in the millions.

Many people were rightly disturbed by evidence to the Royal Commission into institutional child sexual abuse. The Catholic Church was far from the only institution to suffer adverse findings, but it was the particular focus of much of the media coverage and some were looking for scapegoats. Cardinal Pell was targeted by much of the media, particularly by the ABC. He was tried and falsely convicted of child sex abuse and sent to prison. I wrote a personal note to him when he was found guilty and prayed that his conviction would be overturned. His appeal to the Victorian Supreme Court was lost two to one, before he appealed to the Hight Court of Australia. His detractors, including the ABC, continued to vilify him, but a band of believers supported him through his ordeal.

On 7 April 2020, in a seven-to-none judgement by the High Court, the conviction was quashed and Cardinal Pell was set free. By chance, I was attending an Australian Christian Lobby board meeting on Zoom when the news broke. We immediately paused the meeting to give thanks to God for ending the long, drawn-out saga and for setting free this courageous man.

It is an embarrassment that some of the great achievements of the Christian legal tradition, the presumption of innocence, the right to a fair trial and the establishment of guilt beyond reasonable doubt, were not upheld in the lower courts. The vilification continued in some media, apparently unaware of Jesus' warning that "If any one of you is without sin, let him be the first to throw a stone" (John 6:7).

The saga continues. As I write, the unredacted report of the Royal Commission into Institutional Responses to Child

Sexual Abuse has just been published. Cardinal Pell is criticised for having offered "implausible" evidence on the shifting of the notorious paedophile priest Gerald Ridsdale in the early 1980s. Pell hit back, claiming the adverse commentary about him in relation to Ridsdale was not supported by the evidence.

"Justice?" asks William Gaddis in the first sentences of *A Frolic of His Own*. "You get justice in the next world; in this world you have the law."[23]

## The Reverend John Stott CBE

John Stott along with Dr Billy Graham are arguably the two best-known and most respected Christian leaders of our generation. For many years, John Stott was the rector at All Souls Church of England, in Langham Place, Marylebone, at the north end of Regent Street, London. The regency-style building, designed by John Nash, is directly opposite the BBC's headquarters. On the other side of the road is the Langham Hotel, where Rae and I have stayed from time to time whilst in London.

On 19 July 2002, Rae and I were invited to a private dinner for John Stott to be held in the Banjo Paterson Restaurant at Gladesville, Sydney. This was a great honour and I was excited to see the famous evangelical again. My excitement was compounded when I was asked by the organiser, David Bussau, to make a speech and presentation to John Stott on behalf of the eight guests present.

I was unsure what I should talk about and considered speaking about Australian birds, remembering that Stott was a keen ornithologist. In the end, I decided to speak about

23   Attributed to Henry Ergas.

something of which I had a better knowledge: Three of my great teachers—my father; Banjo Paterson; and John Stott.

My father was born exactly 90 years before the dinner. I inherited his love of the bush and of bush poetry, and my fascination with it continues to grow after more than sixty years. My Dad particularly liked Banjo Paterson, who wrote about the country area where we lived. Legend has it that Banjo—the very name of the restaurant where we were dining that evening—met his friend, Clancy, when he was shearing at Jumble Plains, our family property on a tributary of the Lachlan River.

My second teacher, then, became Australia's most famous bush poet, Banjo Paterson. When Paterson was ten, his parents sent him to Sydney from Illalong to live with his grandmother where he finished his education at Sydney Grammar School. During holidays Paterson would go home, where he would go camping with his five sisters and one brother. He became a skilful rider, a wonderful shot, and a real bushman.

In 1889 Paterson's popularity as a poet had reached its peak, and in that year the *Bulletin* published the romantic bush ballad, "Clancy of the Overflow", which is my all-time favourite from Banjo's pen. In 1895, Banjo published the very first book of Australian poetry, *The Man from Snowy River and Other Verses*. This revealed his identity as "The Banjo." The book became a best seller and Banjo became a celebrity.

There was movement at the station, for the word had passed around
That the colt from old Regret had got away,
And had joined the wild bush horses—he was worth a thousand pound,
So all the cracks had gathered to the fray.

After returning from the Boer War in 1903, Paterson went to visit his fiancé in Winton and heard a local legend about a wanted man who drowned himself to avoid being captured. Paterson wrote a song about it, but sold the rights to Angus and Robertson because he didn't particularly like it.

> Oh there once was a swagman camped in the billabongs,
>> Under the shade of a Coolibah tree;
> And he sang as he looked at the old billy boiling,
>> "Who'll come a-waltzing Matilda with me."

When war broke out in 1914, Paterson put his knowledge of horses to good use becoming a lieutenant in the Second Australian Remount Unit, which broke and trained over 50,000 horses. In 1930, Patterson was made Commander of the British Empire and left his newspaper work to write books.

It would be absurd to even begin to recount the influence John Stott, my third great teacher, has had on Christian life in this country, but I shared two personal insights.

First, my pastor for ten years was Simon Manchester. He admires John Stott immensely and believes that he and Billy Graham are the two most influential Christian figures of our age. When I told Simon that we were having dinner that evening with John Stott, Simon's eyes lit up. He recounted with tender fondness his experiences working with John at the retreat John then had in Wales, pouring concrete and digging post-holes. I told Simon, again—as I had the very first day we visited St. Thomas' and heard him preach—that I thought he taught God's Word just like John Stott. Simon was embarrassed at being compared with the great teacher himself.

Second, at the invitation of my then pastor, Rev. Dr. Michael Youssef, John Stott came to Atlanta to teach a gathering of 100 of Atlanta's pastors. On 15 February 1993, I put on a holy face, and trying to look like a pastor, sneaked in and sat at the back of the chapel to listen—thinking that that may be my only chance to hear this famous teacher.

My notes from that day are extensive, but one thing that stood out was John Stott's statement that there are two obligations of exposition. I then shared my notes with him and he was impressed that I had nurtured them for 15 years.

Having been asked to thank John for joining us for dinner, I paraphrased something the famous actress, Tallulah Bankhead, said: "I read Banjo Paterson and the Bible, and I can shoot dice. That is what I call a liberal education."

"John", I said, "I am sure you wouldn't do something as wicked as shoot dice, but I hope you enjoy Banjo Paterson as much as I do. "

I then presented John with a magnificent leather-bound volume of Paterson's complete works that Rae had given to me a few days before. I figured that I could simply go into Dymocks and purchase a replacement. It transpired, however that it was the last copy in captivity. Well, for Fathers' Day 2020 Rae found an antique two-volume set of the complete works of Banjo Paterson which she purchased for me as a replacement. I was thrilled.

The following day, Stott was giving a lecture to a large group of ministers and again I managed to sneak in. Many of Stott's books were available at the conference. Amongst them was a new two-volume biography of Stott by Timothy Dudley-Smith, which I couldn't help but purchase. I asked Stott if he would be kind enough to autograph it for me, but he was reluctant. "This is not my work," he pleaded. He finally relented and signed the two volumes, which I now treasure as perhaps the only signed copies in captivity.

Later that week, Rae and I heard Stott deliver a magnificent oration in the Sydney Town Hall. To this day, we were so glad we attended. This, sadly, was his last talk in Australia for he went to meet his Maker on 27 July 2011.

Like Christians the world over, we mourned John Stott's passing, but were so grateful we had had a little time with this great man. Fortunately, to this day, I still receive each morning a brief theological lesson from the Langham Partnership, extracted from Stott's writings, for which I am very grateful.

## CHAPTER 17

# GOLDEN YEARS

He will sit as a refiner and purifier of silver; he will purify the Levites and refine them like gold and silver.

MALACHI 3:3

The technology we used until recently for testing the gold content of a lump of ore has barely changed in two and a half thousand years. When the Old Testament prophet Malachi foresaw the coming of the Lord around 550 BC, he described Him as "a refiner's fire" (Malachi 3:3), a phrase transformed into a beautiful Aria in George Frederic Handel's *Messiah*. The metaphor is picked up by Peter the Apostle in the New Testament. "You have been grieved by various trials," writes Peter, "so that the tested genuineness of your faith—more precious than gold that perishes though it is tested by fire—may be found to result in praise and glory and honour at the revelation of Jesus Christ" (1 Peter 1:6-7).

Until a few years ago, the process known as fire assaying was universally used to determine the quantity of gold, silver and other elements in a representative core sample from the mine typically weighing around 30 grams. Materials such as borax, soda, silica are added as fluxes and the core sample is placed in a crucible inside an assay furnace, which has been pre-heated to 2,000°F to fuse the contents. When the liquid sample is allowed to cool and solidify, impurities such as silica, lime, iron, copper, zinc form layers according to their density. The heaviest of them, lead, sinks to the bottom with the gold contained within it. The lead breaks off easily by hammering and is placed in a clay crucible called a Cupel which is again placed in a furnace. The lead is absorbed into the cupel, leaving only a tiny gold bead which is weighed.

If the prophet Jeremiah was to return to earth today and find himself in one of many gold mine testing labs, he would not be unfamiliar with the testing process which he describes in some detail in the Old Testament.

In late 2015, when I was 75, I was approached by an investment banker representing the CSIRO, to ask if I might have an interest in commercialising a new technology that replaced the ancient furnace method and revolutionised the testing of precious metals. It was yet another unexpected turn in my business life which, from the day I took over running the family property upon the death of my father, has been one long, steep learning curve with plenty of tips. Almost 60 years later in my mid-70s, I thought my biggest professional achievements were behind me. Clearly God had other plans, however, for what I was reluctant to call my retirement.

Thanks to my background in the mining industry, I recognised immediately the technology's potential and started doing my homework. I invited the inventor of the technology, Dr James Tickner, to stay in our home in Bowral where I took an immediate liking to him. He was extraordinarily intelligent but completely down to earth. When Dr Tickner wasn't advancing the frontiers of metallurgy, he spent his time entering his fruit cakes in competitions and arrived at our home with a delicious example of his work. He told us a story of walking with the judge at the Adelaide Royal Show along the table with all the entries listening to her comments on them. They stopped at one that the judge criticised because the entrant had not ironed the greaseproof paper around the edge of the tin, so that the cake was crinkled and was thereby rejected. Dr Tickner told us he has never forgotten the lesson, and I pass on the tip to any aspiring fruit cake baking champions who might chance upon this book.

Dr Tickner's technology, known as PhotonAssay™, was the result of 15-years of research and development by CSIRO. Instead of testing samples with fire, it uses high powered X-rays to bombard rock samples and activate atoms of gold and other metals. A highly sensitive detector picks up unique atomic signatures to determine the concentrations of these different elements. It enables mining companies to detect rapidly small traces of gold, allowing them to plan more efficiently, and optimise their mining and mineral processing operations.

I developed an approach where we would not operate the PhotonAssay™ units, which we would build having acquired the CSIRO technology. Rather, like the business model used by Xerox for its first photocopier, my plan was to lease the units for a base rent plus a throughput royalty. The financial model ensured that the operators could compete directly with fire assay providers, but have numerous advantages referred to below.

I managed to raise millions of dollars in capital in a matter of months before being invited to make a formal proposal to acquire the technology along with a number of potential competitors. After a tense few weeks, I received a congratulatory telephone call from Dr Nick Cutmore, the CSIRO's research director, to advise that my proposal had been accepted. Nick told me it was the biggest deal that CSIRO had done in ten years. Naturally I was excited, but then the hard work began.

I set up a company, Chrysos Corporation Limited, a name taken from the Greek Χρύσος meaning the spirit of gold. We began negotiations on the detailed terms of the agreement with the CIRO in June 2016. They were tortuous to say the least. I twice threatened to walk away from the transaction, while doing my best to keep our pool of investors informed and committed. A critical part of the process was ensuring that Chrysos obtained outright ownership of all the intellectual property and the related patents. These have since expanded into many countries world-wide.

We also made it a condition that we hired the inventor, Dr Tickner who was previously head of CSIRO's nuclear and data analytics team. Dr Tickner has won two CSIRO medals, the Australian Academy of Science Frederick White prize, and the Eureka Prize for Science in support of Defence or National Security. Dr Tickner is now Chrysos' Chief Technology Officer, where he continues to refine the technology.

After six months of difficult negotiations, we finalised all the documents and closed the transaction on 6 December 2016. The deal was announced by Greg Hunt, then the Minister for Industry, Innovation and Science.

As an Australian innovation being taken to
market by an Australian company, this is another
example of the Turnbull Government's strategic
commitment to catalyse industry innovation
for the benefit of the nation and create jobs,"
Mr Hunt said in his announcement. "In an
industry facing declining ore grades, rapid ana-
lytical technology has the potential to unlock
substantial productivity gains in gold mining
and production, and open up a significant new
market for real-time analysis services in on-site
applications.

Mr Hunt went on to say that the new technology would have
a huge impact on the fire assay business, putting an end to a
laborious and time-consuming manual process that came with
significant OH&S risks. The Chrysos PhotonAssay™ could
analyse samples in one to two minutes, compared to days and
weeks. It reduces preparation costs and time and allows for
larger samples of 400–600g and is two or three times more
accurate. Gold recovery is increased by 1–3%, worth $2 billion
a year to this industry alone.

We began in earnest immediately after we closed the
transaction, building the first unit in China, transporting it
to Perth, setting it up and testing it in the premises of our
first client, MinAnalytical, a subsidiary of Ausdril, Australia's
largest drilling company. The CEO of Innovation & Science
Australia, Dr Charles Day, honoured us by cutting the ribbon
on 7 May 2017, and starting the unit. This was a major milestone for Chrysos.

The mining industry is notoriously risk-averse and cautious when faced with change. We found, however, with this innovation that technical people in the industry "got it" straight away. Drilling companies recognised the benefit of being able to keep the rig running while they test a core brought up from below and then decide on the spot whether to keep drilling deeper, change direction or abandon the prospect altogether. Geologists want to know in real time if they are in a prospective zone, rather than having to come down from the mountain top and wait days for the results as they did before our technology.

Much of our progress can be attributed to our CEO, Dirk Treasure, whom I have grown to respect enormously. Little wonder he was awarded "Emerging Leader of the Year" by Australia's Mining Monthly. None of us would be here were it not for the genius and leadership of Dr James Tickner, the inventor of Chrysos' PhotonAssay™ and now our Chief Technology Officer. Without him there would be no technology to do what we do. As C.J. Dennis said in The Sentimental Bloke, "I dips me lid" to Rob Adamson, my founding partner in Chrysos. Rob was among the first to catch the vision of the potential of PhotonAssay™. He then backed the Company with everything he had at his disposal … financing, guarantees, top people, the provision of administrative support, introductions to a number of our founding shareholders. I shall forever remain grateful to this fine man. When I retired as Chairman, Rob succeeded me and has done a spectacular job in advancing the Company.

In 2020, we finished the financial year with an after-tax profit of over $3 million. Our balance sheet showed net equity of $24.5 million, including $13.5 million in cash. As a testament to our success, Morgan Stanley recently invested $15 million in the Company. The risk I had taken as a founding investor had paid off ten-fold.

Later that year, Chrysos won the prestigious KCA award for the best research commercialisation in Australia.

While some entrepreneurs live for the thrill of making money and draw pride from their ranking on the rich list, I had not established Chrysos to add to my personal fortune. Some might dream of owning a yacht on Sydney Harbour or their own private jet, living the kind of jet-setting life I had enjoyed in my younger days in Egypt, Europe and America. Salvation had been the turning point for Rae and me, however. We had learned the joy of enriching the lives of those around us rather than ourselves. By devoting our wealth to philanthropic causes, on the other hand, we could multiply our contribution to human happiness many times over. Not for nothing did Jesus tell his disciples "It is more blessed to give than to receive"(Acts 20:35).

In 2014, Jim Wallace, the founder and chairman of The Lachlan Macquarie Institute—who was given the vision for LMI by God—and, as chairman of Australian Christian Lobby, Jim and I set out to find new premises for the Institute. After inspecting a number of possibilities, we settled on a small guest house at Murrumbateman, not far out of Canberra. We were able to negotiate a purchase price of $1.2 million and arrange a deferred closing. Great progress so far, but from where would we get the money to complete the purchase?

Jim formed the view that we needed to secure commitments for donations of a minimum of $700,000 before we could exercise our option to proceed with the purchase. We got off to a good start with one person who I knew well committing to contribute $100,000. A small number of other donors also agreed to back our plans.

We were, however, quickly running out of time to meet our target when I organised a meeting with the managing director of Christian Super, thinking that I had developed a sophisticated plan that would ensure an attractive return to the fund. The meeting, however, was a flop and when Jim and I returned to the coffee shop down below, where Rae was waiting for us, we passed on the disappointing news. We were all a little downhearted.

The problem, Rae suggested, was that we had not personally committed, although we had always planned to support the effort. There and then Rae and I made a commitment to contribute $100,000 to the campaign, an amount that was many times greater than anything we had ever donated to any cause. The transformation was astounding. I believe that people who we subsequently approached could somehow "sense" that we were also personally committed. By the deadline we had secured commitments totalling $810,000! It was an incredible lesson.

Importantly, Rae and I believe that God honoured our commitment by providing the opportunity for me to establish Chrysos in partnership with the CSIRO. The financial success of that business would in time give us the joy of contributing far more towards advancing God's Kingdom. Like precious metal in the centuries before the development of PhotonAssay™, however, we must be prepared to be tested by fire.

In late 2018, I spent several weeks in hospital with an acute attack of septicaemia. The specialist told Rae that unless he was able to get the infection under control I would die. I was approaching my 80th birthday and both Rae and the specialist were keen for me to retire. I reluctantly came to the conclusion that they were right.

The following month, I took Jim Wallace on a fishing trip to Montana with a wonderful old friend from Houston, Jeff Rawson. Jeff and J'Anne had built a magnificent house on a knoll with literally 360-degree views of the stunning snow-capped mountains of Montana. It was truly magnificent and while I was not well enough to join in the fishing, I did enjoy the visit with two of my closest friends and our eldest son, Scott.

When I returned I was suffering acute pain. I began an exhausting series of visits to all sorts of specialists, who ordered endless tests, trying to discover what might be the underlying issue. Bone cancer was one speculation by the medical experts. A rheumatologist finally diagnosed the problem as Polymyalgia Rheumatica. This is a rare disease that only strikes nine people out of every 100,000. It arrives unexpectedly and I am told is likely to disappear as quickly as it came within two to five years. The bad news was that the pain was quite nasty; the good news was that the specialist put me on steroids that almost instantly eliminated most of the discomfort.

I felt relieved that the nagging illness had finally been diagnosed and that very night Rae and I went out to a Thai dinner to celebrate. We had barely seated at the restaurant when my phone rang. It was the Chrysos CEO who had rung to tell me that someone wanted to buy one-third of my shares in the company. The proposed price was ten times the original subscription price less than three years previously.

We felt blessed beyond measure and placed more than half the proceeds in a trust to give away. We still own the balance of the shares, which we plan to sell progressively over the coming years devoting the bulk to The McLellan Foundation. It will allow us to donate many millions to Christian causes and have already made a substantial start in funding a new building, McLellan Hall, at the Lachlan Macquarie Institute.

I told our minister that when they had formed the world, God and Jesus sat on a log and God asked Jesus, "What are we going to do with the McLellans in 2019?" Jesus said, "First, we need to get Tony well again, and then we will line up a buyer for his shares knowing that they have committed to contribute the bulk to Christian causes."

It all came flooding back. Rae and I remembered the lesson of the Vine from John 15, referred to in chapter 10. The Bible teaches that if you are faithful, the Gardener prunes you, which of course is painful, but it will ensure that you bear much fruit.

It is tempting to think my glorious ride may be over and that I can start taking things a little easier. When you surrender yourself to God, however, you know that those decisions are in stronger hands than your own. As the Apostle Paul said in his farewell to the Ephesian Elders: "My only aim is to finish the race and complete the task the Lord Jesus has given me, the task of testifying to the good news of God's grace" (Acts 20:24).

# CHAPTER 18

# ADVICE TO THE YOUNGER ME

Start children off on the way they should go, and even when they are old, they will not turn from it.

PROVERBS 22:6

Looking back on my life's experiences, what advice would I liked to have received sixty-five years ago when my father died? What would I have appreciated knowing then, about what it takes to have a meaningful life as opposed to mere existence? After all, Jesus tells us in the Gospel of John that he came not only that his followers might have live, but that they might have it "to the full".[24] This teaching of Jesus does not mean that one will be healthy, wealthy and wise, but that one should seek the most meaningful life possible.

I have much to say to the precocious young Tony, but I decided to distil my advice down to a few key points.

---

24   John 10:19: "The thief comes only to steal and kill and destroy; I have come that they may have life, and have it to the full."

## Focus on one thing

The Greek poet, Archilochus, divided the world into two types of people: foxes and hedgehogs. The fox knows many things, but the hedgehog knows one big thing. Foxes pursue many ends, often unrelated and even contradictory. Their actions are not connected by any aesthetic or moral principle.

Hedgehogs, on the other hand, relate everything to a single central vision; a single universal organising principle that defines what they think and believe.

So, my first advice to the young Tony is to act like a hedgehog and focus on one thing.

## Do what it takes

One of history's most inspirational men, Winston Churchill, once said: "Sometimes doing your best is not good enough; you must do what is required." So go for it young Tony! The world is crying out for leaders—men and women who will do what it takes, especially when the chips are down.

We lived in America when Walter Payton, the famous running back for the Chicago Bears, was at his peak. Payton was a relatively small man to be playing American Football: he was less than 1.8 metres tall and weighed a mere 90 kilos.

But Payton set one of sport's greatest records: the all-time rushing record of 15,294 metres. During his twelve-year career, Payton carried the football over fifteen kilometres!

What is truly impressive, though, is that Payton was knocked to the ground, on average, every four metres of those fifteen kilometres by someone bigger than himself. But he kept getting up, and he kept getting up, and he kept getting up. You can't keep a good man down, although there are those who would like to try.

## Examine your life

Socrates said that the unexamined life is not worth living. I only wish I had been challenged at your age to examine my life—to ensure I was planning to leave this world a better place. Sadly, it was not until later in life did I appreciate that, as Gabriel Garcia Marquez said, "A man has the right to look down on someone only when he is helping him to get up."

At his famous "Day of Affirmation" address at the University of Cape Town, Senator Robert Kennedy said:

> It is from numerous diverse acts of courage and belief that human history is shaped. Each time a man stands up for an idea, or acts to improve the lot of others, or strikes out against injustice, he sends forth a tiny ripple of hope . . .

I implore you, young Tony, examine constantly your life and your bank account, to ensure you are sending out tiny ripples of hope.

## Encourage as many people as you can

Learn to encourage everyone around you—and do it as often as possible.

Giving encouragement is important, as witnessed by the many references in the Bible:

- Paul told his young minister, Timothy that he was to correct, rebuke and encourage.[25]
- Isaiah instructed us to encourage the oppressed.[26]
- In 1 Thessalonians, we read that we are to encourage the timid.[27]
- In Hebrews, we are told that we are to encourage one another *daily*.[28]

So, young Tony, perfect the art of encouragement.

## Get your priorities right

It is a truism that nobody on their deathbed laments the lack of time spent at the office. Yet still we allow trivialities to keep us from important events. Please ensure your priorities do not get mixed. Don't leave your wife lying in a hospital bed as you race off on some "important" mission, as I once did.

## Discipline will have the biggest impact on your pursuit of success

Success stems from self-discipline, perseverance and diligence. Remember, it is up to you to control how conscientious you are; how diligent you are; how persistent you are. And, importantly, how hard you work.

Believe you are an eagle, Tony, and put aside any fears or doubts about your ability to achieve what you have set out to do.

25   2 Timothy 4:2

26   Isaiah 1:17a

27   1 Thessalonians 5:14

28   Hebrews 3:13

## Some other things

- Read "A World Lit Only by Fire" *and* lots of other great books. Commit poetry to your memory and heart, such as the final verse in the immortal rondeau "In Flanders Fields":

> Take up our quarrel with the foe:
> To you with falling hands we throw
> The torch; be yours to hold it high.
> If ye break faith with us who die
> We shall not sleep, though poppies grow
>    In Flanders fields.[29]

- Learn to play the piano.
- Get back on the horse and not just any horse, your own horse.
- Know that humility and low self-esteem are not the same thing.
- Eat fruit in season and grow your own strawberries.
- Barrack for the Waratahs.
- Overcome your fear of public speaking; just get on with it. It is all about storytelling. People don't remember what you said, only how you made them feel.
- Toughen up.
- Make your old friends soon, so you can keep them for 50 years.
- Learn how to reverse a trailer. And how to prune a rose bush.
- Develop your people skills. Your success always depends on other people. Get to know and appreciate as many as

29  Lt. Col. John D. McCrae, *In Flanders Fields*

you can. Ask them about themselves. The key is listening intently, and then paraphrasing back what they just told you. They will then know you heard them and cared for them.

- Talk to your grandmother about your grandfather.
- If you want to be radical, wear a suit and tie; it's a great disguise.

## Fall in love

Tony, ideally you should fall in love only once—and then stay scrupulously faithful. Decide in advance, as Joseph did, that you will not succumb to the devil who prowls around like a roaring lion tempting you in all sorts of ways. Pray for your wife every single day. Help bring your children up well, with a sense of discipline and commitment. Be generous with hugs, expressions of love and affection.

Tell the people you are close to—especially your family—that you love them; in the same way you might want to eulogise a dear, dear friend. And, as a man, don't be afraid to tell another man that you love him.

I want to urge you, Tony, to beware of being swept off your feet by what is called falling in love, assuming that that in itself is an adequate basis for marriage. There are some other critical considerations, such as intellectual and spiritual compatibility. Love is an unreliable emotion, and it has to be checked by the Word of God.

I write these words on Tuesday 19 January 2021 as Rae and I celebrate our 60th wedding anniversary. I want to pay a special tribute to this darling wife of mine. And, through that, to acknowledge her beautiful Christian grandmother who raised Rae from the age of three months; who showed her how to get ahead, and told her that when the chips are down you need to pick yourself up by your bootstraps and get on with it.

These beliefs have made Rae the special person she is; have fortified her in tolerating me; and have brought unquenchable love into our family. Further, without Rae at my side, I could never have accomplished the many things which I have attempted. Without her support, we would never have been able to live in 41 homes in so many countries.

Having benefited from a compelling marriage, I want to close this story of our life by reflecting on what I call the five keys to moral maturity in our marriage.

### First, practice self-control

Aristotle said in the Nichomachaen Ethics, moral virtues come from habit. Whatever we learn to do, we learn by actually doing it: men come to be builders, for instance, by building, and harp players, by playing the harp. By doing just acts towards one another, we come to be just; and by doing self-controlled acts, we come to be self-controlled.

In his letter to the Galatians, Paul told us that "the fruit of the Spirit is love, joy, peace, patience, kindness, goodness, faithfulness, gentleness and self-control" (Galatians 5:22-23). Later, in the midst of his discourse on virtues, we read in Peter's second epistle that self-control stems from knowledge: "and to knowledge, add self-control".[30]

We also know that the opposite is also true: lies keep us bound. James says that if we speak lies to ourselves, we lose

---

30    2 Peter 1:6: "and to knowledge, self-control; and to self-control, perseverance; and to perseverance, godliness"

self-control. We all make many mistakes, but those who control their tongues can also control themselves in every other way.[31]

Indeed, the man who speaks the truth is always in control of himself—in other words, he is self-controlled. Jesus said, "If you hold to my teaching, you are really my disciples. Then you will know the truth, and the truth will set you free" (John 8:31b-31).

### Second: Maintain integrity

Integrity is defined as adherence to moral principles, soundness of moral character or honesty. And the Bible is replete with men and women who acted with great integrity. Joseph, the youngest of Jacob's 12 sons, was sold into slavery in Egypt. Through his obvious abilities and perspicacity—but most importantly his integrity—he became prime minister of Egypt. He faced many trials, including temptation by Potiphar's wife who tried to seduce him. But Joseph remained loyal to his master. The big lesson from that incident is that Joseph had already decided in advance what he would do when faced with such temptation.

As the ancient Chinese philosopher, Mencius, said, "Before a man can achieve great things, he must first of all decide those things he will not do."

I know from personal experience that the devil prowls around like a roaring lion seeking to devour all.[32] He is constantly seeking to destroy or humiliate those in power, by

---

31  James 3:2: We all stumble in many ways. Anyone who is never at fault in what they say is perfect, able to keep their whole body in check.

32  1 Peter 5:8 Be alert and of sober mind. Your enemy the devil prowls around like a roaring lion looking for someone to devour.

tempting us at our weakest points. He tempts us with illicit sex; he tempts us with ill-gotten financial rewards; and he tempts us with pride.

All of us acknowledge the desirability of being physically fit. But we also need to be psychologically fit. In *The Republic*, Plato said integrity is having one's psychological parts integrated—having it all together as we say—and is the psychological counterpart of physical fitness.

What I have learned is that we become what we are as a person, by the thousands of decisions we ourselves make day by day. And one of the saddest things I come across too often is men flouting their marriage vows . . . "will you, forsaking all others, be faithful to her as long as you both shall live?"

Each one of us needs to live day by day, in such a way that we are able to look across the table at our wife . . . and have nothing to conceal. Integrity is doing the right thing even when no one is watching.

### Third: Dream

Martin Luther King, who did so much to bring freedom to the African American people, in his famous "I Have a Dream" speech, delivered at the foot of the Washington Monument, paraphrased the prophet Isaiah[33] when he said:

> I have a dream . . . that one day every valley shall
> be exalted, every hill and mountain shall be made
> low, the rough places will be made plain, and the
> crooked places will be made straight, and the glory

33    Isaiah 40:4-5, Every valley shall be raised up, every mountain and hill made low; the rough ground shall become level, the rugged places a plain. And the glory of the Lord will be revealed, and all people will see it together. For the mouth of the Lord has spoken.

of the Lord shall be revealed, and all flesh shall see it together.

We need to have a dream for our spouses. We need to dream that we will be the kind of person God wants us to be. We need to dream that we will have insight into our wife's or husband's emotions. We need to dream that we will continually strengthen all aspects of our marriage, protecting it from destruction, and increasing the love between us.

### *Fourth: Be Friends*

It may seem trite, suggesting that married couples be friends. But friendship is demanding and requires great commitment. We must always speak frankly to one another, to reveal our inner feelings, to take our partner's criticisms as seriously as their expressions of admiration and praise, to practice absolute loyalty to the point of self-sacrifice.

There is nowhere in all of literature a greater statement of friendship and loyalty than the words Ruth said to her mother-in-law, Naomi, when Naomi planned to return to the land of Judah after their husbands had died in Moab. Naomi begged Ruth to stay with her own people, the Moabites, but Ruth responded with that immortal plea:

> Where you go I will go, and where you stay I will stay. Your people will be my people and your God my God. Where you die I will die, and there I will be buried.[34]

34   Ruth 1:16b-17a

### *Fifth: Have Faith*

Faith is an incredible source of discipline, and power, and meaning in the lives of the faithful, in all major religious creeds. And a shared faith binds a married couple together in ways that cannot be duplicated by any other means.

Believe, like Job did, that God is working a plan for your good. Believe, as Daniel did, that God can keep the lions' mouths open.

I cannot begin to imagine what our marriage would be like without our shared faith. I suppose it would be like what it was before I messed it up.

A shared belief in God and his purposes for us is the strongest glue I can imagine for our marriage. In Ecclesiastes we read that, "a threefold cord is not quickly broken".[35] This indicates to me that the union of a husband, his wife and their shared faith is hard to destroy.

We give thanks for the gift of our three children—Scott, Stuart and Samantha—and their wonderful spouses—Sara, Carla, and Alexi. They make a great six-pack, giving us Sophia and Susanna, Keller and Fiona, and Brooke, Ashley, Chloe, and Magnus, for whom we pray by name every single day. Those of you fortunate enough to have grandchildren will understand what an incredible joy they are, and it is the legacy we leave them that is so important to both Rae and me.

I believe that Rae's great metier is that she completely trusts God and she also trusts me as her husband. With this assurance, Rae submits willingly to me as the head of the household. It is then up to me to accept the call to leadership with repentance and humility—which does not come easily to

35   Ecclesiastes 4:6-9

me. But the Bible tells us that, "Humility and the fear of the Lord bring wealth and honour and life" (Psalm 22:4).

On the question of headship and submission, the Bible instructs us to: "Submit to one another out of reverence for Christ. Wives, submit to your husbands as to the Lord. For the husband is the head of the wife as Christ is the head of the church" (Ephesians 5:21-23a). There is then placed on we husbands a huge burden: "Husbands, love your wives, just as Christ loved the church an gave himself up for her."[36]

In his magnificent address to Pope Francis's humanum colloquium on complementarity, for which he received a standing ovation, Rabbi Lord Jonathan Sacks concluded by saying:

> As Adam and Eve were about to leave Eden,
> Adam gave his wife the first gift of love, a personal
> name. And so, it has been ever since, that when a
> man and a woman turn to one another in a bond
> of faithfulness, we come as close as we will ever
> get to God himself, bringing new life into being,
> turning the prose of biology into the poetry of the
> human spirit, redeeming the darkness of the world
> by the radiance of love.

Rae and I love to visit art galleries, and we have had the good fortune to have spent time in such wonderful places as the Uffizzi in Florence, the Musee d'Orsay in Paris, the Metropolitan Museum of Art in New York, and our favourite, the Prado in Madrid.

---

36   Ephesians 5:25

A few years ago, some American tourists were in the Louvre in Paris, and in a loud and uncouth way were being critical of the spectacular artwork. Disturbed by the noise they were making, an official from the Museum approached the group and in his heavily accented English told them that the quality of the paintings was not affected by their reaction; rather their reaction determined who they were.

Similarly, the way we react to the call of Jesus on our lives does not determine who Jesus is. Rather, it determines who we are . . . and, consequently, what sort of people we might become.

### Finally, Grace to you

For more than six hundred years the Hapsburgs exercised political power in Europe. When Emperor Franz-Josef I of Austria died in 1916, his was the last of the extravagant imperial funerals. A processional of dignitaries and elegantly dressed court personages escorted the coffin, draped in the black-and-gold imperial colours. To the accompaniment of a military band's sombre dirges, and by the light of torches, the cortege descended the stairs of the Capuchin Monastery in Vienna.

At the bottom was a great iron door leading to the Hapsburg family crypt. Behind the door was the Cardinal-Archbishop of Vienna. The officer in charge followed the prescribed ceremony established centuries before. "Open!" he cried.

"Who goes there?" responded the Cardinal.

"We bear the remains of his Imperial and Apostolic Majesty, Franz-Josef I, by the grace of God Emperor of

Austria, King of Hungary, Defender of the Faith, Prince of Bohemia-Moravia, Grand Duke of Lombardy, Venezia, Styrgia . . ." The officer continued to list the Emperor's thirty-seven titles.

"We know him not," replied the Cardinal. "Who goes there?"

The officer spoke again, this time using a much-abbreviated and less-ostentatious title, reserved for times of expediency.

"We know him not," the Cardinal said again. "Who goes there?"

The officer tried a third time, stripping the emperor of all but the humblest of titles: "We bear the body of Franz-Josef, our brother, a sinner like us all!"

At that, the doors swung open and Franz-Josef was admitted. All of us alike will meet death bereft of rank and title. Neither wealth nor fame can open the way of salvation, which is only available through God's grace—given to those who will humbly acknowledge their need.

That, young Tony, is the most important advice I can give you. And may God bless you as you earnestly seek His face.

. . . "To strive, to seek, to find, and not to yield."

**Tony McLellan** began his business career at age 15, managing the family sheep station when his father died. Moving to the city to study, he graduated summa cum laude, and then spent half his working life abroad. His responsibilities included the development of a new city in Egypt. Later he served as the president and CEO of a number of major international corporations, transacting business in more than twenty countries. A proven leader, since returning to Australia, Tony has been elected the chairman of a number of listed public mining companies. He was the founder and chairman of Chrysos Corporation Limited, in partnership with the CSIRO. With a passion for the poor, Tony has served as a director of several not-for-profit organisations, both overseas and in Australia. He is now chairman emeritus of Australian Christian Lobby. Married for 60 years, Tony and Rae are the proud parents of three children and grandparents of two princes and six princesses.

**Nick Cater** is a writer and media commentator on political and cultural affairs. Born and educated in the United Kingdom, he has been a proud Australian citizen for 30 years. He became Executive Director of the Menzies Research Centre in 2014 after a long career as a journalist, foreign correspondent and editor. His book *The Lucky Culture* was published in 2013. He writes regularly for *The Australian*, hosts the Watercooler podcast and appears frequently on radio and television.

# INDEX

Habitat for Humanity Australia, chairman, 163, 213

Menzies Research Centre, director, 14, 232, 273–275

Opportunity International Australia, director, 163, 189, 216, 229–231, 276–277, 281–283

We Care America, co-founder and vice chairman, 162, 271

McLellan, Allan Kenneth (father), 18, 21, 25, 40–41, 287

McLellan, Amy (née Webster) (grandmother), 17–18, 20–21, 41

McLellan, Anthony Scott (son), 49, 64, 66, 97, 135–136, 156, 299, 311

McLellan, George (great grandfather), 17

McLellan, George Robert (grandfather), 17–20

McLellan, Judy (sister), 22, 127–128

McLellan, Mary (née Downs) (mother), 21, 43, 127–129

McLellan, Rae Natalie (née Hand) (wife), 54–61, 67–68, 124–129, 158–160, 180, 306–307, 311

McLellan, Samantha (daughter), 72, 123, 136, 159, 172–173, 311

McLellan, Stuart (son), 97, 135–136, 311

McLellan, Wendy (sister), 22, 127

Melbourne, Civic Square, redevelopment, 68–69

Menzies, Sir Robert, 38, 50, 63, 218–219, 265, 273

Menzies Research Centre, 14, 232, 273-275

Modesto Manifesto, 185–187

Mother Teresa, 192

Munk, Peter
background, 99–100
first meeting with TM, 74–75
Pyramids Oasis project discussion and job offer, 76–77
move to Toronto office of the company, suggestion to TM, 100–101
TM as President of Barrick Resources, proposal, 102–103

offer to pay travel expenses of Rae (wife), 104–105
corporate collapse experience and advice to TM, 114
encouraged TM to join Southern Pacific Hotel Corporation, Board, 116
appreciation of TM's assistance, 131
work as a philanthropist, 143
death, 142

Nasser, Gamal Abdul, 78–79

Nawaf ben Abdul Aziz, Prince, 111

Nelson, Duane ("Swede"), 118

New Zealand, 165, 170

Nile river cruise, 90

Nyngan, NSW, 47, 54

O'Hare, Butch, 258–260

Owens, Jesse, 251–252

Pailthorpe, Michael, 228

PAN Am Jumbo, trips on, 69

Paris, 107–109, 111, 116, 118, 122, 124–125, 241, 312–313

Parker, Jill, 49, 127

Parker, Ron, 127

Paterson, Banjo, 30–32, 57, 287–288

Paulsson, Jan, 111, 118

Payton, Walter, 302

Peak Hill, NSW, 55, 127

Pearson, Noel, 225–226

Pell, George (Cardinal),12, 283–286

Penfold-Hyland, Jeffrey, 71

PhotonAssay, 293

Pinefield Public School, 34

Pooncarie, NSW, 277

Pyramids Oasis Project
background, 76–77
offer of Managing Director position, 77–78
agreement and submission of project proposal, 80–81
completion of first phase, 84–85
nationalisation, 93–97